Psychology Today

HERE TO HELP

the power of
LOVING
DISCIPLINE

Psychology Today
HERE TO HELP

the power of
LOVING
DISCIPLINE

Karen Miles

ALPHA

A member of Penguin Group (USA) Inc.

ALPHA BOOKS

Published by the Penguin Group

Penguin Group (USA) Inc., 375 Hudson Street, New York, New York 10014, U.S.A.

Penguin Group (Canada), 10 Alcorn Avenue, Toronto, Ontario, Canada M4V 3B2 (a division of Pearson Penguin Canada Inc.)

Penguin Books Ltd, 80 Strand, London WC2R 0RL, England

Penguin Ireland, 25 St Stephen's Green, Dublin 2, Ireland (a division of Penguin Books Ltd)

Penguin Group (Australia), 250 Camberwell Road, Camberwell, Victoria 3124, Australia (a division of Pearson Australia Group Pty Ltd)

Penguin Books India Pvt Ltd, 11 Community Centre, Panchsheel Park, New Delhi—110 017, India

Penguin Group (NZ), cnr Airborne and Rosedale Roads, Albany, Auckland 1310, New Zealand (a division of Pearson New Zealand Ltd)

Penguin Books (South Africa) (Pty) Ltd, 24 Sturdee Avenue, Rosebank, Johannesburg 2196, South Africa

Penguin Books Ltd, Registered Offices: 80 Strand, London WC2R 0RL, England

Publisher: Marie Butler-Knight

Editorial Director: Mike Sanders

Senior Managing Editor: Jennifer Bowles

Senior Acquisitions Editor: Paul Dinas

Senior Development Editor: Phil Kitchel

Production Editor: Janette Lynn

Copy Editor: Keith Cline

Cover Designer: Kurt Owens

Book Designer: Trina Wurst

Indexer: Heather McNeill

Layout: Becky Harmon

Proofreading: John Etchison

To Alan, my partner in parenting and life.

Contents

Foreword

It's not easy being a contemporary parent. Modern-day stresses and conflicting ideas about parenthood make the job much more complex than it once was. Add to that the pressure our kids are under from popular culture and heightened competition, and it makes the job even tougher. What can we do as caring parents to offset these complications?

As *The Power of Loving Discipline* explains, parents have two pitfalls to avoid. The strict authoritarian parent cracks the whip: "You will go to bed whether you like the dark or not." The wishy-washy, permissive parent lets the child rule the household: "Can't sleep, honey? Come and watch late-night TV with me." Neither of these options provides the guidance your child really needs. Nor do they foster his or her emotional growth.

In contrast, the loving discipline style gives a child strong but constructive support. It is effective in both preventing and solving a child's behavioral problems. It shows you how to be a careful observer and how to pay attention to your instincts.

Look inside these pages for practical suggestions on productive family meetings, using the right kind of time-out (for both parents and children), and teaching a child lifelong problem-solving skills. You may not know the difference between natural consequences and logical consequences, but this book explains how to use them in a positive framework.

Author Karen Miles knows this subject matter well, both professionally and personally. As a mother of four, she has lived through the obstacles you face today. What's more, she has written more than 300 articles that have appeared in such publications as *Parenting, Family Circle, Reader's Digest, Woman's Day, Family Fun,* and *Baby Talk*. She also contributes to the popular parenting website BabyCenter.com. For this book, the author spoke to some 40 experts who weigh in on the various parenting styles, giving you the best overview of what is available.

What's more, this book will introduce the tools you'll need to tackle parenting today. It will help you understand your child's need to belong, foster mutual respect, provide unconditional love, and look for the message behind his behavior. More than that, you will learn specific tips as well as dos and don'ts on how to establish limits, set expectations, encourage your child, and nurture her fullest potential. *The Power of Loving Discipline* puts theory into practice, showing you the way to help your child grow into the happy, thriving individual you know he can be.

Kaja Perina
Editor in Chief
Psychology Today magazine

Introduction

You know how sometimes when you read something or hear something it just clicks? There's this sense of excitement and validation, of renewal and inspiration. As a parent, I feel that way about the loving discipline ideas in this book.

When our first child, Lilianna, was born over 20 years ago, all I really knew about parenting was that this baby of ours inspired my unconditional love. I began reading everything I could find about parenting, and I wrote about parenting (in large part so I could stay close to her by working as a freelance writer).

Some of what I read didn't click. It suggested that I let her cry herself to sleep, for example, or that I feed her at scheduled intervals rather than intermittently (and frequently) round the clock, which was obviously her need, both for nourishment and reassurance.

But some of it did click. I read about Attachment Parenting and Aware Parenting. As she grew into a feisty toddler, I read and rejected authoritarian discipline ideas and drew from the philosophy and support of experts who advocated more loving, respectful approaches. As our firstborn grew—and was joined by a brother and two sisters—I learned more, both about loving and about parenting.

Our children became adolescents, and, like many parents, I was forewarned as they each approached their teen years. But we continued to build on the unconditional love that began with Lilianna's arrival and were encouraged by the parenting experts I admired. We were rewarded with creative, fun, and accomplished young adults.

In *The Power of Loving Discipline*, you'll hear from many experts who have helped parents raise their children positively, lovingly, with faith in their goodness and commitment to their best interests. These professionals have devoted themselves to learning what's best for children and to helping children and their families grow. There's parenting advice galore out there, and much of it is conflicting. What you'll find here is a current overview of the issue of discipline—what we know, where that knowledge points us, and how best to put it to work.

When it comes to what's in our children's best interests, research points to one discipline style as the clear winner. You'll learn why, and you'll see that within that style there are still many different approaches. You'll also learn about the common threads that run through these loving approaches—all are non-punitive, and all are based on developing a close, loving relationship with your child, for example.

The fact that you're reading this book shows that you take your parenting job seriously. You may feel confused by all the advice you've run across about discipline, or you may have decided that a loving approach is your best bet and you want to learn more. Or perhaps you're just curious to know more about discipline techniques. I hope this book helps you envision the enormous fulfillment and enjoyment available to you in your role as a parent. There's much to know, but children are fascinating and relationship building can be satisfying—and fun—work.

Once the philosophy behind the loving discipline approach "clicks," it will guide you in your daily decision making. You'll find plenty of suggestions here to help you put the ideas to work. Pick and choose among them. Fashion your own personal loving discipline style, based on what makes sense to you and what seems appropriate for your child.

What You'll Find Inside

The Power of Loving Discipline is organized into three parts:

In **Part 1, "Discipline: The Great Parenting Challenge—and Opportunity,"** you'll find the background for learning about disciplining children. It's a big topic, with plenty of research behind it. We'll explore the basic idea of discipline, and we'll look at the long-term effects of various discipline styles on children, which is, after all, the most important aspect of discipline. You'll see where loving discipline fits into the continuum of discipline styles, and you'll get a short introduction to a handful of loving discipline styles on which the rest of the book is based.

In **Part 2, "Loving Discipline Provisions,"** you'll explore those common threads that run through loving discipline styles. You'll see how encouragement, structure, time and attention, and modeling are the core ingredients your child needs to flourish, and how to keep them in mind as you use them to discipline (guide) your child.

In **Part 3, "Loving Discipline Strategies,"** you'll delve into some nitty-gritty loving discipline techniques that will help you guide your child on a day-to-day basis. You'll learn how to build your relationship with your child through communication skills, how to use natural and logical consequences in a loving, non-punitive framework, and how to use positive time-outs in a helpful way. (It's not the time-out you'll find in most parenting books!)

You'll learn how to teach your child valuable skills, too, like communication and problem solving, so that she can grow into the confident, competent, empathetic, loving person you have in mind. As you read this book—and other parenting books— keep your goals for your child in mind. Let them, and your heart, guide you. Use them to test every idea and every technique.

How to Use This Book

In *The Power of Loving Discipline*, you'll hear from parents, parenting specialists who have studied the issue of discipline, and therapists who have worked with children and their families. Direct quotes from parents and other parenting experts provide plenty of food for thought, practical advice, and inspiration. Reading the book cover to cover should give you a pretty thorough understanding of the topic. But you can also tackle a specific chapter on its own—to learn more about a particular technique or idea, for example. Throughout the book, you'll find these helpful sidebars:

Each Q&A features a question from a parent like you and an answer from an expert who is well informed about that particular topic.

PsychSpeak

PsychSpeak explains, in plain English, terms that may be unfamiliar to you. You'll see the term in italics in the text and bold in the sidebar.

GET PSYCHED

Read Get Psyched for inspirational quotes and bits of advice from experts on the topic at hand.

WEB TALK: This sidebar points you to valuable information on the web, for expanding your exploration of a topic or for networking.

you're not alone

The stories in these sidebars are from parents who are learning about and test-driving discipline with their children. Their stories will inspire, amuse, and reassure you.

You'll also find a "What You Can Do" section at the end of each chapter. This checklist suggests things you can do to put some of the chapter's ideas to use right away.

Acknowledgments

I have not missed the delightful irony of receiving so much love and support in writing a book about disciplining children with love and support.

Thank you to the many parenting experts, who, without exception, have been generous and helpful. They are a dedicated group, devoted to the well-being of children and their families. I hope my mention of them in this book will encourage you to further explore the invaluable work they do. (You'll also find information about some of their books and reference to some of their affiliated organizations in the appendix.)

Thank you to all the parents who shared their stories with me, and to those who alerted me to topics and resources.

Thank you to Paul Dinas at Alpha Books, who encouraged me and showed faith in me each step of the way. Every writer should have such an enthusiastic, supportive, and positive editor. Thank you to gracious and talented Lybi Ma at *Psychology Today,* whose vision for this project and belief in its importance drove its creation and completion. Thank you to Janette Lynn, Phil Kitchel, and Keith Cline for their conscientious work on the manuscript.

Thank you to Sarah Smith at *Parenting* magazine, who has always been such a delight, and who recommended me for this project.

Thank you to my friends and family, who have nourished me with their love throughout. Thank you to Christine White and Russell Madden for your friendship and the lovely reprieve you provided when I was in the thick of this book. Thank you to kindred spirit Ann Hahn, whose characteristic thoughtfulness and mothering instincts always ring true. Thank you to my friend and our community librarian, Beth Crow, who so cheerfully helps me find elusive materials and whose positive support brightens so many lives. To the dedicated community volunteers who literally saved my life shortly before I began this book—Mindy Brittain, Steve Metz, and Jim Fisher—thank you for the blessing of each day and each opportunity. To my extended family, Helen and Don Davis, Thomas Burke, and Brandon Wilson, thank you for showing such faith in me and enthusiasm for this project. I love that we're family. Thank you to Bob Leddy, my brother, who demonstrates as great an example of family love and parental devotion as I've found. Thank you to my father, Robert Leddy, who taught me that knowing you're loved goes a long way, and to my mother, Anna Leddy-Burke, from whom I learned how to put that love to work.

My husband, Alan, who loves me as well as our children unconditionally, I cannot thank enough. Your practical and emotional support has been crucial to the writing of this book and to my daily sustenance. The fact that you are the father of my children and my parenting partner is one of the greatest joys of my life. Lucky us.

To our children, who are now wonderful young adults, thank you: Lilianna, I count your radiance and love among my blessings every day. Thank you for your thoughtfulness, for your fierce loyalty to your family, and for starting me on this most wonderful journey. Zak, nothing has made me happier than seeing you grow to become a wise, loving, and thoughtful man of great integrity, a man we all look up to. Thank you for the heartfelt hugs that you've never outgrown. Hannah Mae, I cherish your bright, independent, creative spirit and tender, tolerant heart. Thank you for touching my cheek and teaching me that there are many ways to love. Emma Rose, I treasure your love of life and family, and I admire your great conviction and compassion. Thank you for always insisting on what's right and for always keeping me in your heart. Thanks to all of you for teaching me life's most important lessons and inspiring me to do my best— and most important—work.

Part 1

Discipline: The Great Parenting Challenge—and Opportunity

Discipline can be a thorny, controversial topic. There's no shortage of advice, of course—from other parents, academic experts, religious leaders, politicians, Grandma, teachers, and the next-door neighbor. That's because disciplining our children is an important job—our *most* important job, in fact. How can you sort out what's best for your child and your family?

In Part 1, we explore just what we mean by discipline, and the definition will help illuminate your way through the rest of the book. We look at some of the controversy surrounding the topic, and we think about how your discipline style developed. You'll learn about one classic way of defining discipline styles on a continuum, from strict to lenient (authoritarian to permissive), and you'll learn why a third style—authoritative—continues to gain in popularity today. Finally, we take a look at a handful of the many loving discipline styles that fit (or are closely aligned with) an authoritative style. We hope you pick and choose from these to design your own discipline style—a style in which your child can flourish.

What Is Discipline?

Discipline is one hefty word, carrying a load of serious implications. For some parents it conjures memories of having been shown by gentle example how to act at the dinner table (*"Please* pass the peas" and "Thank you for taking your plate to the kitchen"). For others it brings back a booming parental "Because I said so!" or the humiliation of being spanked for impertinence.

When those of us who are parents hear the word, we also reflect on how we're disciplining our own children and whether we're doing it right. Hundreds of books, articles, and acquaintances advise us, but it seems like they're talking about different things. As a matter of fact, many times they are.

Takes on the Topic

Before you decide which styles are right for you and your child, it's a good idea to zero in on how each expert or approach defines the very word *discipline*. As you'll see in this chapter, there are basically two very distinct definitions.

Your definition—which you may now consciously choose, regardless of how encumbered it's been in the past—will directly impact your relationship with your child and the dynamics of your family, as well as the kind of person she is now and becomes 10 and 20 years down the road. (You'll learn more about how styles directly affect a child in Chapter 5, but throughout the book you'll want to keep your goals for your child in mind.)

The word *discipline* makes many parents uncomfortable, thanks in part to their childhood memories, but also because it seems to be the basis on which we're judged as parents. If your toddler throws a tantrum at the grocery store checkout, you may worry that the person behind you will think you haven't disciplined your tyke properly. If your grade-schooler doesn't get her homework done, won't the teacher know that your discipline about schoolwork isn't making the grade? And when your teen doesn't write Grandma a thank-you for hosting the holiday festivities, will Grandma think you haven't emphasized etiquette enough?

Discipline is tough partly because so many people seem to be watching and judging, and because everything your child does and doesn't do reflects squarely on your ability to discipline her. Of course, discipline is also difficult because there's so much at stake. We worry that if we get it wrong our children will be delinquents or depressed; lack motivation or empathy; be incompetent, unsuccessful in school and work, or apathetic about life and others. To top it off, they'll hate us for the rest of their lives for all the mistakes we've made!

"Parenting is the biggest responsibility and hardest job that someone will have," says clinical psychologist Erik Fisher, Ph.D., author of *The Art of Managing Everyday Conflict.* "There are no hard and fast rules, and everyone has an opinion. There is so much fear that underlies parenting, and wherever there is fear, buttons will be pushed. Discipline is important to the family because of the influence of consistent and inconsistent discipline on the parents and children. Discipline is important to the child because it helps to set the patterns for consistency, inconsistency, self-esteem, limits, and boundaries ... for a lifetime. Discipline is important to the culture because how children are disciplined will influence how they interact in the world," says Fisher. Which means that the way we discipline our children defines what the future looks like, too. No wonder it's a weighty topic.

"You don't have to do very much research or watch too many television programs to catch on to the fact that society gives discipline a very high profile," says parent Ashlie Hand, of Kansas City, Missouri. Indeed, entire television shows have been built around the topic, and daytime talk shows never tire of discussing it! "Parents are overwhelmed today with the number of discipline tactics that are offered through all kinds of media. Everyone seems to have a better way to discipline your children ... It has such an impact on your child's future, and that's a *very* emotional issue," Hand notes.

It is an emotional issue, and a somewhat subjective one. Each child is different, as is each parent and each circumstance. But taking a careful look at what discipline means and making a decision about how best to implement it in your family can smooth the way. There's plenty of advice to go around, but there are also some solid guidelines—based on a plethora of research—upon which you can base well-informed decisions.

"**W**hen my own daughter was caught smoking a cigarette in the back-yard at age 12, I was sure the next step would be car theft followed by heroin addiction. 'There goes my career as a psychologist,' I thought.

"With these concerns, it was obviously impossible to respond appropriately to the relatively minor incident at hand. Impossible—when you're projecting into the future and concocting all sorts of dangerous and illegal behavior—to respond the right way. It may be easy to say the right thing to a child who was caught smoking, but when you have to come up with a way to handle car theft and heroin addiction, the problem is overwhelming!

"We often don't know the best way to act because we see ourselves as a failure as a parent and, as a consequence, our child as having serious behavior problems."—*James Windell, author of* Discipline, A Sourcebook of 50 Failsafe Techniques for Parents

As a noun, the word *discipline* doesn't cause much confusion or stir much debate. When we say that a person is studying math as a discipline, or that a person has good discipline when it comes to working out at the gym, we all know what we mean. When we use it as a verb, however, we're not always on the same page. Here's a look at a handful of definitions from a handful of dictionaries:

Discipline (v):

- to correct, punish, control, penalize, chastise
- to control, direct, correct, govern, supervise, and oversee
- to train to improve strength or self-control
- to train by instruction and practice; especially to teach self-control
- to punish in order to gain control or enforce obedience
- to train, check, condition, correct, sort out
- to use rules and punishment to control behavior
- to impart knowledge and skill—to teach

So dictionary definitions explore the word a bit more for us, but a major question remains: *Does discipline mean "to punish," or does it mean "to teach"?*

It's a distinction you'll want to make, because much of the parenting advice you'll read will be based on one take or the other—and the difference between them is enormous.

Discipline as Punishment

In our culture, discipline is often equated with punishment. And when a parent who thinks of discipline as punishment decides to discipline a child, it's usually retroactive, after an infraction. A preschooler tells a lie and Mom sends him to his room; a toddler throws a rock and is made to sit on a chair; a teen sasses, and the car gets parked for the weekend.

"For many years," Martha Heineman Pieper, Ph.D., and William J. Pieper, M.D., authors of *Smart Love* explain, "the consensus in this society has been that parents need to respond to children's failures at self-regulation with an array of measures designed to manage unwanted behavior by attaching unpleasant consequences, including punishment, disapproval, isolation (time-outs), forceful language ('No!'), or withholding privileges. Parents have been told that by setting rigid limits and meting out significant consequences for breaking the rules they will raise well-behaved kids—those who will stay out of trouble and will not trouble their parents."

Punitive Means of Control Most of the punishments that parents dole out in the name of discipline are designed to make children do what parents want them to do, or not do what parents don't want them to do. The discipline is external; the children are motivated primarily by fear of being punished. And as we'll see later, when that external control is not around, these children often have no internal control to rely on; they have not learned anything about *self-control*. Most experts now agree that the best way to teach a child self-discipline is not to dictate to her, but to give her some decision-making responsibility, to help her learn that she can control herself—and that there's good reason to.

Sometimes parents embrace punitive discipline because they believe it's necessary to keep from "spoiling" their children. The Piepers explain, "Time-outs, restrictions, punishments, and other forms of discipline are based on the assumption that being too nice to children who are 'misbehaving' will encourage and reward their bad behavior. But we point out that discipline interferes with the most consistent and satisfying source of young children's inner well-being: the conviction that they are causing their parents to love caring for them. For this reason, disciplining children makes them more miserable and less able to forgo their wishes. In contrast, loving regulation shows children that, although they may have to give up gratifying a particular wish, they can always count on the pleasure of the parent-child relationship." Importantly, we'll see later that permissiveness is not the only alternative to punitive discipline.

Because the control is external, punishing your child does nothing to teach her self-control or self-improvement. It doesn't do much for your relationship, either! When your child feels that you are being punitive, harsh, dictatorial, controlling, or even simply wielding power over her because you are not her equal, but her superior, there's little opportunity to build a close bond with her. And that bond, say loving discipline advocates, is crucial for successful discipline. A child who is not respected by her parents isn't likely to respect them in return (although she may show compliance, which is something quite different).

In fact, the Piepers have found that a child who is not respected by her parents isn't encouraged to respect herself, either. "Because children adore their parents and believe they are ideal caregivers, when parents routinely impose unpleasant consequences for 'misbehavior,' children develop the need to treat themselves the same way," they explain. A close relationship with your child, on the other hand, not only fosters her self-esteem, it makes parenting rewarding and discipline easier, too.

WEB TALK: Smart Love Parenting Center is guided by the principles of Smart Love, by authors Martha Heinemen Pieper, Ph.D., and William J. Pieper, M.D. Visit to find out about parenting classes, discussion groups and workshops, parenting coaching, and publications such as "Smart Love Answers."

➤ www.smartloveparent.org

The Rod of Tradition We've all heard the call for a reintroduction of "traditional" parenting roles and discipline styles, suggesting that our children are suffering from a lack of punitive discipline. Children are getting away with too much, the refrain goes, and are badly behaved, spoiled, inconsiderate, and ungrateful—all because of wimpy parents. The answer, these experts believe, lies in parents asserting themselves as strict disciplinarians—in control, in charge, and tough.

It's an old but common notion that when discipline (punishment) isn't working, what you need is more discipline (punishment). Loving discipline advocates point out that punishment deprives a child of her needs rather than trying to help her meet

GET PSYCHED

"There are many terrible things in this world. But the worst is when a child is afraid of his father, mother, or teacher. He fears them, instead of loving and trusting them."
–Janus Korczak, author and educator

them. Instead of teaching or showing respect for a child, those who use punitive discipline demean, humiliate, and frighten her. The bottom line is that research shows it doesn't work, unless your only goal for your child is immediate compliance (in which case, it sometimes works). A better approach is to build your ability to discipline your child by fostering your relationship with her.

Making a Connection One reason children misbehave is that they don't feel connected; they don't feel a sense of belonging. Despite the disciplinarians' assertions, punitive discipline does not foster the parent/child connection. Instead, it increases a child's sense of isolation and disconnection from her parent.

"You acquire more influence with young people when you give up using your power to control them!" says Thomas Gordon, Ph.D., founder of Parent Effectiveness Training. "The opposite is also true, of course: The more you use power to try to control people, the less real influence you'll have on their lives."

It's important to note that loving discipline advocates are not proposing a *laissez-faire* approach. In fact, disciplining a child with love and guidance rather than punishment takes an enormous amount of conscientiousness and commitment. Children still need to be taught, they still need structure. But as you'll see throughout this book, they learn best and fare best when it's provided in a loving, rather than punitive, framework.

Discipline as Guidance

So what's the alternative for parents who don't want authoritarian-ruled households, but do want to discipline their children to be competent, well-mannered, and successful—however we may choose to define that for our children?

The alternative way of looking at discipline—one that goes back to its Latin roots—is one of teaching and guidance. And that's the approach we take in this book. We should pay attention to what the research (and our hearts and our children) tell us. The children who fare best are raised by parents who listen to them and care about their feelings and needs, who are not interested in controlling or punishing them, but always have their best interests in mind, and who have faith in their innate goodness.

Here's an interesting definition of discipline, from the Canadian Pediatric Society: "Discipline is the structure that helps the child fit into the real world happily and effectively. It is the foundation for the development of the child's own self-discipline." Discipline isn't a result of being coerced, threatened, or yelled at. Instead, it's the result of positive influence.

When we keep guidance and teaching in mind, we can think about giving up control. When we do that, we empower children to grow and flourish. Our parental role isn't one of dominance, but of wholehearted support.

After you decide what your goals are for your child—self-control, competence, confidence, responsibility, honesty, integrity, success (however you define it: academically, socially, or spiritually, for example)—you can teach her all of these things, not by punitive measures, but by respecting her, encouraging her, and teaching her practical skills such as communication and problem solving.

Building from a Loving Foundation If discipline isn't sitting your child on a chair, taking away a privilege, or yelling at, threatening, or hitting her, what does it look like?

Well, discipline—when you use it in a loving, guiding way— is something you do with your child from the day she's born. You teach her that the world is a friendly place, that her parents will care for her needs, that she is loved, and that she belongs.

In fact, "Getting attached is how discipline begins," says William Sears, M.D., author of *The Baby Book*. We discuss more about "attachment parenting," one loving-discipline style, in another chapter, but basically it involves sensitively responding to your baby's cues and needs from the start. Discipline is easier for attachment parents, says Sears, because "the sensitivity that attachment-style parents develop enables them intuitively to get behind the eyes of their child to see situations from his or her viewpoint." An attachment-parented baby is more receptive to parents because she operates from a foundation of trust, Sears explains.

As your baby grows, your knowledge and understanding of her grows—and hers of you, too. It's easy to take her perspective, and it's easy to understand how she's feeling. "Connected parents and infants grow naturally into a disciplined relationship," explains Sears. "As the relationship matures, attachment parents are better able to convey what behavior they expect of their child and the child is better able to understand these expectations."

There's so much expert parenting advice available. And much of it makes good sense. But what role should my instincts play?

Even if our "instincts" feel right and solid, in reality they can vary tremendously in their dependability. We are all born with instincts to love and care for our children, and when those instincts are reinforced by positive childhood experiences, they are good parenting guides for adults. But instincts can also be distorted by the caregiving we received as children so that responses that feel absolutely "right" to a parent may in reality mirror suboptimal parenting responses from that parent's childhood.

An example is spanking. Many parents are convinced that the spankings they received as children were both deserved and good for them and their instincts tell them to spank their own children, whereas in reality there is ample evidence showing that spankings harm children emotionally and make them more likely to be violent as adults. The good instincts we are born with can also be interfered with by the misinformation about childhood that pervades our culture. For example, the instinct that tells parents to make toddlers share and not grab is based on the erroneous but common belief that adult virtues have to be instilled early if children are to be properly socialized. Given the way children's minds actually develop, they should not be expected to share reliably until they are over four.

The general rule is this: Listen to instincts that tell you to be kind, loving, and understanding, but question and evaluate instincts that tell you to respond critically or punitively.—*Martha Heineman Pieper, Ph.D., co-author,* Smart Love

As your child becomes a toddler, you're disciplining her when you model caring behavior toward your ill neighbor, when you give her choices about which shoes to wear and respect her decision, and when you establish limits and guidelines for her safety and well-being (enlisting her input when possible) and let her experience the consequences of her actions while remaining empathetic. You're disciplining your preschooler when you teach her to wash her hands before coming to the table and when you

GET PSYCHED

"When punishment falls short—and it always does—there are a variety of alternatives that work better. Taking a fresh look at discipline and children's behavior, we can see that closeness, playfulness, and emotional understanding are better bets than punishment, behavior modification, and too much permissiveness."

–Lawrence J. Cohen, Ph.D., author of Playful Parenting

help her view her mistakes as opportunities to learn. Showing your faith in your grade-schooler by letting her complete her own homework or talk with a teacher about a problem is discipline, as is talking with your teen at midnight about her problems with friends and teaching her to put gas in the car when she borrows it.

So discipline isn't something you do *to* a child, in response to misbehavior. It's something you do *with* her. It's not a set of tactics you use on your child to get her to do what you want her to do and to keep her from doing what you don't want her to do. It's the way you interact with her all day, every day, from the time she's born through her childhood. When you and your child have a bond built on mutual respect, she will want to cooperate; it will be much easier to guide her.

"Discipline includes all those things that we do as parents to teach our children how to make better decisions," explains Ron Taffel, Ph.D., author of *Parenting by Heart.* So it includes modeling good behavior and teaching them empathy and problem solving. It means showing them that they have the power to make decisions and therefore control their lives. It means teaching them to take power and act responsibly. "The purpose of discipline is not control," Taffel says, "but cooperation. Cooperation means that your children choose to behave because it makes sense to behave. It feels good to behave. This is the goal of good discipline."

When you get right down to it, everything you do with your child is discipline, because all that you do teaches her something.

Yes, the potential for messing up is everywhere—but so is the opportunity to teach.

Teacher, First and Foremost Taking the teaching definition literally is helpful. A good teacher knows what her goals are for her students, and she plans accordingly. A parent thinks ahead—by making sure her toddler is well rested before a trek to the grocery store, for example, and by problem solving the curfew issue with a teen before it comes up next weekend. A good teacher gears lessons that are appropriate for the age of the child; parents keep developmental stages in mind when they set expectations or present challenges. You wouldn't try to teach a baby to ride a bicycle, and you won't expect her to sit happily in her high chair through a four-course adult dinner, either. Just as you wouldn't require a toddler to iron her own dress, you won't expect her to thank Aunt Liz for the cookies without a little prompting. And teaching your teen the importance of getting enough sleep will be easier if you understand that her biorhythms aren't the same as yours. Yes, there's a lot to know. But keeping abreast of what your child is going through not only helps you be a better teacher, it makes the job more fun, too.

Effective teachers also know that most kids don't get a lesson first time around, and they're willing to repeat them. Good teachers encourage children, practice with them, and inspire them to learn. (They know that learning is not something you can command a child to do.) They demonstrate, and they look for good teaching opportunities. When their methods don't work, they seek other ways of approaching the lesson. Successful teachers focus on strengths, show enthusiasm, and stay optimistic.

When you envision your role as your child's teacher rather than as her controller, discipline is no longer a dreaded aspect of parenting. Instead, it's an exciting opportunity to do your most important, fulfilling work.

So What's Loving Discipline?

When we talk about loving discipline in this book, we're talking about discipline as guidance, as teaching. It's nonpunitive, it's respectful, and it's effective. It's based on what's best for the child, it's thoughtful, and it builds on loving relationships and reflects solid research. Loving discipline makes sense, so much so that when you understand the underlying premise—that discipline is not punishment, but guidance—the rest falls easily into place.

Many experts and many approaches fall under this umbrella. If you are familiar with the work of psychiatrist Rudolf Dreikurs (1897–1972) and psychologist Alfred Adler (1870–1937), you'll recognize the notion that connectedness and a sense of belonging are crucial to a child's well-being. You'll see generous use of their principles of encouragement and democratic parenting, and careful inclusion of natural and logical consequences. If you know psychologist Carl Rogers's work (1902–1987), you'll see underpinnings of his ideas about *unconditional positive regard* and empowering people to reach their full potential. If you've read teacher and psychologist Haim Ginott (1922–1973) and psychologist Thomas Gordon (1918–2002), you'll be familiar with their suggestions regarding communication and sensitivity to a child's feelings.

Chapter 4 provides an overview of some currently popular parenting approaches that fall within our nonpunitive, loving discipline framework: Attachment Parenting, Positive Discipline, P.E.T., Aware Parenting, and Unconditional Parenting.

PsychSpeak

Unconditional positive regard is one of the conditions Carl Rogers outlined as necessary for successful therapy. It means viewing a person in a positive light and accepting that person completely and nonjudgmentally.

In a nutshell, loving discipline is built on mutual respect and cooperation. It fosters a child's happiness and her long-term growth by guiding her to learn life skills and self-control. It encompasses a number of positive approaches to parenting, all of which are nonpunitive, all of which embrace the parents' role as teacher.

What You Can Do

When you understand the different discipline definitions, the rest of the story—all the advice and ideas—makes sense. Learning about discipline and applying what you've learned becomes fun rather than overwhelming.

☐ If disciplining your child means teaching her, you might find it handy to have a curriculum. Make a list of all the things you would like your child to learn en route to adulthood. Cover everything you can think of, from problem-solving skills to empathy. You don't need to do this all in one sitting; keep a notebook of your teaching goals handy and add to it as you think of objectives.

☐ When you're feeling frustrated with your child, think about your curriculum. Is there something on your list that she needs to learn now, with your guidance? Knowing that there's an important goal at stake can sometimes provide the patience needed to see it through.

☐ Keep a journal of your child's development, with an eye toward the lessons she's tackling. For example, when you note that her shoelaces easily frustrate her or that she had a tantrum when you insisted on holding her hand in the subway, it may become clear that she's struggling with her independence right now.

17

☐ Think back to your own childhood. From which teachers did you learn the most? What were their approaches? How did they treat you? Think about these traits as you endeavor to teach your child.

☐ Talk with your child's childcare provider or teacher about discipline approaches. Learn from each other.

☐ Read some of the books by the experts who laid the foundation for loving discipline approaches. (See the Appendix for suggestions.)

Where Did You Get Your Discipline Style?

Whether you're having a "Because I said so" reaction to your preschooler's fourteenth "But why?" or are thoughtfully planning a family meeting to talk about chores, being a parent always involves a discipline style of one kind or another.

Do you have a pretty good idea where you got your style? Do you read parenting books and cull advice that you find useful? Or have you adopted the approach of a friend or relative whom you admire as a parent? Are you simply, because it worked fine, repeating the style with which you were raised? Do you think your style is affected by your personality or mood, or by your child's mood? How about your general circumstance, whether things are going great (you're on a delightful, well-deserved family vacation, for example) or not so good (you've just been laid off)?

There are plenty of possible influences, of course, and most likely your style grows out of a complex combination of these influences. Understanding the factors that contribute to parenting styles can help us evaluate, adapt, or update our own styles where needed to better accomplish our goals in disciplining our children.

Your Inheritance Initiates

Sometimes to our delight (perhaps as we sing a favorite childhood lullaby to our baby), and sometimes to our chagrin (as when we utter a familiar empty platitude), we recognize our parents' parenting styles in ourselves. It's undeniable.

In fact, a good place to start looking for the reasons why you relate to your child as you do is in the past, says Dan Kindlon, Ph.D., assistant professor of psychology at Harvard School of Public Health. "We can't avoid the influence of the people who raised us in the way we parent our kids—for better or worse," he says. In his book *Too Much of a Good Thing,* Kindlon explains how we carry powerful, idealized images of good parents and bad parents inside us, constructed from childhood memories. We react to these images, he says, as if they were living people rather than internalized objects.

These childhood memories are not accurate play-by-plays of specific incidents, Kindlon says, but images filtered through the lens of our childhood personality. "[T]he memories of a child who was the star or hero in a dysfunctional family, perhaps a very responsible and talented firstborn, will have her memories colored by the burden of the adultlike role she assumed in the family. This would be a very different memory filter than that of a child who could never measure up and lived in the shadow of a high-performing brother or sister. A hypersensitive or painfully shy child will remember interactions with his parents differently than an outgoing, extroverted kid for whom childhood was a fearless, playful romp. Even though we can update or remodel our inner parents from time to time, they are always constructed on the foundation that was laid down in childhood."

What role do these inner parents play? Kindlon suggests that they stand right next to us as we raise our children, influencing our parenting approach—and often making parenting more difficult. Even inner parents whom we perceive as "good" examples can be demanding and difficult to please, he points out, with impossible expectations. On the other hand, some parents learn what *not* to do from how they were raised; they spend time and energy trying to avoid being like their bad inner parents. Many times they indulge their children, in ways that are counterproductive to the child's becoming a competent person.

"Visiting our good and bad inner parents," says Kindlon, "can help us gain insight on why we raise our children the way we do." By being conscious of them, he says, we can diminish their influence. "Our inner parents' power to make us feel good or bad comes from inside us, not from anything real; by visiting them, we can begin to come to terms with the incidents that formed them, giving us the perspective to be able to be the kind of parents we want to be, instead of automatically reacting to figments and projections inside ourselves."

GET PSYCHED

"Parents often talk about the younger generation as if they didn't have anything to do with it."
—*Psychologist Haim Ginott, author of* Between Parent and Child

Your parents' beliefs, values, attitudes, customs, and even mannerisms may be contained in your parenting style. Of course, sometimes these are wonderful contributions. Perhaps your parents handed down a generous attitude toward community contribution, or a love of reading. Maybe fun family rituals or a delight in discovery were passed along, or maybe you've garnered specific, practical parenting solutions, such as a massage method to relax a toddler at night or an agreement that teens who borrow the family car wash it on the weekend. We can learn plenty of positive lessons about caring and nurturing children, as well as practical advice, from our parents.

Other times, what we repeat may not be so terrific. Sadly, mistakes such as alcohol and drug abuse, or verbal and physical abuse, are often repeated. But smaller negatives are handed down, too. Maybe your parents expected you to be silent at the dinner table so that the adults could carry on their own conversation. Or they didn't believe in talking about sex with children. It's up to you to filter through the ways your upbringing influences your parenting and decide what is valuable and what is not helpful for your family. There's no reason to wear a style that doesn't suit you.

Overall, of course, parents who themselves were raised in a healthy environment that enabled them to become healthy adults have an advantage when it comes to parenting. In a 1984 study published in *Child Development,* researcher Jay M. Belsky reported that a parent's developmental history shapes his or her personality and psychological well-being, which in turn shapes how he or she functions as a parent. "In general," he concludes, "Supportive developmental experiences give rise to a mature healthy personality that is then capable of providing sensitive parental care which fosters optimal child development." If you didn't have the advantage of a positive childhood environment to influence your parenting, of course, it's even more important that you become aware of the ideas you've "inherited."

you're not alone

A couple involved in the PARENTS FORUM parenting program, asked how they were different from their own parents, responded that they frequently tell their kids they love them. The husband remarked that he often says "I love you" to his son and, ruefully, described his own father's discomfort at hearing him say, "I love you, Dad." This couple said that although they happily do many of the same things their parents did, they realize that the parenting they got is not at all the parenting they want to give, particularly when it comes to communication.

Circumstances Contribute

Like children, we find it hard to do our best when we're discouraged. And stress can be very discouraging. The 2003 American Academy of Pediatrics "Task Force on the Family" reported that family circumstances play heavily and importantly into the way that children are treated in their families. The researchers linked the health and well-being of children with their parents' social circumstances as well as their physical, emotional, and social health. In studying the stress level of parents, they found that stress from financial concerns or health problems, lack of social support, unhappiness at work, and unfortunate life events all can cause emotional distress that results in conflict between parents, which in turn disrupts parenting and the parent/child relationship. The longer the disruption lasts, they reported, the worse the outcomes for the children.

In many families, finances are a major cause of stress, and it's easy to imagine how that worry might spill over into the way in which a parent relates to her child. A special issue of *Child Development*, published in 1994, reported that among poor, single African-American mothers, unemployment increases the punishment they give their adolescents. In addition, these mothers had, overall, a negative perception of their role as mothers. And a 2000 study by Ellen E. Pinderhughes and colleagues, published in the *Journal of Psychology,* reported that parents with low socioeconomic status who faced economic hardship had their ability to use nonpunitive discipline strategies undermined by stress. Instead, the researchers found, stress resulted in increased reliance on punitive discipline.

Other stressors that show an increase in punitive discipline include being a single parent, having a large number of children, living in an unsafe neighborhood, and having an unplanned pregnancy. Like the researchers in the 1994 study, the Pinderhughes team also found that stressors negatively affect parents' perceptions of their children. And they found that parents' worry about the future implications of their child's behavior causes them to react more punitively. ("Will he grow up to be a pathological liar or a thief if I don't stop this right now?" for example.) Finally, a parent's sense that he or she doesn't have control over the child's behavior—and wouldn't be able to prevent the problem behavior in the future, for example—also exacerbates the tendency to be punitive.

Studies also show that things only get worse when socioeconomic conditions worsen. Ellen E. Whipple and Carolyn Webster-Stratton at Michigan State University reported in a 1991 study that parental stress often plays an important role in abusive situations. Physically abusive families, they found, had younger mothers with less education, significantly lower income, a more frequent incidence of alcohol or drug abuse, and a history of child abuse.

GET PSYCHED

"As soon as a child is born, it's time to think about our parenting style, and specifically about the way we react when things don't go smoothly … Some people very quickly become fair-weather parents, supportive and attentive only when their children are easy to be with. But unconditional love matters most when they're not."
—*Alfie Kohn, author of* Unconditional Parenting

And in a 2001 study published in *Child Abuse and Neglect,* researchers Julie L. Crouch and Leah E. Behl reported that parents under stress who believe in corporal punishment resort to physical child abuse more than parents who believe in corporal punishment but are not under stress.

Those most likely to spank, according to Belsky's 1984 study, are younger, single black mothers. These mothers also tended to be religiously conservative and more likely to be living in poverty. Belsky concluded that poor mental health, lower education level, younger age, and conservative religious orientation are all factors in the increased incidence of corporal punishment.

A study by Randal Day and colleagues that appeared in a 1998 issue of *Journal of Marriage and the Family* examined parents' characteristics that influence the increased spanking rates in some households. He found that older parents, with more education (whom he hypothesized would have a higher sense of self-control and be more informed about alternative, nonpunitive approaches), are less likely to spank. On the other hand, parents who are depressed are more likely to spank, as are parents with strong ties to conservative religion.

Some factors can help offset some stressors, however, and thus influence parenting in a positive way. In his 1984 study, for example, Belsky also reported that a parent's patience and sensitivity are increased when he or she has a supportive social network. And a more recent study (2005) by Karen S. McCurdy at the University of Rhode Island confirmed Belsky's findings that stress contributes to physical punishment, but that increased social support decreases its use.

GET PSYCHED

"Forgetting one's human-ness is the first serious mistake one can make on entering parenthood. An effective parent lets himself be a person—a real person. Children deeply appreciate this quality of realness and human-ness in their parents."—*Thomas Gordon, Ph.D., founder of Parent Effectiveness Training*

If you are struggling with financial difficulties, substance abuse, or any other serious stressor in your life, your discipline approach with your child is likely to be negatively impacted. Getting support can make a difference. It's a good idea to be sensitive, too, to how even life's smaller stressors may influence your relationship with your child on a day-to-day basis, perhaps making you less patient or understanding than usual. Kids don't need us to be perfect. In fact, they benefit from watching us acknowledge and deal with problems. And it's always a good idea to let them know that the source of your worry isn't related to them.

Personality Plays a Part

You're probably keenly aware of your child's temperament. From the time he was a baby, you saw signs of whether he was outgoing and eager for change and adventure or shy and reserved, more comfortable with the familiar. The best way to discipline your child depends a great deal on that temperament of his. If he's rambunctious and loud and very confident, for example, he may need a bit more firm directive when it's time to leave the park than his shy, sensitive sibling who tears up when there's a hint of impatience in your voice.

I love my son, but we're very different. I am very active and on-the-go, but he is happy to sit and play with toys or look at books. Does this mean we'll have more trouble getting along?

"No. What matters most for building a strong relationship with your child is your ability to value him for who he is, as a separate being from you. This is a challenge for parents whether they are similar to or quite different from their child. There is simply no perfect 'fit.'

"The good news is that you have taken the most important first step—being aware of and respecting your differences. This will help you encourage your child's natural interests as well as broaden his experiences by engaging in the activities he enjoys while at the same time finding ways he, too, can enjoy movement. For example, together you can act out the story you are reading. If he likes music, encourage him to get up and dance with you. Bring his favorite stuffed animals or action figures to the playground and make pretend games with his 'friends' that involve exploring the equipment.

"The key is not to force him, but to find ways to build more movement into activities he already enjoys. And keep in mind that you can learn a thing or two from your child, too! He can help you slow down and smell the roses."
—*Claire Lerner, LCSW, child development specialist at ZERO TO THREE*

Your own temperament or personality plays a large role in your overall discipline style, too, of course. You'll be more prone to that firm directive if you're a bit impatient, for example. In a 1997 study at the University of Iowa, Grazyna Kochanska and colleagues studied personalities of mothers and concluded that mothers who were negative and disagreeable were more power assertive in their parenting and less nurturant. Their children were less attached to them and had more behavioral problems than children of other mothers.

27

What personality factors affect what style components isn't always obvious. In a 1997 study at the Department of Psychiatry and Human Genetics at Medical College of Virginia, Kenneth S. Kendler and colleagues concluded: "Parenting is a complex, multi-determined set of behaviors that is influenced by parental personality, psychopathology, values, and marital quality, and by a range of child characteristics." The researchers determined, for example, that a parent's warmth is strongly influenced by parental and childhood temperament, whereas a parent's protectiveness and authoritarianism are more heavily influenced by "sociological" factors such as level of education and religious affiliation.

WEB TALK: ZERO TO THREE is a nonprofit organization promoting the development of young children and developmentally appropriate parenting. For articles on issues from adoption to discipline to violence in the home, visit:

www.zerotothree.com

More subtle personality traits than being generally disagreeable, of course, will affect how you relate to your child. Think about likes and dislikes, or your own behavioral tendencies. If you love to read, for example, you may use reading with your child as a way to calm down together, a way to share time at night, and a way to explore new ideas. If you're a very orderly, neat person, you may keep your child to more of a schedule and routine than a parent who likes to fly by the seat of her pants.

The trick is to recognize how your temperament is affecting your style, and to make sure that it's having a positive rather than negative effect on your discipline style. Routine is a good thing, for example; but if you were to require that your baby feed on a strict schedule or that your grade-schooler not finish the last page of his newest library book because the clock says it's time to pick out his clothes for the morning, then the influence of your tendencies might not be in his best interest. You don't need to overhaul your personality, but you can monitor its effect on your parenting style.

Experts Weigh In

Looking at the array of advice and approaches to discipline, it's hard to imagine that there's ever been much consensus. But until relatively recently, a strict, authoritarian discipline style reigned.

Children were seen and not heard in the 1800s (and in some families to this day, of course). A leading pediatrician in 1894, Luther Emmett Holt, president of the American Pediatric Society and author of *The Care and Feeding of Children,* advised parents to keep their babies on firm schedules, and to refrain from cuddling or playing with them. He warned against picking them up when they cried, and he recommended bottle feeding, because he believed it to be most hygienic. John Broadus Watson, based on his work with laboratory rats, suggested that children could be controlled with conditioning. In his 1928 book *Psychological Care of Infants and Children,* he warned against cuddling and kissing children. (It was okay to shake hands with them in the morning, though, he said.) These "don't spoil" approaches were embraced by parents for well over a century, before the pendulum began to swing.

Arnold Gesell, author of the 1943 book *Infant and Child in the Culture of Today,* introduced an appreciation of the importance of child development, outlining the way in which child behavior develops in a very consistent way. The more parents and other caregivers understand these patterns and developmental milestones, he believed, the better they are able to discipline children. (Gesell's ideas are still vibrantly at work today in the Gesell Institute in New Haven.)

GET PSYCHED

"There are many ways to measure success; not the least of which is the way your child describes you when talking to a friend."
–Unknown

In his 1946 classic (still selling today) *The Common Sense Book of Baby and Child Care,* Benjamin Spock told parents, "Trust yourself. You know more than you think you do." He offered a child-centered approach; at the same time he stressed that children are conflicted and need limits. Spock spread the word about characteristic behaviors in children from birth through adulthood and encouraged parents to support and encourage their children every step of the way.

Other recent contributors to more child-centered parenting styles include Bruno Bettelheim, a developmental psychologist and author of *The Informed Heart* (1960), and T. Berry Brazelton, author of *Infants and Mothers* (1969), who introduced "learning by loving and listening," an approach that stresses abundant parent/child interaction. Other child-centered experts include Penelope Leach (*Your Baby and Child,* 1977) and Stanley Greenspan (*The Growth of the Mind and the Endangered Origins of Intelligence,* 1997). All of these parenting experts have profoundly affected the way we discipline children today.

Many, many other experts specialize in discipline today, and you'll hear from a number of them—particularly loving discipline experts—in this book. Of course, although loving discipline approaches are popular today, there's no across-the-board expert (or parental) consensus. In fact, you'll find less consensus on the right way to parent now than in the past. Loving discipline's major critics, it seems, would be those who still advocate strict, authoritarian discipline, such as James Dobson, a popular right-wing Christian minister, and John Rosemond, who calls for a return to a romanticized, punitive parenting style of yesteryear.

Like styles of dress and music, parenting styles have changed. And like styles of dress and music, today seems an era of options. You'll find experts who suggest rewards and punishments and those who find them counterproductive. You'll run across experts who recommend time-outs as a gentle discipline and those who view them as cruel. Some experts will advise you to explain what's up to your kids, whereas others will tell you to lay down the law, sans the talk.

Keep in mind that although there's plenty of solid research about parenting, there's also an abundance of questionable (and harmful) advice. Carefully consider the advice you hear. No, someone doesn't need a Ph.D. after her name to have something worthwhile to contribute; in fact, some of the most helpful suggestions come from other parents. But in our culture, the media often features advice from people who have quick fixes, extreme approaches, and attention-grabbing personalities. Listen carefully to the underlying messages. If you're looking for advice in line with loving discipline, ask yourself whether the person is showing respect for the child. And evaluate whether the advice he or she gives is in the long-term best interest of the child before you use it with your family.

(Re)Defining Your Own Style

Whether you've punted at parenting or spent your pregnancy and parenting years poring over how-to parenting books, you already have a discipline style. The challenge—and opportunity—lies in evaluating that style to make sure it's working for you and your child, now and as he grows and matures. (In fact, it's especially important to adapt your discipline techniques to your child's changing needs.) When you find an approach that works, parenting is a joy.

31

GET PSYCHED

"Parenting isn't as much about doing things to children as it's about parental self control. In other words, if you're having problems with your child's behavior, don't leap to blame your child. Look first at how you can improve your own behavior and attitudes."—*Rod Wallace Kennedy, Ph.D., author of* The Encouraging Parent

You may find the approach that's best for you by wholeheartedly adopting a philosophy you read about. Or you may be comfortable with some aspects of one style and uncomfortable with other aspects of it. You may feel the need to tailor your style to your own child, who is very spirited or very sensitive, for example. Certain characteristics of discipline may even be defined by your community or by your church.

As you learn about different styles, choose what works for you. Our exploration of styles isn't meant to be prescriptive. For example, if you like the ideas you read about Attachment Parenting but have chosen not to breastfeed (which is one of its principles), you can still bond with your baby, carry her, and sleep with her. Or you can just keep in mind how important it is for you to be sensitive to her cues. Or perhaps you're breastfeeding and carrying her, but you'd rather not sleep with her. Maybe you're excited about the cooperative problem-solving ideas you come across, but your grade-schooler nixes them because he hates to sit down and work things out. So you decide to use the technique by writing notes back and forth to each other rather than scheduling a sit-down.

So take ideas and customize them for your family. You don't have to embrace every single tenet of a parenting approach to put it to work for you. You will, however, want to make sure that the ideas underlying the approach you choose are in keeping with your parenting philosophy and your goals for your child. Is it a punitive technique designed to teach obedience, for example, or is it a loving technique designed to guide your child?

Also keep in mind that your choice as a parent isn't between authoritarian firmness and indulgent or neglectful permissiveness. At times it may feel as if you're being judged according to your child's behavior, and the verdict is coming down in terms of whether you've been punitive enough. If a parent is doing a good job disciplining the child, the unwritten rule goes, then the child is well behaved. If the child is misbehaving, the parent has some discipline work (often in the form of punishment) to do. Problem is, this kind of approach, although common, is aimed only at immediate behavior and compliance. And, according to those who advocate a loving discipline approach, *that's not really what discipline is all about.* What it should be about, if we have the best interests of our children at heart, is helping them grow and reach their full potential.

So when you're designing your own style, don't let yourself be pressured by others' expectations for your child's behavior. Take what you know about discipline, what you understand about your child and your goals for him, and tailor your style to meet your and his needs.

Remember, too, that a style needn't include a prescribed answer to every situation. In fact, often there is no "quick fix." A loving discipline style, as you'll see, is about developing a mutually respectful relationship with your child and teaching and guiding him to learn what he needs to know. After you understand the underlying premise, you may find tips and suggestions from loving discipline experts interesting and effective, but you won't need to rely on them, or any "scripts," for daily answers.

Most parents want to be informed, and they realize that we need to learn the best way to parent much the way we need to learn to read or write or cook or play soccer. We learn from experts, we learn from other parents, and we learn from practice.

When you need inspiration or clarity, reread parenting philosophies that support your approach. And when you're stumped, refer to the underlying ideas or specific examples from approaches that have appealed to you. (Try a Positive Discipline technique for dealing with bedtime, for example, or a P.E.T. method of communicating in the midst of a head-to-head disagreement.) Day by day, you'll define and refine your own style.

What You Can Do

All this introspection about how you parent may leave you feeling a bit self-conscious, but it can actually be fun to try to identify what makes you tick as a parent. Besides, it's a good way to become *mindful* and start to make *conscious* decisions about what you want your parenting style to be (and not be). That will benefit both you and your child.

☐ Think about your inner parent as described by Dan Kindlon. Is it a good inner parent that you try to copy, or a bad inner parent that you try to avoid modeling? See if you can recognize his or her influence on you and your parenting style.

☐ Note any messages you've carried with you from the way you were parented. Do you tell your children, "Anything worth doing is worth doing right," for example? Do you still believe that? Think about which messages you want to keep and pass down and which you're ready to replace.

☐ Describe your parenting style, as you perceive it, to your partner. Get feedback. Are your styles similar? Try to come up with compromises where they differ.

☐ The next time you are stressed, ask yourself how that might be affecting your relationship with your child. Explain to your child, when appropriate, that you are upset. Try not to let it influence the way you perceive him.

☐ Talk with your parent(s) about the discipline styles with which they were raised. What do they think about them today? Do they think their parents' style influenced their style in raising you?

☐ Describe the ideal parent. Having a clear picture in your mind (or on paper) of what it means to parent well will help you fashion your discipline style.

☐ Watch and listen to your child as he pretend plays with his stuffed animals or action figures. What kind of parent does he pretend to be?

☐ When you run across a parenting expert whose ideas appeal to you, look for more of her or his work. When a philosophy really clicks for you, keep the author on hand for inspiration.

The Classic Discipline Continuum

There may be as many discipline styles as there are parents. In an effort to get a handle on similarities and differences and understand what works and what doesn't, researchers have categorized and named predominant styles according to common techniques and ideology. It's interesting—and helpful—for parents to look at the array of discipline approaches; it clarifies our role as parents and helps us determine whether our own discipline strategies are a good fit with our goals for our children.

You've likely heard the words *authoritarian, permissive,* and *authoritative* bantered about in the discipline arena. This is the classic categorization of parenting styles, presented in the 1960s and 1970s by researcher Diana Baumrind at the Institute of Human Behavior, University of California, Berkeley. For the sake of argument—and ease of understanding—Baumrind's styles are often viewed on a continuum or a scale. At one end we have the strictly authoritarian parent, and at the other the very permissive one.

This chapter covers both ends of the continuum to give you an idea of the range of styles. While most parents' overall approach can be placed somewhere along this continuum, it's easy for one parent to run the gamut of possibilities in the course of one day (letting little Lindsey pig out on chips late in the afternoon, then sending her to her room for not cleaning her plate at dinner), defying categorization.

As you read about these styles, think of the continuum or scale in terms of limits and love, control and mutual respect, because it's how you mix these ingredients that moves you from one end to the other. Authoritarian parents tip the scale in favor of control and limits, whereas lenient parents crash down on the love side of the scale at the expense of any structure whatsoever. Sitting someplace near the middle, not bouncing back and forth but incorporating both love and limits at the same time, is our third category, the authoritative parent. By the way, although some loving discipline experts remove themselves from the continuum altogether, within this framework most align themselves most closely with an authoritative approach. You'll see why.

Authoritarian Rule

When somebody declares "What that child needs is some good old-fashioned discipline," they likely have the authoritarian parent in mind—somebody who demands respect, somebody who controls the situation and the child. The authoritarian parent generally gets results—in the short-term anyway. He doesn't have to ask twice, and his children always seem polite and well behaved—whether in the longest checkout line at the supermarket or in the midst of the most tedious adult conversation. ("Seen and not heard" is a product of the approach.) Children aren't given choices or voices in decision making. You won't find the authoritarian parent having a family meeting to solicit the children's input on this year's vacation or routine bedtimes, for example.

Because the goal of the authoritarian is the child's perfect behavior, his discipline techniques are geared to garner obedience. Authoritarians have a negative view of children; many strict authoritarian parents view a child as something to be broken, something that needs to be shown, by punitive means when necessary, how to act and who's the boss.

WEB TALK: For news stories and articles about children's development, health, and education, updated daily to bring parents the latest, freshest take on parenting issues, visit:

www.newsforparents.org

To implement discipline, the authoritarian relies on external forces—such as rewards for being "good" and punishments for being "bad." (Of course, not every parent who relies on rewards and punishments is authoritarian.) Much of the authoritarian's motivation stems from a fear of spoiling the child. The strictest authoritarians are often harsh and swift, with no tolerance for a child's explanations or excuses. Major consequences are doled out, but they aren't necessarily fair or even related to the behavior involved. Authoritarians are often comfortable using guilt, shame, humiliation, and fear as motivators, readily issuing verbal (and sometimes physical) punishments.

"When it comes to discipline," explains Positive Discipline expert Jody McVittie, M.D., "many parents believe that children have to suffer to learn. You can hear it in the phrases they use, like 'you'll pay for this,' and 'he'll suffer the consequences.'"

GET PSYCHED

"It's not possible (or even desirable) to stop to analyze everything you say and do. Yet when time and energy allow, trying to understand your feelings and reactions to the demands of parenting can help you make decisions that will make a positive difference for your child." —*Claire Lerner, LCSW, child development specialist at ZERO to THREE, co-author of* Bringing Up Baby

Like other parents, the authoritarian has the best interests of his child at heart, but unlike permissive or authoritative parents, he isn't concerned with fostering a loving relationship with his child. In fact, many authoritarians believe that a close relationship would be detrimental to the discipline process. Parents and children are primarily viewed as adversaries, and a strict hierarchy is maintained. Speaking about children's perceptions of parents, psychologist James C. Dobson, founder of Focus on the Family, explains in his book *The Strong-Willed Child*, "Like a military general before a battle, they will calculate the potential risk, marshal their forces and attack the enemy with guns blazing. When those nose-to-nose confrontations occur between generations, it is extremely important for the adult to win decisively and confidently. The children have made it clear that they're looking for a fight, and their parents would be wise not to disappoint them!"

Control is obviously a major issue in the authoritarian home. So is order. To keep things in order, rules—lots of them—are rigidly enforced. Authoritarians emphasize that children need structure, and they provide it in abundance.

The authoritarian is long on limits, then, and short on *demonstrating* love. Authoritarian parents love their children as much as any other parents. In fact, you'll often hear them say "I'm doing this because I love you," or "This hurts me more than it hurts you." But when children do experience their authoritarian parents' love, it's often conditional. Children learn that if they play the game right, they'll be loved in return for their good behavior. They don't always know that they're loved regardless.

GET PSYCHED

"There is no single effort more radical in its potential for saving the world than a transformation of the way we raise children."
—*Marianne Williamson, author,* A Return to Love

40

The authoritarian style has longevity. In fact, the authoritarian approach predominated in agrarian-industrial societies throughout much of Western history—until the pendulum began its swing to the opposite, permissive style in the 1940s and 1950s. Parenting expert Sue Dinwiddie explains, "Authoritarian parenting is effective in societies experiencing little change and accepting one way to do things. A master teacher (often the parent) instructs the child on each act (such as sowing the seeds and weeding the fields). The child learns by imitating the expert."

Many prominent parenting experts (like Luther Emmet Holt and John B. Watson) have historically supported the approach, too. And, despite the pendulum swing, there are still plenty of authoritarian advocates today. Parents and parenting experts who fear a "breakdown of the family" or point to the folly of permissiveness often call for a revitalization of authoritarian discipline techniques.

Dr. Dobson, for example, recommends that parents teach children to be subservient to authority as soon as possible—with punitive measures, including spanking, if necessary.

In fact, many conservative religious groups today support authoritarian rule, advising parents that they should not be afraid to exercise their authority, to punish children, to exert control. The prevailing thought behind many of these approaches is that it's a parent's responsibility to teach a child to obey, and that in many instances the child "needs" or even "wants" to be punished for his wrongdoings. Children, most authoritarians would agree, require strict, controlling limits to feel secure, to learn obedience, and to respect the established chain of authority. We need this approach, its advocates assert, to prevent chaos in our homes and in our culture.

What if my discipline style doesn't match my ex-partner's?

In every family there are times when parents don't agree about a discipline decision. However, these differences can be especially troublesome when parents have a strained relationship. Ideally, former partners will work together to co-parent their children peacefully and respectfully. Here are some suggestions:

- Set clear limits and expectations in your home. Although you cannot post the house rules in your former partner's house, you can provide appropriate, loving limits and guidance to help your children know what to expect when they're with you. This will promote positive behaviors and help them feel secure.

- Avoid communication through your children. Don't put your children in the middle of your differences with your former partner by sending messages through them.

- Avoid negative remarks. Bad-mouthing your children's other parent can hurt the family, so choose your words carefully.

- Pick your battles. Focus on the issues that are most important to you and your children and ignore minor differences.

- Seek additional support. If you and your former partner are experiencing significant differences, consider enrolling in a parenting class or seeking professional counseling to address your challenges. If you have concerns about your former partner's ability to adequately care for your children, or you need additional support, seek professional guidance. Your family physician can provide referrals.—*Debbie Glasser, Ph.D., licensed clinical psychologist and director of Family Support Services for the Mailman Center for Child Development at Nova Southeastern University*

Despite the staunchness of its advocates, many parenting experts believe that authoritarian rule in the home may well have seen its heyday. As Dinwiddie explains, "This style—with its focus on one correct way (the parent's way) of doing things—mismatches a rapidly changing society that values choice and innovation. Rebellion often results from strict punishment. Not all authoritarian parents spank their children, but those who do model violence as a solution to problems—contradictory behavior in a society which claims to value peaceful solutions. And children raised to follow the "expert" easily copy anyone, including undesirable peers." Perhaps most importantly, parenting research has confirmed and repeatedly underlined the detrimental effects of an authoritarian style on children, as you'll see in Chapter 5.

When a 2-year-old toddles into a room and dumps a lovely vase of flowers on the floor, the strict authoritarian parent might tell her she's a "bad girl," yell at her as he puts her firmly in her playpen, and/or give her a swat on the bottom to ensure she doesn't do it again. When an 8-year-old playing in the yard tosses a softball through the living room window, the authoritarian parent might berate her about how clumsy she is, ground her for a week, and/or take her out of Little League. The teen of a strictly authoritarian parent, home late again with the car, might find herself barred from seeing her new boyfriend, declared irresponsible beyond repair, and stripped of her wheels for the duration of her senior year.

Of course, even parents who use other methods most of the time occasionally fall into authoritarian discipline territory.

GET PSYCHED

"I would never advise you never to yell at a child or never to show your anger. That would be unnatural. We all need to vent our feelings, and children have to learn to cope with that reality. However, if you always—or even mostly—react by becoming angry and doling out punishment when your kids do something you don't want them to do, it will be more difficult for them to become independent, thinking children."—*Myrna Shure, Ph.D., author of* Thinking Parent, Thinking Child

When you "put your foot down" as a parent in the heat of the moment, you're likely stepping onto authoritarian turf. It's easy to do when you're at your wit's end.

Many parenting experts point out that one of the problems with authoritarian discipline is that a parent's job isn't simply to make a child behave; it's to teach a child the attributes that we'd like her to learn before adulthood. Getting back to our definition of discipline as guidance, you can't impose these punitively. And you can't monitor behavior forever.

Sure, if a child is afraid of you she'll likely do what you say. But what will she do when you're not around? And do you want your child to do the right thing because she's afraid of you, or do you want her to have a moral compass of her own? Critics point out that an authoritarian approach forces a child to conform; it does not encourage her to do what *she* thinks is right, and it fosters resistance and/or apathy. "After all," the child reflects, "why does it matter what I think?"

If a parent's focus is on retribution for past behaviors, how will a child learn to make decisions about her future? And finally, but perhaps most importantly, because authoritarian discipline does nothing to foster a sense of belonging or connectedness, it falls short of providing what the child most needs to grow—a strong, loving relationship with her parents.

Permissive—The Nondiscipline Style

In the authoritarian household, the parent is in control. In the overly permissive home, the issue of control is still front and center, but the child runs the show. A parent might be overly permissive for several reasons. There are, in fact, further classifications of permissive parenting styles for each reason.

Listen to Your Instincts

Single mom Cheryl Erwin, of Reno, Nevada, was taught by her church that when her child willfully misbehaved he should be spanked. So when her son Philip was a spunky 3-year-old, she spanked him. Once. Half an hour later, Cheryl found Philip in his room, hitting himself and saying, "I hate myself. I'm a bad person." It was at that point, Cheryl says, that she began searching for a different way to parent her son. "This isn't what I want my son to learn," she told herself. "While taking Positive Discipline classes, I discovered that my child's defiance was developmentally appropriate, and I learned how to deal with it in a productive way. I changed my parenting style. It takes some confidence to use a long-term process rather than a quick fix, but the stakes are high. Philip—now a wonderful 21-year-old studying Spanish and economics—was well worth it."

Permissiveness via Indifference The indifferent parent allows his child to do whatever she pleases because he's unwilling or unable to meet his parenting responsibilities. He is psychologically unavailable to the child, so establishing a close bond is not a priority for him. He may also respond to parenting and to his child's needs as an inconvenience; by avoiding the parenting role, he avoids the inconvenience as much as possible.

An indifferent parent isn't interested in the needs, development, or emotions of the child; so when the child makes a demand, he takes none of these into account. The goal of the indifferent parent is to terminate the child's demands as easily and quickly as possible. And so the parent may initially establish few, if any, rules or guidelines, then give in easily to protests and/or avoid conflicts and decision making altogether.

We've all run across parents like this, although they're few and far between. This is the parent who ignores his child as she demolishes the pediatrician's waiting room. He's the parent who defines no curfew, looks the other way when his child is caught cheating, and barely acknowledges his child's efforts on the Little League field. The child of an indifferent parent, of course, doesn't fare well. Neglect is not a viable discipline technique; there is not even an effort to teach.

Permissiveness via Indulgence The other permissive style is what researchers call "indulgent-permissive." Children whose parents use this style also have few restrictions, rules, or expectations, and their parents are abundantly tolerant of their impulses. These permissive parents differ in motivation, however. Many were raised by authoritarian parents and are determined not to repeat their stifling mistakes.

Sue Dinwiddie suggests that two other influences helped push the pendulum from authoritarian to permissive styles. One was a backlash against the horrors of populations blindly following totalitarian regimes. The other was the influence of Sigmund Freud's theories of psychoanalysis, which led to a concern that parents not inhibit their children in any way. Whatever the shaping influences, most indulgently permissive parents value the ideals of freedom and nonconformity. And most, unlike indifferent parents, are acting out of genuine love for their children and a desire to make them happy.

Also unlike the authoritarian or indifferent parent, the permissive parent's relationship with his child is a close one. He freely demonstrates his love with affection, time, and attention. Sometimes, however—in trying to be his child's friend rather than parent, for example—he can come up short when the child needs guidance. He might give in easily and often, even on crucial decisions, in the name of understanding and empathy. He may allow a child to make decisions she's not capable of making, such as what time to toddle off to bed, or how much television to watch after school. The child in a permissive household rarely has any chores to do. She may feel that she's loved, but being loved, she believes, means being protected, taken care of, and granted every wish. And many permissive parents are okay with that.

This desire to keep children perfectly happy often leads to a lack of structure in the permissive household. In fact, according to findings by the National Association for the Education of Young Children, the permissive parent views structure—rules, schedules, standards, and expectations—as challenges to the child's individuality and freedom. The problem is, without any framework, a child often feels insecure; she doesn't know what to expect or what, if anything, is expected of her. She's likely to be confused rather than pleased by the lack of rules and expectations in her life. There's no good and bad in terms of her behavior, she has no responsibility, and she isn't challenged to do her best or even think about things in terms of right and wrong. In a nutshell, she flounders.

In an effort to make childhood as painless and enjoyable as possible, permissive parents often try to protect their children not only from rules and regulations, but from emotional suffering of any kind. "Parents have been led to believe that letting their

> **GET PSYCHED**
>
> "No research has ever suggested that children fare better when their parents are aloof than when they are accepting, when their parents are lenient rather than firm, or when their parents are psychologically controlling rather than supportive of their psychological autonomy."
> —Laurence Steinberg, Ph.D., author of The 10 Basic Principles of Good Parenting

children experience emotions such as frustration, anger, and sadness will harm them," explains Jim Taylor, Ph.D., author of *Positive Pushing.* "Based on this belief, parents have felt the need to protect their children from feeling bad. They rationalize failure, distract children from experiencing emotions deeply, try to placate negative emotions, and create artificial positive emotions."

Indulgent-permissive parents are loving parents, but they're not competent parents. And as you'll see in Chapter 5, research shows that their children don't usually do well in the long run. With good intentions and loving hearts, these parents shower their children with affection, but they don't consider that the child's long-term growth requires much more than that.

Research shows that children need an environment in which they have ample opportunity to learn and grow from successes *and* mistakes. Because the child of an indulgent-permissive parent never gets to try and fail (or succeed), she never has the satisfaction of learning to be a competent, independent little tike, big teen, or adult. Learning to face adversity, to take responsibility, and to make choices are important tasks of childhood. In addition, without any responsibility, a child lacks not only self-discipline but also a sense of being valued. So permissive discipline is an oxymoron. The permissive parent isn't guiding or teaching a child, he's simply watching over her.

When the toddler in our earlier scenario dumps the vase full of flowers on the floor, the overly permissive parent may delight in her playfulness and encourage her as she starts pulling apart flower petals or playing in the spilt water. Or he may quickly scoop the toddler up and console her, concerned that she might become frightened or upset by the mishap. As the water soaks into the carpet, he might run to get his toddler a consolation cookie.

The permissive parent of the 8-year-old window-shattering home run hitter just thanks God that she didn't get hurt. He hugs her and tells her not to worry about a thing, that it was just an accident and that he'll have the window repaired in no time, no problem. There was no rule about ball playing in the yard, and she's too little to understand about glass windows and softballs not being a great match.

If the overly permissive parent is still up when his teen comes home late, he's likely not to mention the time at all. He may simply say "Good night, sweetheart" or "I was so worried about you, but silly me, you're just fine!" or, seeing the worried look on her face, he might console her—"You must have been having a good time. I'm so glad. Now don't worry about it. Is there any gas left in the car, or do I need to get some on my way to work in the morning?"

Authoritative Style

It's easy to see discipline in black and white: strict or permissive, punitive or lax. Given those choices, it's no wonder parents have a hard time deciding how to discipline their children. And it's no wonder some waffle back and forth.

Since her initial research, many experts have confirmed what Baumrind published about parenting styles: that children raised at neither end of the continuum but by an approach she called "authoritative" not only had much better relationships with their

49

parents, they fared much better in the long run than other children, too. Kids of authoritative parents have better social skills than kids raised by permissive or authoritarian parents, and they're more confident, content, secure, and self-disciplined.

Experts have tweaked the definition of the term *authoritative,* giving the approach or others like it names such as *informed permissiveness* and *democratic discipline,* and founded new styles within the basic guidelines of this approach. And like all styles, it's still controversial. Because it's a democratic style, and because it requires building a mutually respectful relationship between parent and child, for example, it's no surprise that it's often criticized by authoritarians for being too lenient. On the other hand, parents with a more indulgent style bristle at the fact that parents of this approach frequently set parameters for a child's choices and maintain a firm consistency.

But today a large majority of parenting experts, with more than a decade of solid research to back them up, agree that an authoritative approach is the most successful discipline style for raising children.

Love and Limits Many of today's loving discipline styles are built on a few key components of authoritative discipline. Authoritative parents set clear limits and standards for behavior. They provide structure for the purpose of supporting and encouraging their children, not controlling them. In the authoritative home, there is freedom, but within boundaries. There are choices, but they are not unlimited, and there is order. The child feels safe choosing because she has parameters. She must choose in ways that are respectful to others, for example, while taking responsibility for her actions. Rules are set in a positive way, for everyone's benefit, and in a way that balances the rights of the child with the rights of the parents and others.

Parents who discipline authoritatively try to be consistent and at the same time flexible. Some rules are negotiable, some aren't. (Your preschooler may never play in the street, but maybe she can skip her nap to play with Grandma who's visiting today.)

Authoritative parents make reasonable demands (based on their knowledge of their children's developmental stages, for example), and they make them firmly, consistently, and kindly. In Baumrind's words, the authoritative style is a "warm, engaged, rational parent-child relationship." Experts who talk about the authoritative style today often use the catchphrase "with love and limits." But it's not a balancing act, warns Positive Discipline expert Jody McVittie, M.D. "It's not a dance back and forth— some strictness, some love, some kindness, then some firmness. It's using them both at the same time, setting limits kindly.

GET PSYCHED

"Assertive-democratic parenting is the best for today's fast-changing information age where choice is constant and there is no longer just one 'right way.' Children raised by this style learn to accept responsibility, make wiser choices, cope with change, and are better equipped to succeed in a work-force which relies on cooperative problem solving."—*Sue Dinwiddie, author of* Let Me Think! Activities to Develop Problem-Solving Abilities in Young Children

Open, Respectful Communication   A strong relationship with the child, built on two-way communication, is the basis of the authoritative approach. Authoritative parents listen to their children empathetically, sharing reasons and eliciting input. They encourage their children to acknowledge and express their feelings, and they consider their point of view when making decisions. At the same time, authoritative parents express their own point of view, too. They use open communication, rather than lectures, directives, and punitive measures, to discipline and teach. By developing a warm, respectful relationship with their children, authoritative parents foster trust and cooperation in return. From that foundation of trust and support, the child can flourish.

Child's Growth So authoritative parents strive to discipline their children, in the purest sense of the word, as teachers. They are assertive and confident with their children, but not controlling or restrictive. They give children choices whenever possible so that they may learn from their decisions, and they allow fair consequences to occur, within a supportive framework.

Within this framework, children raised by authoritative parents can solve problems, deal with conflict, and grow. Authoritative parents strive to teach specific skills such as listening and attributes such as empathy and conscientiousness. At the same time, authoritative parents know that pampering or spoiling their children—protecting them from the ups and downs of daily life, relieving them of responsibility—is detrimental. What's crucial for the child is the freedom to experience life and make decisions, to take responsibility and to deal with problems—all within the environment of parental love, encouragement, empathy, and support.

So how do those children we met earlier fare in the authoritative home? Well, on a good day, an authoritative parent wouldn't *put* a vase of flowers where a 2-year-old—programmed to explore—would spot it. If he does, he'll quickly realize his mistake and use a technique like distraction to avoid the mess.

The 8-year-old ballplayer will be met with concern and empathy. The authoritative parent will make sure first of all that the child isn't physically hurt or emotionally shaken. He'll explore with his child how she feels about her mistake and talk about the consequences with her. Together they may decide that Slugger will have to do some extra chores this weekend to help earn some money to pay for the new glass, and maybe she won't be able to play ball in the yard anymore. Whatever is decided, it won't be punitive, and it'll make sense. Regardless, the parent doesn't say "I told you so," explode in anger, or belittle the child. The child already feels bad about her mistake, and rubbing it in does nothing to help her learn the lesson.

Why do children misbehave?

- The child is attempting to fill a legitimate need. Obvious needs are for food, clothing, shelter, safety, and love. Additional needs are for physical closeness, individual attention, a stimulating but predictable environment, opportunities to play, freedom to make choices, and respect from others.

- The child lacks information. The word *discipline* comes from a Latin word meaning "to teach." Children have much to learn about our complex world. They must learn that windows are breakable, that teeth can get cavities, and that busy streets are dangerous. Even teenagers, sophisticated as they may appear to be, still have much to learn so they can make wise choices.

- The child is suffering from stress or unhealed trauma. When children feel stressed, frightened, frustrated, angry, jealous, confused, or insecure, they often become obnoxious, uncooperative, or even violent. Sometimes there is no immediate cause for a child's painful feelings. The child may be suffering from earlier, unhealed trauma (such as a difficult birth, hospitalization, a death in the family, or abuse). Children with traumatic experiences such as these often harbor pent-up feelings of rage or terror, which can lead to behavior problems.—*Aletha Solter, Ph.D., developmental psychologist and founder of the Aware Parenting Institute*

you're not alone

Sometimes just paying attention to the fact that you're using a discipline style puts you on the right track. After taking a class in Positive Discipline strategies, one mother said, "I realized that I needed to change my behavior if I wanted my kids to change theirs. ... I realized I was trying to micromanage the life of a 17-year-old and was also confusing what I needed to know with what I wanted to know. It was very difficult at first to back off. ... It was worth the effort, though, because the relationship soon improved, and after several weeks my daughter began to volunteer information about what was going on in her life that she wouldn't have told me before. Now when there is a conflict between my children and myself, I try to remember to stop before I react and evaluate how I am handling the situation. I look for the most positive approach, and I try to act rather than react."

The authoritative parent is probably waiting up for the late teen, who is likely sorry to have worried her parents. He'll listen to her reason for being late and talk with her about how the right to drive the car means accepting the responsibility to be back on time and to return it with at least as much gas as you found in it. Together they might make an agreement about what will happen if there's a next time. If this *is* that "next time," then he'll empathize about the child's loss of privilege, but firmly adhere to it.

Many successful parenting approaches fall within the parameters of authoritative discipline. The next chapter discusses a handful of them.

Are You Style Savvy?

Take this quiz and find out.

Choose the parenting style shown in each example.

AUTHORITARIAN   AUTHORITATIVE   PERMISSIVE

☐ ☐ ☐ 1. Diedre's mother tells the toddler that she may not have a cookie before dinner. She offers Diedre the choice of carrot or celery sticks instead.

☐ ☐ ☐ 2. Nora swats her brother over the head with her schoolbook when he tells her she's too dumb to understand world history. Dad cancels Nora's upcoming sleepover.

☐ ☐ ☐ 3. Daniel screams "I hate you!" when Mom tells him he can't ride his bike without a helmet. Mom washes the preschooler's mouth out with soap.

☐ ☐ ☐ 4. Toddler Phillip bangs into Grandma's end table, upsetting the candy dish onto the carpet. Dad tells him, "Don't worry kiddo, Grandma will get that with her vacuum."

☐ ☐ ☐ 5. Lactose-intolerant Tara is 10 and forgot to bring her juice thermos to school—for the third time this week. Because they only serve milk with school lunches, Mom swings by the school with Tara's thermos, even though that means she'll be late for work.

AUTHORITARIAN
AUTHORITATIVE
PERMISSIVE

☐ ☐ ☐ 6. Sophie's mother is fashion-conscious and has fun choosing outfits for her grade-schooler. Every night, while Sophie sleeps, her mom chooses the next day's outfit—complete with accessories—for her.

☐ ☐ ☐ 7. Nell cries the minute Mom closes her bedroom door at night. Mom comes back in, sits on the bed, and asks the toddler what's wrong. Mom doesn't let Nell get up and watch *Late Night* with her, but she retrieves a flashlight for Nell to keep next to her bed. Then she gives her a little backrub and leaves the bedroom door open when she leaves, assuring her that she'll be back to check on her in a few minutes.

☐ ☐ ☐ 8. Despite their agreement about refueling, Raven brings the car home without any gas again, and Dad has to get up earlier to fill up in the midst of rush hour on his way to a morning appointment. Dad tells Raven she may not borrow the car for the next two weeks.

☐ ☐ ☐ 9. Max forgets to bring his snack plate to the kitchen at bedtime. In the morning, his bedroom carpet is crawling with ants. Mom tells him he must vacuum the house and wash the dishes for a week.

AUTHORITARIAN
AUTHORITATIVE
PERMISSIVE

☐   ☐   ☐   10. Rubin swears repeatedly at the playground when he can't nail a skateboard move. Mom turns to the elderly couple next to her on the bench and explains, "He's trying so hard!"

Answers: 1. Authoritative, 2. Authoritarian, 3. Authoritarian, 4. Permissive, 5. Permissive, 6. Authoritarian, 7. Authoritative, 8. Authoritative, 9. Authoritarian, 10. Permissive

What You Can Do

After you're aware of these classic discipline groupings, it's easy to see them at work all around you. Thinking about them—and how you feel about them—can help you decide what works best for your family.

☐ Think about where you fall on the discipline spectrum. You don't need to classify yourself with a term, but it's likely you have a pretty good idea whether you're to the left, right, or dead center when it comes to disciplining with love and limits. How would you have handled the toddler, grade-schooler, and teen mentioned previously?

☐ Talk with your parents about their discipline styles. What techniques did they use and did they find them effective? How did these techniques align with their long-term goals for you? What would they change if they could relive their early parenting years?

☐ When you attend daycare meetings or parent/teacher conferences, find out what discipline styles and techniques are being used. Ideally, your child will meet with consistent approaches at home and at daycare or school.

☐ Talk with all your child's caregivers about discipline. If you're not comfortable with rewards, you won't want your sister or babysitter doling out cookies to your toddler for picking up her toys.

☐ Put yourself in your child's position. Listen to what you say to her and how you say it. What would she say your discipline style is?

☐ When you watch television or movies or read a book that depicts parents and children interacting, see whether you can spot particular parenting styles.

☐ When you hear or read parenting advice (in books or the newspaper, from friends or relatives, for example), try to put it in context of parenting styles. If the advice is a good fit with your style, you may want to try it out. If not, don't feel obligated.

☐ Describe the perfect parent. What changes might you make in your discipline style to bring you closer to this ideal?

☐ Draw a line on a piece of paper and write "strict" at one end and "lenient" at the other (or authoritarian and permissive). Now think about the ways you disciplined your child today, and place each incident on the line. It's not important that you always respond to every one of your child's behaviors in a prescribed way, but he needs you to be pretty consistent. When you run the discipline gamut, being a harsh disciplinarian one minute and a lenient (likely feeling guilty) spoiler the next, it's hard for your child to know where he stands.

☐ Does your discipline style change when you're in a good mood or a bad mood? Think about specific instances when a change in style affected your child. What might have been the outcome otherwise?

Loving Discipline Approaches

Our look at the classic continuum showed why so many parents and parenting experts today are looking for discipline techniques with an authoritative style. Children need guidelines and they need love. At the same time. It's almost that simple.

Of course, the minute you decide to parent with that (or any) tenet in mind, myriad circumstances and myriad questions come to mind. How do I convey my love to my child while telling him he absolutely may not ride his bike without a helmet? And if I pick up my baby every time he cries, it's all love and no limits, isn't it? Sometimes your instincts will guide you to good answers (pick up the baby); other times you'll second-guess yourself and try various options until you throw up your hands ("then don't ride your bike!").

We explore some practical, loving techniques in Part 3 of this book, but first let's look at the ideas behind these techniques. Understanding the underlying values will help us better implement the ideas—and it's a great inspiration, motivation, and validation when you find a parenting philosophy that's aligned with your own.

There are many terrific, loving discipline approaches in the authoritative family. This chapter explores five of the most influential discipline schools today: Attachment Parenting, Positive Discipline, Parent Effectiveness Training, Aware Parenting, and Unconditional Parenting. There are others; in fact, new ones seem to pop up every day. Don't be intimidated by the numbers and the variety. Instead, enjoy and benefit from the work that's been done to help you be the parent you want to be. Read what these styles are based on; pick and choose what appeals to you. Test drive ideas. Then come up with your very own customized, loving style.

Attachment Parenting

Attachment theory, as it's called, was first presented by researchers John Bowlby and Mary Ainsworth, who suggested that an infant explores his world best from the secure base provided by an attachment figure, namely Mom. Ainsworth and others tested and expanded upon these ideas. In one 1970 study, for example, she and co-researcher Silvia Bell found that when mothers were in the playroom, their infants would more heartily explore the room and play with toys than they would when Mom left or when a stranger came in. Ainsworth and colleagues further explored the idea of maternal sensitivity to an infant and how this sensitivity might foster the baby's development. In a 1972 study involving mothers' responsiveness to crying, for example, they found that "an infant whose mother's responsiveness helps him to achieve his ends develops confidence in his own ability to control what happens to him."

Attachment theory has been popularized by the work of William Sears, M.D., and Martha Sears, R.N., who coined the term *Attachment Parenting* and followed up with specific Attachment Parenting philosophy and techniques in their parenting books, including *The Baby Book* and *The Attachment Parenting Book*.

Although attachment techniques seem to focus on infancy, advocates suggest that the strong, secure bond established from the get-go carries over into the quality of relationships that a child will have in the future. And many of the methods have expanded to include older children, too. Advocates also point out that the basis of trust built by the parent's sensitivity and responsiveness to the baby's needs forms the basis for loving, effective discipline every step of the way.

The ideals of Attachment Parenting, as outlined by Attachment Parenting International, are as follows:

- Preparation for childbirth. Informed decisions about childbirth and peaceful pregnancy and education regarding childbirth and breastfeeding should all be part of childbirth preparation.
- Emotional responsiveness. When a parent picks up a crying baby, for example, she is doing more than meeting his physical needs; she is demonstrating an understanding of his emotional needs, too.

> **GET PSYCHED**
>
> "While it is true that each baby's potential is genetically predetermined, how close the infant comes to reaching his potential is greatly affected by the responsiveness and the nurturing of his care-giving environment."—*William Sears, M.D., author of* The Baby Book

> **WEB TALK:** The official site of Attachment Parenting International includes information about Attachment Parenting, co-sleeping, and attachment-related news topics:
>
> www.attachmentparenting.org

- Breastfeeding on demand. Baby-led breastfeeding is the ideal way to meet a baby's nutritional needs and his need for contact. (Parents who bottle-feed their babies can still practice Attachment Parenting, however, by holding the baby while feeding, engaging his attention, etc.)

- Baby wearing and nurturing touch. Babies often feel more secure when held close, or put in soft carriers next to the parent's body. This helps meet the baby's need for closeness, stimulation, security, and movement. Infant massage provides an enjoyable opportunity for both parent and baby to have skin-to-skin touch.

- Shared sleeping. Nighttime parenting simply means that it's also important for parents to be responsive to their baby during the night. Safe bed sharing enables a parent to respond to her baby's nighttime needs. She might sleep with the baby next to her, in her bed, or she might keep him close by in a crib that attaches to the side of her bed, for example.

- Avoid frequent and prolonged separations from baby. Because your baby needs your presence, separations interfere with the attachment process. When parents need to be away from their baby, they should be respectful of the impact by providing consistent, loving caregiving and by spending time to lovingly reconnect with the baby when reunited.

- Positive discipline. Positive, nonviolent methods of loving guidance and the use of developmentally appropriate boundaries and limits promote self-control and empathy. The long-range goal of discipline is to teach your child how to make good decisions as he grows, and that's easier to do from the foundation of a strong bond.

"The infant who is the product of Attachment Parenting learns that his needs will be met consistently and predictably.

The child learns to trust. Trust is the basis of authority, and a trusted authority figure disciplines more effectively," explains Sears. Parents who use Attachment Parenting are empathetic to the child's point of view and they understand child development, so that they may view the child's behavior in terms of what's developmentally appropriate.

- Maintain balance in family life. Parents need to take the time for exercise, they need to take quiet time, ensure good nutrition, and seek support systems as needed.

Q&A

Won't this kind of attachment attention spoil my baby?

Parents have been led to believe that the practices that make up Attachment Parenting may spoil the infant and keep him from learning to be independent. Attachment Parenting does not mean overindulgence or inappropriate dependency. The possessive parent or the "hover mother" is one who keeps an infant from doing what he needs to do because of her own needs. This has a detrimental effect on the development of both infant and parent. Attachment differs from dependency. Attachment enhances development; dependency may hinder it. Parents will be happy to know that current research has finally put the spoiling theories on the shelf—to spoil. Infants of the Attachment style of parenting actually turn out to be sensitive children who are much easier to discipline. As one sensitive mother of a well-disciplined child proudly exclaimed, "He's not spoiled, he's perfectly fresh."—*William Sears, M.D., author of* Growing Together, A Parent's Guide to Baby's First Year

For older, school-age children, Attachment Parenting International outlines these eight ideals:

- Understand your child's developmental and cognitive levels. If you understand your child's normal behavior, his temperament, and how he learns best, you can nurture his desire to learn.

- Stay emotionally responsive. Respect and acknowledge your child's feelings. Be empathetic and listen well. Provide a safe environment in which your child can express himself.

- Strive for optimum physical health. Model good nutrition and exercise and provide good health care.

- Maintain a high-touch relationship. Your child still needs your affection.

- Develop and maintain positive sleep routines. Keep in mind that older kids might still like to snuggle. Provide routines for bedtime (such as reading and talking together).

- Be present and available for the child. He still needs your presence to feel safe and secure and cared for. Provide supervision as needed.

- Use positive discipline. Remember that the ultimate goal of discipline is to help your child develop inner self-control and self-discipline.

- Maintain balance in your family life. Value both family time (such as meals and activities together) and individual time with one child or your parenting partner.

Positive Discipline

Positive Discipline, popularized by the work of Jane Nelsen, Ed.D., and colleagues, is based on the teachings of Viennese psychiatrists Alfred Adler and Rudolf Dreikurs. One of the basic principles of the approach is that children are social beings, "hardwired" to connect, and that fostering that connection—with family, school, and the community—encourages good behavior.

In an effort to make the connection, to belong and feel significant, children sometimes adopt mistaken or inappropriate goals as a rationale for misbehavior. "A misbehaving child is trying to tell us 'I don't feel I belong or have significance, and I have a mistaken belief about how to achieve it,'" explains Nelsen. These mistaken goals are as follows:

- **Attention.** The child believes she counts only when she's being noticed.
- **Power.** The child feels she belongs only when she's in control.
- **Revenge.** The child hurts others as a way of striking back when she doesn't feel a sense of belonging.
- **Assumed inadequacy.** The child believes she can't belong and acts helpless and unwilling to try.

When parents understand that the underlying reason for the misbehavior is the child's discouragement, they can help the child find positive ways to feel that he belongs and that he is significant. Ways to do this include encouragement, training, building on strengths, and providing a supportive, loving environment.

WEB TALK: For positive solutions to disciplining children, parents, caregivers, and educators will find plenty of direction at www.positivediscipline.com

Effective discipline, then, helps children feel that they belong and are significant. It's nonpunitive, mutually respectful and encouraging, and effective long-term. It takes into consideration what the child is thinking, feeling, learning, and deciding about himself and his world—and what to do in the future. And it teaches important social and life skills, such as self-discipline, responsibility, concern for others, problem solving, and cooperation.

The Positive Discipline approach lies firmly on authoritative parenting ground, based on firmness with dignity and respect, freedom with order, and choices within. Mistakes are seen as opportunities to learn, and an atmosphere of love and cooperation builds the child/parent relationship.

Positive Discipline in Schools

The concepts and tools of Positive Discipline can also be practiced in classrooms and schools. According to Terry Chadsey, career educator and certified Positive Discipline lead trainer, and Jody McVittie, M.D., certified Positive Discipline lead trainer, the ways the techniques are integrated include the following:

- Making mutual respect and encouragement top priorities in classroom and school communities.
- A focus on solutions rather than punishments to address misbehavior.
- Regular class meetings in which students learn and practice critical life skills as they solve real classroom problems.
- The creation of a community in which every student is respected and contributes to the school community. Academic success for every student depends upon this sense of community.

you're not alone

"My 14-year-old daughter, Shawna, was invited to a birthday party at which the kid's dad was going to be taking them to an R-rated movie. She hasn't been allowed to see R-rated movies, so it was no surprise when I told her she couldn't go. Instead of trying to get her to understand how I felt about it, I tried to understand how *she* felt and to show her empathy. It didn't change the fact that she couldn't go, but she accepted it and cheered up much faster than she normally would have. She even shared with me that she really didn't care about seeing the movie but that she was embarrassed to not be able to do what the other kids could do.

Chadsey and McVittie encourage parents to engage school principals in a discussion about their approach to discipline by asking such questions as these:

- How do students learn and practice problem-solving skills?
- What do school staff believe about inappropriate behavior? How do they respond to inappropriate behavior?
- How does the school help misbehaving students (of any race, gender, or class) rebuild a sense of connection to the school community?
- What kind of discipline data does the school collect? Does the school know if discipline is different based on race, class, or gender?
- What steps is the school actively taking to improve the culture and community for all students?

Parent Effectiveness Training

Parent Effectiveness Training (P.E.T.) is a system—often described as a movement—developed by psychologist Thomas Gordon,

"I told her I remembered kids who couldn't do what the rest of us were doing in school and how I had always felt bad for them. I told her I would try to lighten up about some R-rated movies in the near future, but that it would be irresponsible to let her go to this movie. We both felt that we had communicated well and that we had been heard and understood. What could have been a typical adversarial argument was instead honest communication that, I think, brought us closer together.—*Laura Myers, Mukilteo, Washington*

Ph.D. The basis of the approach is the belief that children don't "misbehave"; they behave in ways that satisfy their needs at that particular time. So the toddler who sits on the sidewalk instead of hurrying along may be fulfilling his need for rest or for exploring the ants in the sidewalk crack. And the teen who wants a tattoo or stays out late may be fulfilling his need for peer approval or his need to show his independence.

Unlike authoritarians, who often get their needs met at the expense of the child, and unlike indulgent-permissive parents, who meet a child's needs at their own expense, P.E.T. strives to meet the needs of both parent and child. It teaches parents to be effective with skills that develop a warm relationship built on mutual love and respect rather than control. The nonpunitive approach is based on the following two-way communication skills that enable parents to positively influence a child's behavior.

Active Listening Like other loving discipline methods, P.E.T. stresses that parents must demonstrate their love to their children—by communicating nonverbally and verbally, by showing empathy, and by active listening. Active listening means tuning in to what a child is feeling, showing acceptance, and then showing real understanding of what the child has said or indicated (active listening can also apply to nonverbal communication).

GET PSYCHED

"Of all the effects of acceptance, none is as important as the inner feeling of the child that he is loved. To accept another 'as he is' is truly an act of love; to feel accepted is to feel loved. And in psychology, we have only begun to realize the tremendous power of feeling loved: It can promote the growth of mind and body, and is probably the most effective therapeutic force we know for repairing both psychological and physical damage."—*Dr. Thomas Gordon, author of* Parent Effectiveness Training

I-Messages This is a nonblameful way of explaining to a child that his behavior is causing a problem for the parent. It consists of three parts. The first is to convey a nonblameful description of the behavior of the child. The second is to state the feeling created by what's happening. The third is to state the concrete, tangible effect of the behavior.

So, for example, instead of telling a child, "Stop making all that noise!" (which is a classic "you-message," as in "You stop ...!") you might tell your child, "I can't hear Aunt Liz on the phone when you bang your drum in this room. I'm worried that I'm missing something important she wants me to know. Or "I feel bad because I'm not giving her the attention I want to give her."

I-messages are more effective than directives at motivating a child to change his behavior, and they are healthier for the parent-child relationship. Ideally, the child will want to change his behavior out of consideration for the parent, and so the method teaches self-discipline and empathy rather than obedience.

"Parents can raise children who are responsible, self-disciplined, and cooperative without relying on the weapon of fear," Gordon explains. "They can learn how to influence children to behave out of genuine consideration for the needs of parents rather than out of fear of punishment or withdrawal of privileges." I-messages give a child the opportunity to take responsibility for his behavior. They also encourage the child to give constructive I-messages to the adult.

No-Lose Conflict Resolution Conflict is a part of life; what's important is not how many conflicts occur in the family, but how they get resolved. This, explains Gordon, "is the most critical factor in determining whether a relationship will be healthy or unhealthy, mutually satisfying or unsatisfying, friendly or unfriendly, deep or shallow, intimate or cold." Because parents get locked into an either/or (authoritative or permissive) approach to discipline, they see their relationship with their children as a power struggle, with parents or kids winning the battle.

Instead, Gordon suggests a "no-lose conflict resolution" technique. This six-step problem-solving session encourages parents and children to cooperatively find mutually agreeable solutions to problems. A child who participates in problem solving is more motivated to carry out the solution, gains skills in problem solving, and has less hostility and more loving feelings toward his parent.

> **WEB TALK:** To learn more about Parent Effectiveness Training (P.E.T.), including the six-step problem-solving session, visit
> www.gordontraining.com

Aware Parenting

Aware Parenting is a philosophy of child rearing developed by Swiss/American developmental psychologist Aletha Solter, Ph.D., author of *The Aware Baby, Helping Young Children Flourish,* and *Tears and Tantrums.* The approach consists of attachment-style parenting, nonpunitive discipline, and tools for helping children heal from stress or trauma.

> **WEB TALK:** For information about raising children lovingly and meeting their needs without rewards or punishments, visit the Aware Parenting website at
> www.awareparenting.com

Here, as outlined by Dr. Solter, are some of the basic tenets of Aware Parenting. Aware parents:

- Fill their children's needs for physical contact without worry about "spoiling" their children. Aware Parenting supports natural childbirth and early bonding, plenty of physical contact, prolonged breastfeeding, prompt responsiveness to crying, and sensitive attunement to a child's needs.

- Accept the entire range of emotions and listen nonjudgmentally to their children's expressions of feelings. They realize that they cannot prevent all sadness, anger, or frustration, and they do not attempt to stop children from releasing painful feelings through crying or raging.

- Offer age-appropriate stimulation and trust children to learn at their own rate and in their own way. They do not try to hurry children on to new stages of development.

- Offer encouragement for learning new skills, but do not judge children's performance with either criticism or evaluative praise.

- Spend time each day giving full attention to their children. During this special, quality time, they observe, listen, respond, and join in their children's play (if invited to do so), but they do not direct the children's activities.

- Protect children from danger, but they do not attempt to prevent all of their children's mistakes, problems, or conflicts.

- Encourage children to be autonomous problem solvers and help only when needed. They do not solve their children's problems for them.

- Set reasonable boundaries and limits, gently guide children toward acceptable behavior, and consider everyone's needs when solving conflicts. They do not control children with bribes, rewards, threats, or punishments of any kind (including spanking, time-out, or artificial consequences).

- Recognize that stress and trauma are primary causes of behavioral and emotional problems.

- Recognize the healing effects of play, laughter, and crying in the context of a loving parent/child relationship.

- Take care of themselves and are honest about their own needs and feelings. They don't sacrifice themselves to the point of becoming resentful.

- Strive to be aware of the ways in which their own childhood pain interferes with their ability to be good parents, and they make conscious efforts to avoid passing on their own hurts to their children.

Unconditional Parenting

Conventional discipline techniques focus on a child's behavior and depend on a parent's control. They're designed to make a child feel loved conditionally, when he does what parents demand or expect.

Unconditional Parenting, on the other hand, focuses on the child rather than the behavior. The approach stresses working *with* the child rather than doing things *to* him. In his book *Unconditional Parenting*, Alfie Kohn underlines the damaging effects of parental control and conditional love. Instead, he suggests parents foster their child's growth with respect and unconditional love.

WEB TALK: To learn more about Alfie Kohn's perspectives on Unconditional Parenting, rewards and praise, competition, and other parenting issues, visit ➚ www.alfiekohn.org

The main tenet of Kohn's approach is that parents need to make sure that their children feel their unconditional love. Think about how your words and actions might be interpreted by your child, he suggests. A child needs to know that—no matter what he does and no matter how he acts—you will never stop loving him. "Give children affection without limit, without reservations, and without excuse. Pay as much attention to them as you can, regardless of mood or circumstance. Let them know you're delighted to be with them, that you care about them no matter what happens," Kohn explains.

Q&A

What's wrong with rewarding good behavior?

Giving your child a reward for good behavior or a job well done seems, at first glance, like a positive, supportive parenting technique. But it's a technique based on control and conditional love, and it does your child no favors in the long run.

Parents use rewards to try to get children to do what they want them to do. Because your child will comply in exchange for your attention, affection, and support, rewards (including praise) usually buy temporary obedience. But they do nothing to help your child's intrinsic motivation. In fact, research shows that the more we reward people for doing something, the more they tend to lose interest in whatever they had to do to get the reward. The reward, or the praise—not the activity—becomes the goal.

Share your child's successes with him—from learning to use the potty when he's ready to acing his chemistry final—but don't drive those successes with rewards or praise. Provide positive feedback by noting his successes appropriately—but keep in mind that you don't want seeking your praise to be his sole motivation any more than you want him to be only avoiding your disapproval. And help him build his sense of competence by showing your faith in him and your unconditional love for him—yes, even when he misses the potty or the honor roll by a mile.—*Based on the ideas of Alfie Kohn, author of* Unconditional Parenting: Moving from Rewards and Punishments to Love and Reason

Another important aspect of Unconditional Parenting is that parents need to relinquish controlling behaviors. Give up unreasonable rules and structures, for example, be flexible in the needed structure that is provided, and enlist the participation of your child whenever possible. Do you really need that rule about which subject your teen should tackle first when he does his homework? Yes, your toddler who has been playing in the mud needs to wash up before bed, but there's no harm in letting him decide between a bath and a shower. And while you may decide that set bedtimes and limits on television viewing are necessary, it's easy to involve your preschooler or grade-schooler in ironing out the specifics and implementing the decisions.

One of our goals as parents, Kohn explains, is to help our children become independent thinkers who can develop and follow their own values. And the way to do this, he suggests, isn't by raising kids who know how to obey—or even by raising kids who have internalized our values—but by giving children opportunities to make choices. Making decisions for themselves empowers children, offering them occasion to learn and feel autonomous. The extent of these choices will depend on the child's age, of course, but there's no reason not to let a child make choices he's capable of making. Whatever activities or tasks your child is currently doing, you might ask how he wants to do it, or where, or when, or with whom.

Trying to appreciate our children's perspective helps us figure out what's really going on with our kids, and it makes us more patient with them—which enables us to do a better job delivering that unconditional love. "Few things that parents do can equal the positive impact of trying to picture how our words and actions are experienced by our children," Kohn explains.

One loving mom pulls it all together with respect, empathy, communica-tion, choices, problem solving, knowledge of child development, encour-agement, and support!

"Last winter, when my son Michael was 6½, we went to a local toy store to get a gift for someone. He asked if he could have a cool, shiny ring that he saw, and I said no, since we were there to buy just one thing. Later that day, he went to a friend's house to play for a while. When I picked him up, he was gathering his things and the friend's mom said, 'Oh, Michael, don't forget your cool ring!'

"I knew just what ring she meant. I looked at Michael, and the deer-in-the-headlights look combined with a sort of forced bewilderment, told me I was right. I told him quietly, 'I believe I know where that ring came from, and we will talk about it when we get home.' I knew there was nothing to be gained from shaming him in front of his friend.

"When we got home, I asked Michael to sit with me on the couch. I told him, 'You need to know that taking something that doesn't belong to you is not okay. I think you already know it is not okay.' Then I said gently, 'I wonder if, maybe, that ring looked so sparkly and cool that you just really wanted it. When something that special is right in front of you, sometimes it's hard to make the right choice.' I was holding him on my lap as I talked with him, and I wasn't conveying any anger or shame. I knew enough about child develop-ment to know that even at age 6, impulse control is still really difficult, espe-cially with an object of desire right at eye level. I was able to empathize with him while still maintaining the line that the behavior was not okay.

"The next day, I told Michael that he would need to make things right with the toy store, to apologize. I gave him the choice of saying something in per-son or writing a note. (He has a very introverted temperament, and I knew from experience that talking to someone he didn't know would be mortify-ing.) He chose a note, as I expected. He asked what he should say, and I prompted, 'Well, if you owned a toy store, and a child took something from the store, what would you like him to say to you?' He thought for a moment, then said, 'I'm sorry?'

"So Michael wrote a note saying, 'I'm sorry I took the ring. Love, Michael.' He put it into an envelope and decorated it with hearts. Then we drove to the toy store, and I asked to talk with a manager privately. I explained to her briefly why we were there, and Michael handed her the note. To her eternal credit, she knelt down to his level, and said, 'This was very brave of you to write this note and bring it to me. I want you to know you are always welcome here. I'm glad you like to come here, and in the future, if you want something, you'll just need to pay for it, okay?' Her positive, gentle, nonshaming tone really was the perfect end to this scenario.

"I believe Michael learned that it is possible to make restitution when you make a mistake, and that he is not a bad kid just because he made a mistake. In addition, he received practice in empathy, a skill that must be built gradually and by example.

"I told Michael that for a while, he would need to stay near me whenever we shop. He asked why, and I explained that it's my job to help him follow the rules, and I can help him best if he is close by. I was expecting him to protest, but he just nodded—and the next few times we went shopping, he stayed by me without complaint. I felt a strong sense of calm coming from him, like he knew that he needed help and he felt secure with the limit I set.

"Knowing normal developmental stages was a great help to me, and knowing that Michael is not necessarily headed for a life of crime helped me keep a sense of perspective so that I could react constructively rather than hysterically. I try to keep in mind, 'Teach rather than criticize.'"—*Katherine Kim, St. Paul, Minnesota*

Common Ground

Each of the loving discipline styles we've looked at in this chapter is distinct. Yet there are some similarities, some things we can look at as common denominators of a loving style. You might say they are child-centered in that they all have the long-term best interests of the child at heart. Every one is nonpunitive, holding fast to the notion that children learn through support and encouragement, not though force or rewards. Limits and guidelines are deemed necessary, but always provided in a loving, supportive framework. The parent/child bond—built on trust and respect, love, acceptance, and empathy—is the basis for discipline.

What You Can Do

Thinking about the philosophies of different parenting approaches encourages some introspection about your approach. It also enables you to pick and choose from an array of ideas—experiment with a P.E.T. method of communication that's new to you, try holding your infant close in a baby sling while you do a few chores, show your child empathy next time you're inclined to tell him "chin up."

- ☐ Take time to enjoy your child's current skill level or understanding of something before you suggest he reach for the next level. Let him revel in his new ability to jump off the diving board, for example, before encouraging him to try a dive. Give him time to enjoy reading books at his current reading level before introducing more challenging materials.

- ☐ When you play a game with your child, let him take the lead. Ask him what rules he wants to use for this game of checkers, or what number he wants to play to in ping pong.

- ☐ Next time your child comes to you with a problem, see whether you can help him come up with a solution or two rather than providing an instant answer.

- ☐ Are you carrying around any painful emotions from your own childhood? Do you think it affects the way you parent?

- ☐ When you must impose limits on your child, look for the choice within the limits. If he has to write a thank you, let him choose the note cards or the paper. If he dreads going to the dentist, ask him whether he'd rather Mom, Dad, or his big sister take him.

- ☐ Think about the ways you bonded with your child after birth. Were you surprised by how quickly you fell in love, or were you worried about how long it took? Bonding is an ongoing process; what ways do you continue to strengthen your bond with your child?

☐ When your child talks to you, take a minute to repeat or summarize back what he said. Ask whether that's what he meant, or ask a clarifying question. He'll appreciate that you're listening carefully.

☐ When your child acts inappropriately, try to identify a need that's not being met.

☐ When you're uncomfortable with your child's behavior, try stating your feelings using "I-messages" rather than "you-messages."

How Discipline Affects Children

For decades researchers have been studying the effects of various parenting styles on children: Which approaches foster a child's self-discipline, self-esteem, academic success, and empathy? Which don't? Or worse, which have negative consequences? "The study of parenting is an area of research in which the findings are remarkably consistent, and where the findings have remained remarkably consistent over time," says Laurence Steinberg, Ph.D., professor of psychology at Temple University in Philadelphia.

In this chapter, we take a look at some of that research, to give you an idea of the work being done and the clear direction it indicates for concerned parents.

Parenting Style Does Matter

Occasionally you'll hear an assertion that experts put too much emphasis on what parents do, especially from the "I turned out all right" crowd. Even some experts question just how much influence parents really have on their children, most notably Judith Harris in her 1998 book *The Nurture Assumption: Why Children Turn Out the Way They Do.* Psychologists agree that a host of factors—culture, genetics, environment, economy, the media—play a role in shaping children as they grow.

But the factor that preoccupies most parents—and over which they have the most control—is the effect of the parenting decisions they make. Many researchers certainly share the interest, and the conviction that, yes, parenting style matters; thousands of studies have examined the implications. Some take a panoramic view of effects, whereas others zero in on specifics.

Overall, researchers have found the best results among children with authoritative parents and the worst results among children of parents who are permissively unengaged. In a paper published in 1996, Barbara Radziszewska and colleagues looked at the relationship between four different parenting styles and their effects on adolescents' depressive symptoms, smoking, and academic achievement.

The four styles were autocratic (with parents making the decisions), authoritative (joint process, with parents ultimately deciding), permissive (joint process, with the adolescent ultimately deciding), and unengaged (in which the adolescent simply decides). The researchers concluded, "There is consistent evidence that the authoritative style ... is associated with the best outcomes in many domains of child development, including psychosocial functioning, school competence, emotional well-being, and behavioral adjustment, while the unengaged style ... correlates with poor adjustment and problem behavior (like drug and alcohol use, school misconduct, delinquency) and is therefore considered a risk factor in child development."

Many studies confirm that children raised by permissive parents (who may act out of indulgence or neglect) fare the worst overall. These children tend to have the lowest self-esteem, social competence, and confidence and the highest rates of anxiety, problem behaviors, and depression. They are the least motivated and lack a sense of responsibility and respectfulness toward others.

They don't cope well with stress and become easily angered. They tend to be less mature and more domineering.

Scores of studies also report the shortfall of authoritarian parenting. In general, when parents are demanding, controlling, and less responsive and accepting, children have lower self-esteem and confidence, more anxiety and depression, and less social competence than peers parented by authoritative parents, who are both firm and kind.

Compared to children raised by authoritarian or permissive parents, children raised by authoritative parents are most likely to be confident, self-reliant, and competent. They are most apt to succeed academically and socially, and most able to cope with stress. They're also at lowest risk for substance abuse and violent behavior.

How do researchers explain these differences? Each study draws its own conclusions, but authors Jean Illsley Clarke and Connie Dawson suggest some insightful explanations in their book *Growing Up Again: Parenting Ourselves, Parenting Our Children,* in which they examine the underlying beliefs of children raised by parents with different discipline styles.

Clarke and Dawson explain that children of authoritative parents come to understand that there are some rules that need to be followed; that they can learn from their mistakes; that they are good people and nothing they do will change that; that they are lovable and capable; that it's okay to grow up and still be dependent at times; that they can think things through and get help doing so; that they can continually expand their ability to be responsible and competent.

On the flip side, they explain, children who live with punitive parents think that they are not wanted; that they are not cared about; that rules are more important than their needs; that they are bad people if they don't do things right; and that they need to be perfect. They believe that others can think for them, and they decide to comply, rebel, or withdraw. They sometimes feel pressured to try harder, to be strong, or think that they can't be good enough, so it's hopeless to try.

Controlled by their parents, other researchers concur, children of authoritarian parents often have trouble learning self-control, and they are less motivated. When they are motivated, children of authoritarian parents tend to do things to obtain rewards or avoid punishments rather than because the actions are intrinsically right or wrong. Their relationships with their parents and with others tend to be distant. They are often afraid to try new things, are insecure, and have low self-esteem.

On the other hand, because they are treated with respect and taught to approach problems in a reasoned, confident manner, children of authoritative parents develop confidence and competence in both social and academic arenas.

The links between style and effect are logical ones, then. Here's a closer look at a handful of them.

Relationships

Authoritative parents most often have mutually respectful relationships with their children; these warm, reasoning relationships are instructive both in terms of how good relationships work and how satisfying such relationships can be.

Dorothy Briggs, in *Your Child's Self-Esteem*, shows the path to resentment and rebelliousness among children who have been raised with an authoritarian style. This approach, she explains, teaches children not to trust their own opinions and abilities to make decisions. The children learn that their parents lack faith in their ability to work cooperatively with the family. These children often grow up to be alienated from their parents, because they have been trained to be submissive to authority, which leads to frustration during adolescence. They can become hostile, too, as they hold resentment and guilt inside. Children of authoritarian parents often avoid close relationships with others because they don't want to repeat a similar, smothering relationship again. They tend to be more distrustful and withdrawn. By the time they are adolescents, they are often resentful and rebellious.

The messages that a permissive parent sends about relating to others depend in part on whether the permissiveness stems from indulgence of the child or from neglect. Children of permissive parents may feel patronized, incompetent, undermined, manipulated, discounted, unloved, angry, scared, hurt, distrustful, or rageful. They may conclude that they must take care of other people's feelings and needs, or they may conclude that they don't care about anyone but themselves. Children who are indulged learn that they can get away with anything and often feel that they deserve whatever they want.

Authoritative parents stress the importance of a strong bond with children, and this, too, pays off in terms of the child's ability to form relationships. Frederick J. Morrison and Ramie Cooney, authors of *Parenting and Academic Achievement: Multiple Paths to Early Literacy,* published in 2002, analyzed children's secure attachment to a caregiver in relationship to the child's well-being. Infants who are secure in their attachment, for example, have the capacity to use caregivers as a source of reassurance and support for their explorations. Preschoolers with secure histories are more engaged and positive with their peers. In middle childhood, children with secure backgrounds form more desirable, successful friendships, and they function well in groups. In adolescence, these children are effective in mixed-gender groups, and they are able to take leadership roles. Children with secure attachments to caregivers are rated more socially competent by teachers, and they have more effective relationships with adults in general.

In a study of 631 children with behavior problems published in a 2000 issue of the *Journal of Clinical Child Psychology,* researcher Elizabeth Stormshank and colleagues found that punitive parenting practices are associated with higher rates of all child disruptive-behavior problems. "Low levels of warm involvement were particularly characteristic of parents of children who showed elevated levels of oppositional behaviors," they conclude. Physical aggression by parents is linked with physical aggression by children, and disruptive behavior in early childhood (such as aggressive, hyperactive, and oppositional behavior) is predictive of later negative mental-health outcomes (such as substance abuse, academic failure, and criminal behavior).

In a 1974 study published in the *Journal of Personality and Social Psychology,* researchers J. Merrill Carlsmith, Mark R. Lepper, and Thomas K. Landauer concluded that parents who use power-assertive methods with their children—by raising their voices and issuing orders, for example—obtain immediate compliance, but reduce their children's cooperativeness on subsequent occasions. More and more frequent power assertion becomes necessary as time goes on, and finally the power-assertive methods lose effectiveness, unless they escalate to levels where they produce fear in the children.

GET PSYCHED

"In spite of words to the contrary, it appears that parenting experiences, especially during the first five years of life, but also throughout childhood, do have important and enduring effects on children's development. These effects are sometimes subtle and involve interactions with other factors and may be limited to specific contexts. But the effects endure."
—*Kenneth A. Dodge, Ph.D., director of the Center for Child and Family Policy at Duke University*

In his 2002 paper "Mediation, Moderation, and Mechanisms in How Parenting Affects Children's Aggressive Behavior," Kenneth A. Dodge at Duke University states, "Rather than pit genes versus parenting, or even parents versus peers, it is more fruitful to examine how parenting exerts an influence on the child." The most important "how," he says, is through acquired messages about how the social world operates. These messages, stored in the brain, drive behavior. "Children learn the schema of hostility partially from interacting with threat in the form of rejecting and harsh physically assaultive parenting," Dodge explains. In contrast, children learn to become nonviolent from interacting with a parent who inspires security, confidence, and hope."

> **GET PSYCHED**
>
> "Some of the things we say when we take out our anger and other emotions on our children injure them and damage the way they perceive themselves … angry statements can linger in a child's mind well into adulthood."
> —*James Windell, author of* The Fatherstyle Advantage

Self-Esteem

The way you convey your expectations to your child and the way you relate to him day in and day out can profoundly affect how he feels about himself.

Some of the early research on parenting styles concludes that children of authoritarian parents tended to be anxious and withdrawn, whereas those of authoritative parents are consistently more self-confident and content. In one 1967 study titled "Antecedents of Self-Esteem," researcher Stanley Coopersmith reports that mothers whose children have high self-esteem tend to use more reasoning and verbal discussion, whereas those whose children have low self-esteem more often use arbitrary punitive discipline.

Marilyn Lynn Campbell Comstock, in a 1973 dissertation on the "Effects of Perceived Parental Behavior on Self-Esteem and Adjustment," wrote that parents who make firm demands that are perceived by children as reasonable are more likely to foster high self-esteem in the children than parents who dictate demands that are seen as unreasonable. The parents who make reasonable demands "give directions in ways that leave a degree of choice and control in the hands of the children," according to the researcher. And at the University of Georgia, researchers Michael H. Kernis, Anita C. Brown, and Gene H. Brody report in their 2000 study of 11- and 12-year-olds that children with unstable self-esteem are more likely to have parents who are perceived to be critical and controlling and less likely to acknowledge positive behaviors or show approval. Children with stable self-esteem, on the other hand, are more likely to have parents whom the children perceive as good problem solvers.

GET PSYCHED

"If parents would worry more about not paying enough attention to their children and less about spoiling them, the world would be a better place."
—*Laurence Steinberg, Ph.D., author of* The Ten Basic Principles of Good Parenting

Some authoritarian parents make the argument that parents who foster such close attachments to their children are impeding their independence. But research does not bear this out. L. Alan Sroufe, in a 26-year study on individual development published in 2002, found that children who do not have secure infant attachments are *more* dependent as they grow, sitting on pre-school teachers' laps, for example, or becoming more involved with camp counselors than peers. Those with secure attachment histories, on the other hand, are more competent, show fewer behavior problems, and recover more quickly in times of stress.

Academics

It's easy to envision how parenting styles profoundly affect a child's sense of self and his behavior in interactions with others. But how does that sense translate when it comes to something as tangible as school success?

In large part because of the support and encouragement that children of authoritative parents receive at home, they do better academically. According to Morrison and Cooney, "Authoritative parenting has been frequently associated with the promotion and maintenance of higher levels of academic competence and school adjustment, while the detrimental effects of neglectful or nonauthoritative parenting on adolescent outcomes, such as poorer classroom engagement and homework completion, appear to accumulate over time." The researchers make the point that all aspects of parenting directly or indirectly shape the growth of a child's literacy skills. So, for example, by contributing to a child's social development (his independence, sense of responsibility, self-regulation, and cooperativeness), warm and responsive parents also foster a child's academic success.

The link between parenting style and academic success isn't newfound. In a psychological monograph published in 1945, researchers Alfred L. Baldwin, Joan Kalhoun, and Fay Huffman Breese reported that the IQs of children with democratic parents increase significantly (a mean of more than eight IQ points) over the years, whereas the IQs of children with autocratic parents decrease slightly, and those of children with permissive parents remain about the same. "It would appear that the democratic environment is the most conducive to mental development," they concluded.

Children of democratic families are also rated by teachers as more original, playful, patient, curious, and fanciful. They score higher in emotional adjustment and maturity and hold more positions of leadership in school. On the other hand, children of autocratic parents score low in interaction with peers, often being dominated when they do interact. These children are more obedient and lack spontaneity, affection, curiosity, and originality. "By the time the child from the democratic home has become of school age," conclude the researchers, "his social development has progressed markedly; he is popular and a leader; he is friendly and good natured; he seems emotionally secure, serene, unexcitable; he has had close attachments to his parents and is able to adjust to his teachers."

Researchers Philip A. Cowan and Carolyn Pape Cowan from the University of California at Berkeley point out that parenting behavior is not the sole factor in determining school success, but it is a key ingredient. In a study about parents' role in academic achievement and behavior problems, published in 2002, they state, "When mothers or fathers of preschoolers were warm, more responsive, more structuring, and more encouraging of their child's autonomy—that is, more authoritative—then children were more likely to have higher academic achievement on tests and were less likely to be described by their teachers as having acting out, externalizing problems or shy, withdrawn, depressed, internalizing behaviors in kindergarten and first grade."

Studies have directly linked both authoritarian and permissive parenting styles negatively with grades, whereas authoritative parenting is linked positively with grades. In fact, parents who are consistently authoritative have children with the highest mean grades, whereas those who are inconsistent (combining authoritarian with other parenting styles) have children with the lowest grades. Although other factors weigh in, researchers Sanford M. Dornbusch, Herbert Leiderman, and colleagues conclude in their 1987 study that parenting style is a more powerful predictor of student achievement than parent education, ethnicity, or family structure. And in a 1992 study, Dornbusch and fellow researchers Laurence Steinberg and Nancy Darling sum up, "The longitudinal analyses presented ... indicate that authoritative parenting indeed leads to school success."

Steinberg and Julie D. Elmen, in a study published in 1989, tested the hypothesis that authoritative parenting facilitates school success among 120 families with a firstborn child between the ages of 11 and 16. They found that separate aspects of authoritativeness each made a contribution to a child's academic success. Authoritative parents help a child develop a healthy sense of autonomy as well as a positive approach toward schoolwork. "School success is enhanced by authoritative parenting at least in part because authoritative parenting contributes to youngsters' psychosocial development," they concluded. A year later, the researchers followed up on the students in their study, to determine whether the differences were maintained over time. They found that the benefits of authoritative parenting are maintained at the same high levels, but that the deleterious consequences of neglectful parenting accumulate.

Empathy

Many studies show that children are able to show more *empathy* when their parents have been nonpunitive and responsive and when their parents encourage them to talk about their feelings. Explaining the effects of a child's behavior on others, along with the importance of being kind, also promotes empathy, even in young

PsychSpeak

Empathy is the capacity to understand and share another's feelings and perspective. Sometimes this includes the ability to communicate these empathetic feelings.

children. On the other hand, when parents reject or withdraw from children, or when they are inconsistent in the way they react to children's emotional needs, children are less empathetic.

When faced with a distressed playmate, preschoolers who have been raised with secure attachment to their parents are more likely to show concern and helpful, supportive behavior (such as getting a teacher to help a child who's been hurt) than those who weren't, according to a 1989 study by Roberta Kesten-baum, Ellen A. Farber, and Alan L. Sroufe.

And a study by Paul Hastings, Carolyn Zahn-Waxler, and col-leagues in the September 2000 issue of *Developmental Psychology* reports that aggressive, disruptive children are able to show con-cern for others in their early years, but the ability decreases as the children reach school age. In fact, some of the children who were aggressive but able to empathize at preschool age displayed anger, avoidance, and even amusement at others' distress two years later. The study showed important links between parenting style and a child's ability to empathize. Mothers who are overly strict and harshly punitive, who don't reason with their children or establish reasonable and consistent rules, and who strongly show their anger or disappointment with their children are likely to have a detrimental effect on their children's ability to empathize, the researchers found. On the other hand, mothers who are warm, avoid harsh punishments, use reasoning, and set appropriate guidelines have children who show more concern for others. One explanation for these results, say the researchers, is that "angry, authoritarian parenting could be interpreted by the children as a lack of care or concern on the part of their par-ents."

you're not alone

"My parents were wonderful in many respects, especially on the creativity side, but they were screamers and yellers with each other and with me and my brother and sister. There was even some chair throwing, I am sad to say.

"Well, no surprise, I became a parent much like the ones I had, complete with hands, and occasionally furniture, used in anger. In the treatment program that helped one of my sons through his adolescent difficulties I learned a different sort of discipline and saw its positive effect on my youngest son.

"It sounds so simple, but it wasn't: I learned to use words instead of hands (or chairs) to manage conflicts and discipline my kids. I see the effects of my transformation in my sons today. They are truly gentle men. It brings tears to my eyes, thinking back on how we hurt each other in the past, physically and emotionally, but these are mixed with tears of joy, knowing the warm and loving relationships we have today."—*Eve Odiorne Sullivan, PARENTS FORUM founder, Cambridge, Massachusetts*

Substance Abuse

Researchers have found that authoritative parenting can help prevent risk behaviors in children. Studies show that children who have a sense of connection at home and children whose parents are both responsive and firm engage in risky behaviors significantly less than other children. In fact, according to a 2001 National Survey of Families and Households by William Aquilino and Andrew Supple, parent-adolescent relationships influence the well-being and behavior of young adults in predictable ways, with coercive parental control (rather than more democratic family settings) associated with more substance abuse in young adulthood. In a nutshell, parents who parent authoritatively have children who are statistically much less likely to smoke cigarettes, drink alcohol, or do illegal drugs.

GET PSYCHED

"We don't yet know, above all, what the world might be like if children were to grow up without being subjected to humiliation, if parents would respect them and take them seriously as people."—*Alice Miller, Ph.D., author of* For Your Own Good

A national longitudinal study on adolescent health found that most health-risk behaviors were reduced by "parent/family connectedness and perceived school connectedness." Researchers interviewed 12,118 children in grades 7 through 12 in their homes. The study backed up earlier findings that a child's perception that he is cared for and connected to his parents provides a protective factor against an array of risk behaviors. The researchers also conclude that although the physical presence of a parent at key times in the home reduces the incidence of risky behaviors, especially substance abuse, it's consistently less significant than parental warmth, care, and connectedness with the child.

How an adolescent perceives his parents can balance out peer pressure. In a study of 4,263 sixth, seventh, and eighth graders published in 2001, researcher Bruce Simons-Morton and colleagues conclude that whereas "deviant peers" promote smoking and drinking behaviors, parental involvement, expectations, and regard discourage these risky behaviors. "Teens who perceive that their parents provided higher regard by indicating that they like them, respect them, take them seriously, listen to them, and give reasons for rules and decisions that involve them were less likely to smoke or drink. This finding underscores the importance to early adolescents of how they perceive their parents to regard them."

WEB TALK: To read articles about education, behavior, family topics, parenting news, advice, and moms' journals, visit
↑ www.ParentCenter.com

Spare the Rod

Not all authoritarian parents spank their children, but parents who do use physical punishment fall within the autocratic, controlling, authoritarian parenting category. The devastating effects of physically punishing a child have been examined extensively in research.

According to "A Review of the Research on Corporal Punishment" by Children's Hospitals and Clinics of Minneapolis/St. Paul Primary Prevention Committee in 2003, the behaviors significantly associated with corporal punishment include the following: decreased likelihood of long-term compliance; increased aggression in childhood; increased risk of physical abuse; decreased quality of parent/child relationship; decreased quality of mental health in childhood; increased delinquency and antisocial behaviors in childhood; increased likelihood of abuse of future spouse; increased aggression in adulthood; increased criminal and antisocial behavior in adulthood; decreased mental health in adulthood.

Many studies attest to the fact that physical discipline increases antisocial and delinquent behavior. In fact, according to a study conducted by Murray A. Straus and colleagues at the Family Research Laboratory at the University of New Hampshire and published in 1977, the more a child is spanked, the higher the later level of antisocial behavior. (In this case, the researchers followed up two years later.) They conclude that the long-term effects of corporal punishment are actually the opposite of what parents intend.

GET PSYCHED

"If we are ever to turn toward a kindlier society and a safer world, a revulsion against the physical punishment of children would be a good place to start."–*Dr. Benjamin Spock*

Q & A

Is it ever okay to spank a child?

"Of all the forms of punishment that parents use, the one with the worst side effects is physical punishment. Physical punishment has been proven to have a harmful effect on children's development. That's why you should never spank, hit, slap, or otherwise physically punish your child.

"The main side effect of physical punishment is excessive aggression. Children who are spanked, hit, or slapped are more prone to fighting with other children. They are more likely to be bullies and more likely to use aggression to solve disputes with others. Who can blame them? Their parents have taught them that hitting someone else is an acceptable way to solve a problem.

"Excessive aggression is a serious enough problem in its own right, but it also leads to other, equally serious, difficulties. Children who are overly aggressive are more likely to be rejected by their classmates, to get into trouble in school, and to develop early conduct problems. All of these place a child at risk for academic difficulty, forming friendships with antisocial peers, and delinquency.

"Physical punishment is also a poor choice because it easily escalates out of control and ends up in a serious injury to the child. Few parents who hit their children actually intend to injure them. But some parents have a difficult time controlling their anger once they start in on a spanking, and others simply do not know their own strength. If you regularly spank or hit your child, sooner or later she is going to get hurt."—*Laurence Steinberg, Ph.D., professor of psychology, Temple University in Philadelphia*

Experts encourage parents who say that spanking "works" to consider both immediate and long-term ramifications. It may "work" to stop undesired behavior today, but it doesn't teach a child not to behave badly tomorrow. And the price is often paid all the way into adulthood.

Elizabeth T. Gershoff published her findings on the effects of corporal punishment on children's behaviors in a 2002 issue of *Psychological Bulletin*. In her review of 88 studies (which she culled from a survey of 300), the researcher found that spanking does increase a child's immediate compliance. She also found that a child who is being spanked for misbehavior does not internalize rules about the misbehavior. Children who are spanked, in fact, show increased, not decreased, aggression. Gershoff found that corporal punishment is associated with increased antisocial behavior, especially for boys, and especially for children between 10 and 12 years of age. (And boys are more likely to be spanked.) Gershoff also concludes that corporal punishment leads to an increased risk of adult criminal behavior, an increase in abusive behavior as an adult, and an increased risk of victimization from abusive relationships in adulthood.

Adults who were spanked as children often suffer diminished mental health as adults. Gershoff points out that a child who is spanked once isn't headed for a life of crime because of the spanking, but as the frequency and severity of the corporal punishment increases, so does the risk of negative outcomes.

> **WEB TALK:** The Center for Effective Discipline is devoted to eliminating corporal punishment. They provide resources for discipline at home and at school. Read their materials at
> **www.stophitting.com**

In her books on the influence of childhood on the lives of adults, psychotherapist, researcher, and author Alice Miller, Ph.D., makes the point that we have become accustomed to abusing children and that children repress this abuse. She asserts that adults who abuse children have themselves been traumatized as children—without exception. In *The Body Never Lies,* Miller examines the affect of childhood trauma, anger, humiliation, rage, and powerlessness on adults. This suppression of emotions as children (and through adulthood), she says, makes us physically and psychologically ill.

To those who are comfortable with the use of corporal punishment because they believe it causes no harm, Miller says, "The consequences of early, invisible injuries are so severe precisely because they derive from the trivialization of childhood suffering and the denial of its importance."

What You Can Do

Regardless of what your parenting style has been, you can make the decision now to react to your child in ways that will affect her positively—today and as an adult.

- ☐ Think about your goals for your child. Based on the research in this chapter, is your parenting style a good match for your goals?

- ☐ Can you identify any specific effects your parents' discipline style had on you as a child? As an adult?

- ☐ Help teach your child to be empathetic by pointing out how others feel when they are physically or emotionally hurt.

- ☐ Ask your child's teacher or daycare provider how your child reacts to others' misfortunes. Is she helpful and caring?

- ☐ Find a parenting chat group where you can discuss discipline concerns with like-minded parents.

- ☐ Share what you've learned about parenting styles and their effects with your partner. See if you can agree on the best approach for your child.

- ☐ If you spank your child, think of a specific alternative you'll use instead of spanking (comforting your child, taking a time-out together, calling a friend to step in for you so you can have some time alone, for example). Visualize using it successfully.

Part 2

Elements of Loving Discipline

The key components of successful discipline are the same as those needed to build a supportive environment for your child. In Part 2 we explore what those components are. We discuss the importance of structure (versus control) in your child's life and give you helpful guidelines for providing it. We also show you how to supply your child with encouragement, modeling, and positive attention—all within the framework of a loving, authoritative style.

Encouragement

"Encouragement is more important than any other aspect of child rearing," says Rudolf Dreikurs, who laid the foundation for Positive Discipline techniques. Other loving approaches follow this same philosophy, recognizing that encouragement can turn around problem behavior and build a child's confidence, self-respect, autonomy, motivation, and self-discipline.

But many parents are more certain of how to punish than they are of how to encourage. Superficial or overblown praise is not encouragement, for example. Nor is criticism, however constructive we think it is. Encouragement means helping your child see that he "can do" and that mistakes are opportunities to learn. It means supporting his efforts and respecting, accepting, and loving him unconditionally. And it means surrounding him with an environment that's conducive to his growth. "Encouragement is providing opportunities for children to develop the perceptions that 'I'm capable. I can contribute, and I can influence what happens to me or how I respond,'" explains Jane Nelsen, author of the *Positive Discipline* series. Here are some guidelines for encouraging your child.

Foster a You-Can-Do-It Attitude

It's so easy to convey to a child that we don't have faith in him, that he's too little, too inexperienced—by offering to help him when he doesn't need help, by stopping him from attempting things that are "too hard," or by criticizing his efforts. "Half of the job of encouraging a child lies in avoiding discouragement, either by humiliation or by overprotection. The other half lies in knowing how to encourage," Dreikurs explains.

Show Confidence Show your child that you have confidence in him whenever you can. You won't be able to let your toddler take the wheel of the car, of course. But when he wants to pour his own juice, perhaps it is worth the cleanup to show your faith in his ability. Find unobtrusive ways to offer support. Maybe you'll exchange the big pitcher in the refrigerator for a smaller one before his next try. Or maybe you'll show respect for his struggle by offering a suggestion: "I find it's easier if I hold the glass when I pour into it. You might want to give that a try." Or if you've got a first-grader plugging away at his worksheet, you might offer, "It's so hard to get those lines to look nice, isn't it? Maybe a ruler would help." It's good for your child to know you're there if you need him (and you might have a worthwhile idea or two), but you have every confidence in him, too.

To get closer to your child's perspective, think about the kind of approach you appreciate from adults who are teaching you something or who are in a supervisory role, such as at work. In a 2005 study at the Mayo Clinic in Scottsdale, Arizona, students in their medical residencies were asked what attributes they thought were

GET PSYCHED

"Families that communicate love encourage children's competence and self-confidence. The rewards come not just in cognitive matters such as reading, writing, and speaking, but in our children's capacity to care about others, deal with their feelings and respond to stress. When we show our love, we communicate the highest part of our character."—*Rod Wallace Kennedy, author of* The Encouraging Parent

most important in the faculty with whom they worked. The students stressed the importance of a faculty member's ability to answer questions clearly, and they felt (more strongly than the faculty did) that it's important for quality educators to be "readily available and able to provide a safe, nonjudgmental, non-threatening learning environment." It makes sense that, no less than medical residents, children need exactly this kind of encouragement to learn and grow.

You'll also give your child a vote of confidence every time you call attention to his strengths. "Your penmanship is so good on this paper; it makes it a joy to read," you might say, even if your child is shaky on the content. "Look at how well organized your CDs are," you might offer when you notice that one touch of order in his messy room. "You certainly are good at sharing," you might tell him when he gives his little sister a chance to throw the Frisbee. Noticing a strength is nurturing it. And when your child's confidence grows in one area, it's likely to expand into others.

To help your child succeed at home, take the time to teach him everyday skills. Make sure he knows how to fold the laundry or make the bed before you put it on his chore chart. Show him what you expect it to look like when he's finished. Encourage him to help you cook, balance the checkbook, garden, and decorate. Giving him opportunities to contribute will help his sense of belonging and foster his competence.

Sometimes children become discouraged because they can't live up to expectations. So make sure that your child knows you don't expect perfection, and help him set reasonable goals. When you do set expectations (for chores, for example), set them high enough to show respect for what your child can accomplish, but not so high that he becomes discouraged. Find ways for your child to contribute meaningfully, but not in ways that are beyond his reach. One way to sap a child's motivation is by setting the bar so high that he feels doomed to failure.

Be Respectful We offer children encouragement every time we show them that we respect their feelings, opinions, and preferences. So give your child age-appropriate choices whenever you can. Ask your toddler which socks he wants to wear and which snack he would prefer after rest time. Let your preschooler choose his books from the library and your grade-schooler decide how much to save from his allowance for his new bike. Respect your teen's hairdo preference (you don't have to like it to be respectful!) as well as his aversion to gym class.

Asking children for advice conveys respect, too. Get your child's take on the paint color for the living room or the destination for the family vacation. Ask him how he thinks the family might help out Aunt Cordelia while Uncle Ed is in the hospital, or what he thinks the rules should be about television viewing on school nights. Family meetings (see Chapter 8) provide a good opportunity for soliciting your child's input.

The fact that you take time to talk with your child, to listen to his point of view, to share ideas and feelings, shows him that you respect and value him. Use good communication skills (see Chapter 10) to build your bond with him. Conveying that you love and respect him is a great contribution to his confidence level.

you're not alone

"Trips to the grocery store were a real challenge with my twin boys when they were preschoolers—until I enlisted their help. I gave each boy a handheld basket and several coupons. Their job was to find the products and bring them back to our main grocery cart. As they did this, I'd compliment them on finding the right thing, or I'd tell them I appreciated how hard they looked if they couldn't find it. Or I just thanked them for being such big helpers. This became such a habit that I thought nothing of it until one day an older woman stopped us outside the supermarket and said how refreshing it was to hear a mother talking respectfully to her children instead of yelling at them! I used this method with many tasks, and it helped me avoid behavior problems while it helped the boys gain confidence. They are both now seniors in college and doing extremely well!"—*Linda Olson, author of* New Psalms for New Moms: A Keepsake Journal

Allow (Encourage!) Mistakes One reason it's important to focus on effort is that when we convey to our kids that effort is important, we also begin to convey that when they fail at something, what's at stake is not their value as a person, but simply their skill level. A mistake or an attempt that doesn't succeed does nothing to affect your child's value. It just means that he has a chance to improve. And if your child accepts his mistakes not as personal failures but as opportunities to learn, problem solve, and grow, then he's much, much less likely to become discouraged. "Courage is found in one who can make a mistake and fail without feeling lowered in his self-esteem," explains Rudolf Dreikurs. "This 'courage to be imperfect' is equally needed by children and adults. Without it, discouragement is inevitable."

We talk in more depth about modeling in Chapter 9, but this is a perfect illustration of how valuable your example is to your child. Let him see you make mistakes and talk about what you learned from them. Tell him after work when you made a blunder, 'fess up when you're the one who left the refrigerator door open or when you forgot to tape a favorite program for him. Also talk about how you're going to improve next time; outline what measures you'll take. "Next time you ask me to tape something for you, I'll set the timer to remind myself," for example, or "Next time I have a report due at work I'm going to get there half an hour early to review it." When your child makes a mistake, or comes up short, ask him "What will you do differently next time?"

WEB TALK: For articles on child development, gentle discipline, education, breastfeeding, and other issues of importance to nurturing parents, visit www.parentingweb.com

The logical next step to building on mistakes, then, is problem solving, and your child needs your faith in his ability to do this just like anything else. So resist the urge to tell him what to do, even in the midst of trouble. Instead, encourage him to think about it, to discuss it, and to come up with possible solutions.

In talking about how to prompt a child to problem solve a sibling dispute, Lawrence J. Cohen, author of *Playful Parenting,* says, "Encouraging children without butting in too much is a delicate balancing act. I'll often say things like, 'I'm sure you guys can work this out. Anyone have any ideas?' Or, 'This isn't working. Everyone is fighting over turns and nobody is getting to play. What can we do so everybody gets a turn?' Notice how these last few comments propose half a solution—you have to include everyone, you have to be safe—but then leave the other half of the solution up to the children involved," Cohen explains. "I have found that children are remarkably responsive to encouragement to figure things out on their own, as long as they can count on our support. They may end up with solutions similar to those we would have chosen, but it's different when they do it. Their solutions are more creative. Their apologies are more sincere, and their compromises are more acceptable to everyone."

you're not alone

"Our 7-year-old daughter, Maya, who understood that mistakes are one way to learn, had a habit of saying, 'Take chances, make mistakes, get messy!' One day her 2-year-old brother was waving a pole around wildly in the house. I became worried about a small, delicate, glass-blown piano on my dresser, but instead of moving it or redirecting our son, as I should have, I told him, 'Be careful, Eli, you could break something.'

"Sure enough, 'Crash!', he accidentally knocked the piano to the ground, breaking the front of it into tiny pieces. My mouth fell open in distress, but before I could say anything, in walked Maya, who sized up the situation and said, 'Eli, that was a big mistake! Good thing it's okay to make mistakes or you would be in big trouble!' I let go of my breath and sighed, 'Yes, good thing,' took the stick away from Eli, told him I felt sad that my piano was broken, and started cleaning up the mess. Eli replied quietly, 'Sorry, Mommy,' and really meant it.

"I decided to keep the piano on my dresser, even though it now has a jagged hole in front. It reminds me how much more beautiful my children are than my treasured glass piano and how thankful I am to be constantly learning from my children how to love them more." *—Parent Cindy Wenner, Bothell, Washington*

Distinguish Between Encouragement and Praise

Generously encouraging a child is not the same thing as praising him. And although abundant praise sounds like a loving, Positive Discipline technique, it's not always such a good idea.

Are we splitting hairs? Well, the difference between encouragement and praise may seem subtle, but it's actually quite significant, explains psychologist Debbie Glasser, Ph.D. The concern is what effect each will have on your child down the road. "Praise can be a powerful way to acknowledge children's successes," says Glasser. "However, when children are regularly praised for their outcomes, they can become dependent on more praise and feel easily frustrated when their performance isn't perfect." And that dependence on praise is what's at issue.

In fact, some experts go so far as to say that praise is always detrimental, in part because it fuels discouragement. "If the child sees praise as a reward, then lack of it becomes scorn. If the child is not praised for everything he does, the child feels that he has failed," explains Dreikurs. Most experts, though, agree that the key to effective praise is moderation.

Praise is judgmental. No matter how positive, it's still contingent on your approval. And too much praise can backfire. Every child needs to hear the words "I'm so proud of you" from his parents. This is a positive and important message. But it's also external validation. And if you talk with your child that way all the time, your child may learn to do things for your praise rather than for internal benefits such as the satisfaction of a job well done or energetically attempted, having fun, or being helpful or cooperative, for example. "A steady diet of praise and rewards inspires children to believe 'I am okay only if others say I'm okay,'" says Nelsen.

Another problem with praise is that it's often directed at the person and his value rather than the activity. Why is this a problem? When you tell a child "You're great!" or "What a good boy you are for hanging up your coat," you have judged and approved of him, not just his hanging up his coat. So when he doesn't hang up his coat, is he a bad boy? To counteract this, be concrete in your encouragement. "I appreciate that you called to tell me you were leaving Jenny's to go for ice cream." Or "I like how you tidied your closet by matching all your shoes up on the shelf."

When you thank your child for what he's done, or for his efforts, you are providing the best kind of positive feedback. Your appreciation highlights the specific benefits of his action or conduct as well as the fact that he has helped you—and made you happy!

Although there's no such thing as too much encouragement, we've all heard praise overused. A child who hears that every picture he draws is "fantastic!" or "the best drawing I've ever seen!" or every soccer game he plays is "the best soccer you have ever played!" knows the praise is insincere. He knows that not every picture can be the best—perhaps that he didn't even try very hard on this one. And he knows that athletes have good games and bad games, and he's no different. "Instead of developing a strong sense of self-esteem," Glasser explains, "the child who receives this kind of praise may feel unable to trust his parent's feedback. Instead of feeling good about his efforts, he may feel frustrated. And instead of learning how to enjoy the process of creating art or playing with peers, he may become overly concerned about his performance."

Unlike praise, encouragement can be offered regardless of the outcome. For example, explains Glasser, when a child is first learning to ride a bicycle, parents often offer praise when he rides independently. But there are so many opportunities to encourage his efforts even when he isn't yet riding on his own. In fact, encouragement can be offered even when he falls down. "A.J., you rode for a few minutes! That must have felt exciting!" Now A.J. can feel proud of his efforts and progress, instead of feeling discouraged that he can't ride without assistance yet.

When you find yourself sincerely praising your child, don't slap your hand over your mouth. But if you want him to reap the most benefit for your positive feedback, think about ways to offer plenty of encouragement as well. "There's a place for praise in every child's life," explains Glasser. "Find the balance between praise and encouragement that feels most comfortable for you. When that winning goal is scored, go ahead and offer plenty of praise. Just remember that winning goals are not scored every day."

Q&A

I'm confused. Why isn't praise always a good thing?

Used correctly, praise is one of the most important tools parents have in their quest to build good behavior in their children. Praise can focus attention on children's accomplishments and show them the power within themselves to accept challenges and solve problems.

Good praise describes behavior and helps your child understand what you expect while encouraging him to work for his own satisfaction rather than yours. Saying "You must be proud of the hard work you put into your math grade," helps him understand that it was his effort that resulted in the grade. This link between effort and outcome encourages him to believe in himself and in his power to affect his own life.

Bad praise focuses on the person and can lead children to place too much value on the judgments of others. When you say, "I'm proud of you!" the message he hears is that he must please you. "Good effort on cleaning your room," is good praise: "Good boy!" is not and suggests that he can also be a bad boy. Make praise honest and appropriate with the focus on behavior rather than the person. Remember, your child is always a good person, although his behavior may not always be good.—*Jerry Wyckoff, Ph.D., author of* Discipline Without Shouting or Spanking

Give an *E* for Effort Another way to encourage a confident attitude is to support your child's interests and help him experience the satisfaction of making a good effort, whether or not the result is a resounding success. Attend his extracurricular events and find ways for him to build on his interests, whether they be in airplanes, comics, or collies.

When you talk about his activities, try to focus on effort and improvement rather than final accomplishments. "You really seemed to learn a lot working on that project," you might comment to your budding inventor, regardless of the grade he gets on his science fair project. "Look at all the bright colors you chose for this drawing!" you might tell your preschooler. When your high schooler improves his free-throw percentage but still misses a crucial shot, you might point out that he still helped the team by racking up 7 out of 10 free throws. This kind of recognition will fuel his continued efforts.

Even when you don't think your child's efforts will pay off the way he'd like them to, point out the value. "I'm so glad you're applying for that job. The interview will be great experience for you, no matter what happens." Your child needs to know that you love him regardless of his performance and that the outcome isn't what matters most.

> **GET PSYCHED**
>
> "Each child needs continuous encouragement, just as a plant needs water. He cannot grow and develop and gain a sense of belonging without encouragement."
> —*Rudolf Dreikurs, M.D., author of* Children: The Challenge

Is Your Child Encouraged or Discouraged?

One way to tell whether or not a child needs more encouragement is to take a look at his sense of self-worth or self-esteem. Use this questionnaire, based on Stephanie Marston's work in *The Magic of Encouragement,* to think about whether your child needs more encouragement in his life. ("Yes" in the first half and "no" in the second indicate higher self-esteem.)

- ☐ Is your child proud of his accomplishments?
- ☐ Can he act independently?
- ☐ Can he assume responsibility?
- ☐ Can he tolerate frustration?
- ☐ Does he approach challenges with enthusiasm?
- ☐ Does he feel capable of taking charge of situations in his own life?

☐ Does he have a good sense of humor?

☐ Does he have a sense of purpose?

☐ Can he postpone gratification?

☐ Can he ask for help when he needs it?

☐ Is he active and energetic?

☐ Does he spontaneously express his feelings?

☐ Is he relaxed and able to manage stress?

☐ Does your child play it safe by avoiding situations that require taking risks?

☐ Does he feel powerless?

☐ Is he overly sensitive?

☐ Does he constantly need reassurance?

☐ Is he easily influenced by others?

☐ Does he frequently use the phrases "I don't know," or "I don't care"?

☐ Is he withdrawn?

☐ Does he blame others for his failures?

☐ Is he isolated or preoccupied? Does he have few friends?

☐ Is he uncommunicative?

☐ Is he clingy and dependent?

☐ Does he complain constantly?

☐ Does he have a general negative attitude?

Hanging In There When *You're* Discouraged

Maintaining an encouraging atmosphere can be tough when a child isn't behaving well—but, of course, that's when he most needs it. That's not to say that you'll always be able to get through to him; sometimes he'll need to calm down first. But other times you might be surprised at how far a little encouragement goes.

When your toddler or preschooler is upset, try getting down to his level. Look him in the eyes. Offer him a hug or a hand or a lap to calm down in. Invite an older child to sit and talk with you about how he's feeling. You can often defuse an angry situation quickly with a simple, encouraging gesture or word.

Q&A

I try to stay positive and encouraging, but sometimes I'm just too angry with my child to maintain it. Then what?

No matter how much you love your child, or how many parenting books you've read, you're bound to feel amazing anger and rage as well as amazing love toward your child at one time or another. Oftentimes we feel not only angry, but helpless, too. "How is it that I can't get my two-year-old to stop whining?" you ask yourself. And of course anger has a way of mounting. But having angry feelings is not the same as following through on them. When you're so angry that you're no longer rational or you're afraid you're going to say or do something hurtful, you first need to protect yourself and your child from your intense feelings. The best way to do this is by taking an adult time-out until your anger subsides. Once you've calmed down, let your child know that your loving feelings have come back. "Boy, I was upset. I feel better now. I still love you." If you said hurtful things when you were angry, tell your child you feel bad about it. "I'm sorry. I was really upset. It wasn't your fault (or it wasn't anything you did). You were just in the wrong place at the wrong time!" It's important for your child to see that you, too, can make mistakes, and that you can apologize and be close and loving again.—*Nancy Samalin, author of* Love and Anger

To be encouraging, of course, it helps not to get discouraged yourself. So try to focus on the positive in your child and his behavior. "When you spend 85 percent of your time and energy

GET PSYCHED

"Parents are, in effect, mirrors: What we reflect back to our kids becomes the basis for their self-image, which in turn influences all areas of their lives."–*Stephanie Marston, author of* The Magic of Encouragement

focusing on the 15 percent that is negative, the negative will grow and the positive will soon disappear," explains Jane Nelsen. On the other hand, if you focus 85 percent of your time and energy on the positive, it won't be long before the negative disappears and the positive will grow to 100 percent because that's all you see. It is very encouraging to yourself and others when you focus on the positive."

So, for example, when you walk into your child's room and mention those tidy CDs, you're encouraging him to expand his tidiness by appreciating the island of organization in his otherwise messy room. If your child is disruptive at preschool, focus on his good leadership qualities or good sense of humor. When he learns to appreciate these as good qualities, you may be able to explore together how to use them in a positive way.

When you focus on the positive instead of reacting to the negative, not only do you encourage positive behavior, you also avoid fueling the negative. If a child needs attention and the only way he gets it is by doing something ornery, he's perfectly willing to do it. On the other hand, when you encourage his contributions and efforts, you'll encourage his sense of belonging and desire to do well. You don't have to follow your child around telling him how wonderful he is all the time (in fact, that's a bad idea!), but do give him a word of encouragement when he shares, or reads to his little brother, or takes his plate to the kitchen after snack time.

One decidedly discouraging thing you can do is to criticize your child. (When it comes to children, there's no such thing as "constructive criticism.") When your child loses his watch, resist the urge to tell him that he should have taken better care of it, put it in his backpack, not taken it off, not worn it in the first place .... Instead, show empathy and talk about what he might do now. "It is extremely difficult to avoid criticizing children for losing, breaking, or forgetting things," says Nancy Samalin. "But when we are able to act as their allies instead of blaming them, they will be more motivated to avoid such mishaps." You might also explore what he might do next time—by asking him questions in a supportive, empathetic manner.

Know Your Child

To successfully encourage your child, you need to understand his temperament, his developmental stage, and his current state of mind. (Always remember to consider how much sleep he got last night, how school went today, and whether he's hungry or feeling ill, for example.) That's one reason there's no one-size-fits-all-every-day discipline style.

Temperament If you have more than one child, you likely know how amazingly different one child can be from another. From infancy, some children are more outgoing and active, whereas others are quieter and more withdrawn. Some don't like change of any kind, whereas others relish it. Some babies keep their temperamental tendencies as they grow into children, whereas others have a change of heart.

Tailor your discipline to wherever your child is now. With loving, nurturing discipline techniques, that's not a hard thing to do. It's not a matter of talking more or less harshly or finding stricter or less severe punishments. But you may need to put more energy into maintaining consistent limits with some children than others, for example, and some kids may need active reassurance every step of the way while others just need to see you on the sidelines whenever they glance your way. Your shy preschooler might want you to hold her hand as she approaches the new kids at the playground, whereas her sister might be offended if you're even in the vicinity.

Your child is his own person. Not like his big brother, not an extension of you or your partner. You don't want to mold him, but you want to use what you know about him to help you be encouraging, to help him grow his strengths and fulfill his potential.

Ages and Stages Understanding your child's developmental stage can help you set reasonable expectations and appreciate his accomplishments. Perhaps most importantly, it can help you create an environment in which your child can be appropriately challenged and find success. Nothing is more encouraging than that.

Many helpful books and magazine articles are devoted entirely to childhood ages and stages, year by year. If you want to know more about just what the world is like from your child's point of view right now, pick one up that addresses his age. By understanding what tasks your child is tackling, you'll be better able to set reasonable goals for him and provide him with a safe, challenging, rewarding environment.

For example, when your baby is between the ages of 1 and 2, he's becoming more aware of himself as a separate person, yet

GET PSYCHED

"The baby reaches each developmental floor already equipped with certain competencies. How his competencies develop into skills depends on the baby's interaction with the environment that he finds on each floor."
–William Sears, author of Growing Together

he's often frightened about losing the security of babyhood. Your affection and reassurance will get him over the hump, as will established bedtimes, mealtimes, and other routines that he can count on. He also likes to affect his world, so blocks that he can stack (and knock down), shapes and colors to sort, and containers to empty and fill are perfect playthings during his first year or so.

WEB TALK: For reliable, thorough, and accessible information about developmental milestones, health topics, discipline issues, and much more, visit

www.BabyCenter.com

After your child has a second birthday under his belt, he can learn to take turns playing, and he begins to understand the concepts of "yours" and "mine" (which will explain a few squabbles). With his growing physical prowess, he'd love a tricycle and simple mechanical toys this year. He also wants you to help him with his vocabulary—which is growing by leaps—by talking with him about every little thing.

You'll want to keep your 4-year-old's rich fantasy life in mind when you bring him books from the library and encourage his efforts at counting when he makes his highest block tower yet.

You get the idea. You don't have to study child development or memorize every cognitive and physical milestone to understand your child. Usually just tuning in to him sensitively will keep you in touch. But for added insight, it's fun to read up on what he's up to.

GET PSYCHED

"Now, to discipline any child effectively, especially the younger ages, it is essential to know what may reasonably be expected of that child. A good disciplinarian needs to understand the rapidly changing behaviors which characterize the different early ages. An extremely effective way of handling a 2-year-old might be utterly ineffective with a 4-year-old."—*Louise Bates Ames, Ph.D., author of* Raising Good Kids, A Developmental Approach to Discipline

Knowing your child's developmental stage also helps when choosing discipline techniques. When you understand your toddler's struggle with independence and his concurrent need to feel secure, you'll not only be more patient with him, you'll be better at coming up with solutions, too. Maybe you'll buy him Velcro shoes so he can put his own shoes on without the frustration that always ensues with his tie-on sneakers, for example. And when he does have a meltdown, you'll understand that even though he's fighting you, he's scared, too, and still needs you nearby.

What You Can Do

Opportunities to offer encouragement fill each day. Keep encouragement in mind as a positive, nurturing discipline technique, and it will soon become a habit.

- ☐ Write your child encouraging notes and put them in his lunch box or on the bathroom mirror.

- ☐ Encourage your child to be encouraging—to his siblings and to his friends, for example. Point out opportunities and make specific suggestions, or, if he's old enough, ask him how he thinks he might offer encouragement.

- ☐ Ask your child every day—at dinner or bedtime, for example—what new thing he tried today. Give him credit for his efforts.

- ☐ Talk with your child's teachers not just about his grades and his behavior, but about his efforts, too. Include him in the conversation.

- ☐ Think about an adult who offered you encouragement as a child. How was the encouragement given? Did you find it helpful? What emotions does the memory stir?

☐ Think about an incident when you felt angry, upset, not at your best. Would you say you were feeling discouraged?

☐ Check out a book on your child's developmental stage. Don't use it to push your child, but do let your pediatrician know if you think your child is lagging far behind in any particular area.

☐ Keep a journal of your child's important efforts and his accomplishments. This will show him that you value both.

Structure

Being a nurturing, positive, loving parent means that you nourish your relationship with your child with affection and respect. It also means that you provide the framework that she needs to learn and grow. And that framework involves setting limits, being consistent in your discipline, and providing a routine on which she can depend.

The Temptations of Parental Control

When we talk about the need for parents to provide limits for children, we're not talking about controlling children. In much the same way that our culture confuses discipline with punishment, we also tend to confuse limits with control. But children don't need parents to exert control over them; in fact, it's detrimental to their growth.

Loving discipline involves teaching and guiding children to flourish. And the methods used—encouragement and support, modeling, providing time and attention, communicating in a way that builds your close relationship—have nothing to do with punishment. Not so with a parent who disciplines via control.

Parents who exert control over children rather than support their autonomy are often interested in obedience. We've talked about authoritarian discipline style; it's the authoritarian who uses punishment—and rewards—to affect a child's behavior to garner her compliance. Working from a position of power and dominance, it's how he "teaches" her to obey. Other coercive measures the authoritarian parent may take include spanking, yelling, criticizing, humiliating, guilt tripping ("How could you do this to me after all I've done for you?"), threats, deprivation (taking away a privilege or an object of desire), and manipulation. If the controlling parent is successful, the child will be compliant and submissive.

Other parents exert their control by putting too much emphasis on a child's performance. It's great to participate in your child's life, and it's perfectly natural to want your child to do well because it will make her happy. But sometimes we want our children to do well because it reflects well on us (or we think it does), or because we're a bit shortsighted about what's best for the child in the long run.

GET PSYCHED

"Today's parenting requires giving children many opportunities, but not becoming overly concerned about particular outcomes, such as the highest grades, the best test scores, or always winning in sports or other contests. There's more long-term value to children learning self-control and problem solving than in their besting their peers in childhood competitions."–*Wendy Grolnick, Ph.D., author of* The Psychology of Parental Control: How Well-Meant Parenting Backfires

"There's a fine line between being involved in your child's life, which is good, and controlling your child's life, which is not," says Wendy Grolnick, Ph.D., who has studied parental control for more than a decade. "Unfortunately, almost all of us who are parents get invested in how well our children are doing in every single one of their activities. We push them to be the best at everything and act as if their ability to win determines their future survival, which is definitely not the case."

"Reading was a big struggle for our son when he was in first and second grade. We spent hours focusing on reading together, we tried a phonics program, and we became more and more stressed as we became more and more worried. 'Try harder!' we pushed. His teacher suggested he might be dyslexic or have ADD, so we even put him on a waiting list to be tested. Then we decided to stop pushing so hard. We took a step back and gently encouraged our son to simply do the best he could. No rewards or promises for doing well in reading, just support for his efforts. It took time, but as we continued to relax and encourage, he continued to steadily improve. By the time he reached seventh grade, he was moved to the advanced reading class and scored a 'commendable' rating on his state reading test. Because we simply supported and encouraged him, the achievement was all his."–*Parent Jill Dutton, Van, Texas*

Another way we control children is by doing everything for them. Yes, we've arrived at the opposite end of that parenting spectrum, with the permissive parent controlling the child with indulgence. Remember when we talked about permissiveness we said that the permissive parent was long on love and short on limits. We didn't say he was short on control!

When you put away your teen's outfits for her every day and fix her homework for her so it's perfect, or do her chore for her so she doesn't get in trouble with your partner, you're exerting unnecessary control over her life. Sometimes we think of this as overfunctioning out of love, but it doesn't help our children develop their autonomy or their sense of responsibility. Again, we think it's in the child's best interest; we want things to run smoothly for her. That's shortsighted.

Why Controlling Doesn't Work

There's nothing wrong with being in control *of yourself*—how you relate to your child, how you provide for her, how you create a warm home environment. But an abundance of research substantiates the fact that children are better off when their parents don't exert control *over them*.

In fact, Wendy Grolnick found in her research that parents who interfere too much in their children's academic, social, or athletic lives actually handicap the children in developing the life skills they need. What's helpful, she says, is parents who are *autonomy-supportive,* parents who provide plenty of resources and facilitate their children's participation in a wide range of activities. What is *not* helpful is pushing children to succeed at every turn.

PsychSpeak

Autonomy-supportive means helping children feel like the initiators of their own actions by attempting to understand their viewpoints, providing choices, encouraging independent initiations and problem solving. Autonomy-supportive parents involve children in decision making and take into account the children's thoughts and feelings. By contrast, controlling parenting involves using pressure and coercion and solving problems for children.

Control Doesn't Mean Willing Compliance In a study published in a 1974 issue of *Journal of Personality and Social Psychology,* researchers J. Merrill Carlsmith and colleagues concluded that parents who use power-assertive methods with their children—raising their voices and issuing orders—obtained immediate compliance, but reduced their children's cooperativeness on subsequent occasions. As time went on, the researchers found, more and more frequent power assertion was required to gain compliance.

Marilyn L. C. Comstock, in a 1973 dissertation on the "Effects of Perceived Parental Behavior on Self-Esteem and

Adjustment," found that parents who make firm demands that are perceived by children as reasonable are most likely to foster high self-esteem. These parents "make demands and give directions in ways that leave a degree of choice and control in the hands of children."

Analysis of longitudinal data from the National Survey of Families and Households, published in 2001 in the *Journal of Family Issues,* shows that coercive parental control is associated with lower well-being and increased substance abuse in adolescence. In their findings, researchers William S. Aquilino and colleagues described punitiveness and psychological overcontrol as forms of "coercive control," while the preferred "democratic parenting" was characterized by "a clear statement of rules, use of reasoning, and allowing children to participate in rule setting."

As you've seen in Chapter 5, strict, punitive discipline does not produce disciplined kids; in fact, it actually *causes* problem behavior rather than preventing it. For one thing, controlling, punitive discipline is external; it does nothing to teach a child self-control. "Parents who use force frequently complain their children are liars or are sneaks—both natural responses to being coerced to do things we don't want to do," explains psychotherapist James Windell. Experts who work with children of controlling parents commonly report that the child feels either enraged or defeated. "Often the result of control is either that kids become submissive, obedient, and compliant or that they go to the opposite extreme and rebel against any and all authority," explains Barbara Coloroso, author of *Kids Are Worth It!*

That's not to say your child will always be happy—or even grudgingly agreeable—with the rules and structure you provide.

GET PSYCHED

"It seems a fact of human nature that people lose their feelings of self-respect when they comply with others who order them around or make demands for immediate action. Adults greatly resent being ordered around, and there's no reason to believe that children react differently."
—*Psychotherapist James Windell, author of* The Fatherstyle Advantage

Your preschooler may well adamantly refuse to go to bed when his big brother is still up because it seems terribly unfair to him. And your toddler may not even begin to understand that getting his hair washed—which he abhors—is necessary.

There will be many times throughout his childhood that you will need to make decisions for your child that he is unable to understand or unwilling to accept. The key is to minimize those decisions—when it's necessary for your child's safety or well being, for example—but never make them on a whim or because you simply want to exert your control.

When a parent exerts control over a child, he weakens the parent/child relationship, which is the basis of successful discipline. We want to help our children to be happy and productive and responsible, but when we act in controlling ways we lose our influence. Experts have pointed out that exerting power over a child actually lessens a parent's ability to guide or help her. You cannot successfully discipline a child who is withdrawn or deceptive or rebellious because of the way that you've treated her.

"On balance, the kids who do what they're told are likely to be those whose parents don't rely on power and instead have developed a warm and secure relationship with them," explains Alfie Kohn. "They have parents who treat them with respect, minimize the use of control, and make a point of offering reasons and explanations for what they ask."

"In order for children or students to accept an adult's experience, wisdom, or values, they must like, look up to, and respect the adult," agrees Thomas Gordon, author of *Parent Effectiveness Training*. "Conversely, we know that kids grow to dislike, hold a low opinion of, and treat with contempt those who would try to coerce them, bridle them, or deny their right to get their needs met. On the other hand, we also know that kids will seek out, listen to, believe, and model themselves after those whom they like and admire, who treat them with respect, who trust them, who refrain from bossing them around, who are easy to talk to."

WEB TALK: To learn skills for building a close relationship with your child and with other parents, visit The Parents Leadership Institute at www.parentleaders.org

It Brings Out the Worst Gordon studied the results of the use of control by those in positions of authority, and he concluded, "Parents and teachers are paying a terrible price for using power: They are causing their children or students to develop habits, traits, and characteristics considered both unacceptable by most adults and unhealthy by mental-health professionals." In a nutshell, victims of control commonly fight, escape, or give in.

Based on surveys taken in his P.E.T. and T.E.T. (Teacher Education Training) classes, Gordon compiled a list of coping mechanisms children use when adults try to control them:

- Resisting, being negative
- Rebelling, disobeying, being insubordinate, sassing
- Retaliating, vandalizing
- Hitting, being belligerent, being combative
- Breaking rules and laws
- Throwing temper tantrums, getting angry
- Lying, deceiving

- Blaming others, tattling
- Bossing or bullying others
- Banding together, organizing against the adult
- Withdrawing, daydreaming
- Competing, needing to win, needing to look good, making others look bad
- Giving up, loafing
- Escaping, staying away from home, running away, quitting school, cutting classes
- Not talking, ignoring, using the silent treatment, writing the adult off
- Crying, feeling depressed or hopeless
- Becoming fearful, shy, hesitant to try anything new
- Needing reassurance, seeking constant approval
- Getting sick, developing psychosomatic ailments
- Overeating, excessive dieting
- Being submissive, conforming, being dutiful
- Drinking heavily, using drugs
- Cheating in school, plagiarizing

This list, Gordon points out, shows that control creates the very behavior patterns that parents and teachers *most dislike* in children. And of course, it often feeds the cycle, causing parents to be even more controlling, more punitive.

It Doesn't Teach Responsibility   Another important issue raised by the exertion of control is the way in which it diminishes responsibility. Based on the disturbing results of his famous experiments at Yale University in the 1960s, psychologist Stanley

Milgram concluded, "The disappearance of a sense of responsibility is the most far-reaching consequence of submission to authority."

In Milgram's experiments, participants were directed to give electric shocks to "learners" whenever they gave a wrong response. The "learners," unbeknownst to the participants, were actors who would never feel a real shock, but would purposely give an occasional incorrect answer and pretend to feel increasing pain when the participants "shocked" them. Almost two thirds of the participants obeyed the orders to continue to shock the learners, even when they groaned and shrieked as if in agony. Many of them displayed stress and protested about the fact that the person was being hurt, but most continued shocking the learner anyway. When asked about their behavior after the experiment was over, some participants said they believed that what they were doing was wrong, but they felt compelled to obey authority.

> **GET PSYCHED**
>
> "As a society we must urgently adopt the goal of finding and teaching effective alternatives to authority and power in dealing with other persons—alternatives that will produce human beings with sufficient courage, autonomy, and self-discipline to resist being controlled by authority when obedience to that authority would contradict their own sense of what is right and what is wrong."—*Thomas Gordon, Ph.D., author of* Discipline That Works

If we want our children to be strong, independent, ethical adults, we can't teach them to be compliant. For a child to learn to take responsibility, you have to give up control, you have to give her a say in her autonomy. If you teach her, with control, to comply, she does not learn to think for herself. On the other hand, if you let go at every safe possibility, you'll allow her to develop into her own person.

Loving discipline experts do not advocate permissiveness; in fact, they keep the need for structure, rules, and limits in mind.

But they also look for safe opportunities to empower children. Letting go of control can be as simple as allowing your toddler to wear her favorite pink socks with every outfit or respecting your preschooler's decision that she's had enough to eat at dinner. Honor your grade-schooler's wish to move her bed to the middle of her room, and let your teen go out for debate club rather than track (no matter how many medals *you* won, or wish you'd won, or how fast she is). There will be plenty of times when your child won't be able to follow through on her preferences, of course; just consider yourself her ally in minimizing them.

It Doesn't Improve School Performance Studies in the education arena have shown that children do better in schools where cooperation, rather than obedience, is fostered. In a study of 90,000 middle and high school students, the National Longitudinal Study of Adolescent Health researchers found that students who feel "connected" to school are more likely to have "improved attitudes toward school, learning, and teachers; heightened academic aspirations, motivation, and achievement; and more positive social attitudes, values, and behavior." The researchers suggested class meetings, self-direction, and daily attention to the "hopes, concerns, desires, and fears of students." Published in 1997, their findings concluded that "We learn best from those with whom we are in caring, mutually respectful relationships."

Many more studies of teacher/student relationships validate these findings. Researchers Edward L. Deci and colleagues compared teachers' behavior that supported autonomy to teachers' controlling behaviors. In a 1981 study, published in the *Journal of Educational Psychology,* they stated that children who are taught by teachers with controlling styles report significantly lower intrinsic motivation to learn and lower feelings of competence and self-worth. And in 1997, researcher Rolland Deslandes and colleagues found that improved school grades among ninth graders were associated with firm, warm, involved, and democratic teaching methods.

A parent's approach to a child's schoolwork plays an equally vital role, of course. Golda S. Ginsburg and Phyllis Bronstein, in their study of fifth-grade students, published in a 1993 issue of *Child Development,* found "over-controlling parental styles characterized by high parental surveillance of homework, punitive reactions to grades, and use of extrinsic rewards for achievement to be correlated with lower academic performance and decreased motivation to learn." (See Chapter 5 for more studies that link academic achievement with authoritative parenting.)

When children do poorly in school, or become involved with drugs, vandalism, drunk driving, and other self-destructive and socially unacceptable behaviors, it's common to hear a rally cry for more control by parents and teachers. But more control may just fuel the problem. And certainly it doesn't solve it.

As Gordon explains, "The more I have learned about the principal causes of the behaviors that damage youth and weaken our society, the firmer my belief that our best hope for prevention is another kind of strategy—namely, helping adults who deal with children learn a new way to manage families, schools, and youth-oriented organizations. And that strategy will require teaching adults the skills required to govern their family, their classroom, their group more democratically, less autocratically—not the other way around as some are urging us to do."

Although it's hard for some parents to relinquish control, when they do they often find that the result is positive for them as well as their kids. Managing every aspect of a child's life every minute of the day is a stressful, tedious, time-consuming job. It's an impossible job. And it's not rewarding. What's rewarding is watching your child learn to take responsibility, to discover her own likes and dislikes, her own strengths and weaknesses. Best of all, when you stop controlling and instead support and nourish your child, your relationship with her grows into one that will support your discipline efforts and foster her growth.

> **GET PSYCHED**
>
> "The dominant problem with parenting in our society isn't permissiveness, but the fear of permissiveness. We're so worried about spoiling kids that we often end up overcontrolling them."—*Alfie Kohn, author of* Unconditional Parenting

Dependable Discipline

So your child does not need you to control her. But she does need you to provide consistent limits. What's the difference between limits and control? In a loving framework, limits are imposed only when necessary, and the child's perspective is taken into account. (In fact, the child is given a say in limit setting whenever appropriate.) Limits are nonpunitive and supportive of the child's long-term best interests. It may help to keep in mind a picture of your child as her own individual, someone whom you respect and support, but not someone whom you need to fulfill your own dreams and desires, except by becoming fully and gloriously herself. Your goal is to empower her, not coerce her.

What kinds of things might you have limits about? You and your family will want to decide what your important issues are. Perhaps it's a rule that family members never make fun of one another. Or that hitting is not allowed. Maybe you've decided together on a half-hour television limit per day, or Saturday morning chores.

Although it's hard for some parents to set limits, it's harder still to consistently follow them. For one thing, kids don't like it. When you remind your child that her television time is up, for example, she's not going to thank you. When she complains and acts miserable, you can seemingly fix it all simply by giving in. Saying "Oh, okay, one more program" instantly makes the child happy, after all. But, as we've said, your goal is not your child's immediate happiness but her long-term best interests. Which means that you turn off the television.

Inconsistency makes kids unsure of you and of themselves. When you tell your child to "Please hang up the phone and come to dinner," and then proceed to eat dinner without her, you're giving her a mixed message. Can she ignore you when you tell her to come to dinner or not? When it comes time for the next rule, why wouldn't she test it?

It's especially easy to be inconsistent when you're tired or upset with your child. When you throw up your hands and say "I don't care, do whatever you want!" out of exasperation, she gets the message—you don't care. It takes a lot of energy to be consistent, especially if your child is used to your waffling. Some ways to help make it easier:

- Choose your battles. You've heard this before. If you don't make a big deal about everything, you won't have so many things to be steadfast about. After you set a rule, however, you need to follow through or your child won't know where she stands. And she'll try to find out.

- Enlist your child's help in making rules. If your child helps make the rule, she's more likely to follow it. And when you follow through on it consistently, you're showing respect for her part in developing it.

- Give yourself a pat on the back. Remember to encourage yourself when you're able to be consistent during a tough time. Parenting is a skill and it takes practice.

- Ask for backup. Your partner, a friend, or a relative can support you when you feel like giving in even though you know you shouldn't.

- Be on the same page. Make sure you and your partner are consistent when it comes to limits. You don't want your child running back and forth between you, and you don't want to give in because you know your partner will anyway.

- Say what you mean. If you mean "no," say "no," not "maybe." If you're not sure, take some time to think about it, if you need to, but say "I need to think about it. I'll tell you in 10 minutes," for example.

- Act sure of yourself. Your child knows when you're not and she needs you to be confident, at least most of the time.

- Give your child a choice. You can do this while still standing firm. "You may lower your voice and stay, or you may leave," for example.

- Don't be guilt-tripped. Don't let your child guilt you into changing your mind. ("You never let us have any fun!")

- Let your child be angry or disappointed. Acknowledge and give your child permission to express her feelings: "I know you're disappointed that we can't go to the zoo today." Also realize that it's okay for her to feel unloving toward you. Better that you follow through and she be angry with you than not follow through.

- Don't be too rigid. Just note that you're making an exception: to read longer tonight so you can finish the new *Harry Potter* book, or to mow the lawn on Saturday instead of

Friday after school so you can take Grandma to dinner for her birthday, for example.

Although it's a good idea to make sure your child understands and even helps develop rules from the get-go, you won't want to get too caught up in lengthy explanations when it's time to follow through. In *Loving Your Child Is Not Enough*, Nancy Samalin explains that these kinds of explanations don't work because we often give them in an attempt to change our kids' minds and make them agree with us. "We hope they'll buy the explanation and not be angry with us. But after a thousand explanations, children still want what they want as much as they wanted it before. And we just have to deal with not giving them what they want."

Q & A

How can stepparents provide consistent discipline?

In stepfamilies—especially new stepfamilies—stepparents should leave discipline up to the biological parent. If they enter the family and quickly try to control their stepchildren by establishing new rules and disciplining the stepkids, the stepkids will resent them. The children will likely say, "You're not my mommy!" or "You're not my daddy!" Unfortunately, however, many new stepparents feel very powerless. They often feel "left out" of the tight bond between their new spouse and his or her children. They make the mistake of trying to take control and trying to create new rules and traditions. This not only sparks resentment in the kids; it can create tremendous stress between the new stepparent and his or her spouse, and between the new stepparent and his or her stepkids, as well as their biological mother or father.

Sometimes, stepparents are alone with their stepchildren and are in charge of discipline. In this case, the biological parent should very clearly state that the stepparent is in charge. The stepparent should follow his or her spouse's rules and style when disciplining the stepkids, even if the stepparent does not agree with the spouse's parenting philosophy.—*Lisa Cohn, co-author (along with William Merkel, Ph.D.)*, One Family, Two Family, New Family: Stories and Advice for Stepfamilies

Clean Getaways

"I decided I had my last argument and nag session about dirty rooms with my preteen twins, Greg and Marly. I put out the new and simple rules: *If you would like to go out to an activity on the weekend, your room must be clean. You may choose not to clean and stay home, or you may choose to clean and go out. The word 'clean' will be defined by your parents and expectations demonstrated and understood.*

"The kids agreed this sounded fair. I went over with each of them what 'clean' meant (clothes picked up, room vacuumed and dusted, nothing stuffed over, under, or behind anything). They could have their room in any condition they wished until the weekend when they wanted to leave the house for an activity. No nagging by me—it was entirely up to them. In typical twin fashion, each child approached these new family rules differently.

"Greg enjoyed his messy room. I never said a word. When the first Friday arrived, he was still smiling and wallowing in his mess. He watched a few movies, played with his things, talked on the phone and ate snacks on his bed. Saturday found him not smiling anymore after a phone call from friends asking him to go play ball. He asked if he could go and I said, 'Sure, anytime you like after your room is clean. Let me know when you'll be needing a ride.' I would not engage in his 'But Mom's!' Eventually the room was clean, and he was off.

"Marly is very social and staying put was never an option. Her room was ready for its first inspection on a Thursday, since she was going home with a friend after school on Friday. By the third week when she asked to leave and meet friends at the local drive-in, I said, 'Sure' without checking her room. I foolishly thought she had it down.

"After Marly left, I did check her room. Let's just say it did not pass. I got in the family wagon, pulled up in front of the drive-in, and honked the horn and smiled. She knew why I was there, but could not believe I was serious. To avoid further embarrassment, she jumped in the car and we headed back to her room. If I remember correctly, we had only a few more incidents. The secret to the success was follow-through on my part—and no nagging! I had read from numerous parenting books to mean what you say, so I also drew a lesson from that."—*Tami Eiford, parent educator, Bellingham, Washington*

Of course, following through with loving kindness means that when your child balks, you don't resort to yelling or scolding or threatening, or any other coercive methods. You remain firm and kind. If you do this consistently, your child will come to trust and understand limits.

Being consistent means more than just sticking to rules, however. It means providing a consistent emotional climate, an environment that's supportive, helpful, loving, friendly, and open. It means consistently taking time to listen to your child, to spend time with her, to be positive and upbeat as often as you can.

It also means making a commitment to your discipline style. Be firm and loving. Don't become authoritarian when you lose your temper. And don't become permissive when you're tired. At the same time, it's important to evaluate how things are going and to make changes when necessary, as your child grows and her needs change.

The Reassurance of Routine

From the time a child is an infant, she benefits from routine. Of course parents need to respond to a baby's cries for food or comforting without concern for a schedule. But bathing her at about the same time each day, taking her for an afternoon walk, and singing or reading to her at night are all routines that in time coax her into her own schedule and help her learn that there is some order and dependability in this world. As she gets older, if you raise her with certain routines, they can become good habits. You might teach your toddler that beds get made before breakfast, for example, and your kindergartener that homework gets done before play. Your grade-schooler can learn that thank you notes get written promptly for gifts and other kindnesses, and your teen can routinely check in on her younger brother after school. Routines become a matter of course and provide your child with a framework for her day.

Routines make life easier for you, too. When everyone in your household is into a routine, there's no need to nag or reorganize every hour, or wonder who's going to do what when. Chores get done; mealtimes, mornings, and bedtimes run more smoothly; and everybody, generally, feels more comfortable.

Everyone feels chaos at home now and then. But some homes are more chaotic than others, and that's not a great growing environment for kids. If you haven't put much stock in routines, it's never too late. Just make sure that you convey the routine clearly to your child. "This is how we're going to handle bedtime from now on. First you can choose a book and put it on your bed while I run the bath." Get your child's input. Maybe she'll suggest reading to the baby, too, or telling you a story sometimes instead of picking a book. It'll be more fun for her—and easier for you—if she has a say.

GET PSYCHED

"Routine is to a child what walls are to a house; it gives boundaries and dimensions to his life. No child feels comfortable in a situation in which he doesn't know exactly what to expect. Routine gives a feeling of security. An established routine also provides a sense of order from which freedom grows."–*Rudolf Dreikurs, M.D., author of* Children: The Challenge

Chaos happens. Schedules get crazy, the house gets messy, dinner is served late, and alarm clocks fail to go off. But for your home to run smoothly and for your child to have a secure base from which to venture (as well as a welcoming place to return), you'll want a semblance of order at home. In fact, cleanliness and organization can bring security and comfort and an appreciation of order and beauty. Need more incentive? A recently concluded 25-year study of children's homes indicates that your child will be better educated and better off financially if your home is clean! Researchers at the Institute for Social Research found that children raised in homes that were rated "very clean" by the researchers generally received one to two years more education and made 40 percent more money than children from homes rated "so-so" or "dirty." Researcher Rachel Dunifon explains, "Keeping a clean and organized home reflects an overall ability and desire to maintain a sense of order in a wide range of life activities."

Of course, sharing cleaning chores with your child will instill these organizational skills even better than taking care of them yourself. Making her part of the family routine when it comes to chores will also encourage her sense of belonging, of family team spirit. Let her know that you count on her to do her part. Keep in mind that routine doesn't have to mean drudgery. Put on her favorite music while she sweeps, rake the leaves and jump in them together, organize the basement a little bit at a time together and use the proceeds of your clean-out garage sale to buy a new DVD player for the family or take a family excursion.

What You Can Do

Believe it or not, giving up controlling behaviors and substituting limits, routines, and organization can be downright refreshing. It's not a one-day project, of course, but a process.

- ☐ Think about any controlling behaviors you might have toward your child. What drives them—a desire for her compliance or her success? What would happen if you gave up these behaviors?

- ☐ Do you feel that anyone exerts control over you, at work or at home, for example? Any chance that you in turn exert control over your child?

☐ Do you remember being told as a child that it was your job to obey? Or do you remember doing what a parent or teacher told you to do just because you were expected to obey? Do you remember how it made you feel?

☐ Talk with your child about whom she might obey. Would she do what a teacher told her, no matter what? A stranger who was an adult? A relative? Explore the idea that you respect her right to tell right from wrong.

☐ What is the tone at your child's school? Is it a warm, friendly environment or a punitive, adversarial one? Consider getting involved and introducing some ideas from Teacher Effectiveness Training (T.E.T.) or some Positive Discipline techniques to your child's school administration.

☐ Think of ways to make routine chores fun. Use a chore jar, for example. Every Saturday morning (or whatever time you've scheduled family chores), have each family member choose a chore from the jar. Swapping is allowed!

☐ Read up on organizational techniques for families. Invest in some basic supplies, like a large calendar for scheduling and file trays for family members' papers.

☐ Teach your child to organize her things—her toys when she's little, her backpack when she heads off to school.

☐ Write down the rules of your household and review them with your child. Have her help you think of them. If there are too many, whittle them down to the most important half dozen or so. If you don't have any, have a family meeting to develop a list. Review them occasionally as a family.

Time and Attention

Perhaps the most universal advice parents with grown children give is to enjoy your parenting years now, because they fly by. Doesn't seem likely as you rock a colicky baby for the second hour or calm a toddler's third tantrum in one afternoon, does it? But the cliché holds; your kids *will* be grown before you know it. Now's the time to take the time. Question is, what's the best way to spend it?

There are several good bets for using time to build your bond with your child—which, loving discipline advocates point out, is the basis of good discipline. One is to make the most of your time together each day, in the course of your normal routine. Another is to carve out special, one-on-one time with your child regularly. And finally, family time, including family meetings, is a practical way to share problem solving, planning, and enjoying being part of the family team.

Good Intentions

We know our kids need us, and we have high expectations for ourselves as parents. Parents consistently rate the ability to balance work and family life high on their list of priorities. And

GET PSYCHED

"If we can enjoy our children even five more minutes a day and yell or criticize five minutes less, we are moving in the right direction."–*Nancy Samalin, author of* Loving Your Child Is Not Enough

according to a national study directed by KidsPeace Lee Salk Center for Research, "Almost all parents (94 percent) see a direct relationship between the amount of meaningful time adults spend with children and the major issues facing youth today, such as discipline problems, violence, substance abuse, and other dangers to their health and happiness."

In that same study, parents indicated that they wish they could spend more time with their children—engaging in physical activity; talking to them about their problems; eating nutritious, family-strengthening meals; and getting involved in their children's educations. The consensus seems to be that we're not doing enough, that parents today are too harried, too overscheduled, too preoccupied with work and worry to spend much time playing with kids.

Actually, we're doing better all the time, at least in terms of clock numbers. According to a study by sociology professor John F. Sandberg and Sandra L. Hofferth at the University of Michigan, working parents spent more time interacting with their 3- to 12-year-old kids in 1997 than stay-at-home moms did 16 years earlier. And fathers spent more time, too, working or not. In fact, children received 10 more hours each week of parental attention in 1997 than they did in 1981.

And here's a bit more encouragement: Although the stat is often relayed negatively (11 percent don't), according to the U.S. Census Bureau, a full 88 percent of children between the ages of 1 and 5 are read to by a family member at least once a week. And three quarters of parents have talked seriously with their children about drugs, tobacco, and alcohol in the past year.

On a scale of 1 to 10, with 10 being extremely healthy and happy, adult caretakers of children rate the overall health and happiness of U.S. children at only 6.2. But, interestingly, they rated their own children at 8.5. So maybe we're doing better than we think—or than others think!

Of course, there are sobering facts, too. About half of American parents haven't talked with their children in the past year about sexual pressures or sexual activity, and although more than half of parents report that their children are worried about war and terrorism, less than a third of them have talked with their children about the topic in the past year.

Whether or not you're encouraged by the statistics, the fact that we want to spend more time with our children means that we care, that we know it's important, and that we're striving to do better. One practical way to do better is to make what time we do spend with our kids count.

The Question of Quality

Something else parents often hear is that it doesn't matter how much time you spend or don't spend with your child; what matters is that the time you spend together is "quality time." Of course, the amount of time does matter; we owe our children more than meager minutes a day. But at the heart of the concept of quality time is an understanding that kids need their parents to bond with them. When you spend quality time with your child, you know what it feels like.

"Quality time has nothing to do with *what* you and your child are doing when you are together," explains Laurence Steinberg, Ph.D. "Quality time is all about *how* you do it. Quality time is defined by your state of mind, not by a set of activities. It's time where you are really engaged with your child." You and your

GET PSYCHED

"Meeting my child's basic needs heads off most behavior problems. And learning about child development usually helps me understand what's going on with him. Mostly, though, positive discipline means just enjoying my child, delighting in the little things he learns and does each day, always looking for the good and genuinely appreciating him for who he is."
–*Katherine Kim, St. Paul, Minnesota*

child might watch a television program together, for example, without so much as a sideways glance or an impromptu observation. On the other hand, you might share a favorite or popular program and talk about it meaningfully—the moral implications of the character's actions, the messages delivered by the commercials, what you each did and didn't like about the plot.

Basically, quality time is time when you connect, and every time you connect you get to know your child a bit more and build your relationship a bit stronger. It might help to keep in mind the wonderful Latin root of the word *attention* or *attendere*—meaning "to stretch toward." When you pay quality attention to your child, then, you're stretching toward him.

Some parents make the mistake of thinking that quality time needs to be educational. Although love of learning is a great thing to foster in your child, too much of an educational slant might turn him off. If he sincerely enjoys learning about the stories embedded in the night sky, great—share it with him during your quality time. But if he doesn't, play connect the star dots instead—or just wish upon the brightest one.

Another easy mistake to make is thinking that to spend quality time you need to go someplace special or do something extravagant. But it's just as easy to share quality time over an after-school snack. Special outings are great once in a while, but they don't really have much to do with quality time. Again, you can do them with or without a real focus on your child. If you take him to an amusement park and spend most of the time on your cell phone while he rides, you missed the opportunity. Take a walk around the block and leave the cell phone at home, and you've bonded.

Of course, you can't possibly make all of your time with your child quality time. Nor would you want to. Sometimes your child may want to be left alone—to play, to daydream, to do his school-work, or to write in his diary. Encourage him. And your child can learn that when you're rushing out the door and grabbing a bite to eat and he asks you a question, of course you can't give him your undivided attention. He doesn't need your undivided attention every minute.

I understand that my child needs my attention, but sometimes he goes overboard, needing every minute of my attention to the exclusion of everyone and everything else. How should I handle this?

"You may feel like a tightrope walker as you try to find the balance between paying enough attention to your child to help her feel a sense of belonging and significance, but not too much to develop unhealthy dependency. A little hint that might help: set up 'special time' for 10 to 20 minutes daily. When your child wants 'undue' attention you can say, 'Honey, I'm busy right now, and I can hardly wait until our special time together.' During this 'special time,' be sure to give your full attention doing something you both like to do.

"One other key: Allow your child to have her feelings (upset, disappointment) when she can't have your undivided attention all the time. Avoid rescuing and fixing. Have faith in her that she can handle these feelings and will feel more self-confidence when she does."–*Jane Nelsen, author of the* Positive Discipline *series*

Don't try to fake it, though. Your child can tell when you're really listening to his recap of last night's dream and when you're thinking about your deadline at work. Sometimes you'll be distracted, so just own up. As much as you can, let go of those deadlines when you're communicating with your child; when you can't, however, admit that you're preoccupied, and explain why.

It's a good idea to *make time* for your child: that is, not just give him whatever time's left after everything else is done. But don't assume that quality time will happen only when you've scheduled a date for it. Fact is, you never know when you'll have a quality moment.

Daily Opportunities

Even if you go your separate ways during the workday, even if your day seems brimming with errands and must-do activities, there are ways that you can spend valuable time with your child. Children often open up—relating stories about hurt feelings at school or fears about performance—not when you ask them point blank, but in the midst of washing dishes or sorting the laundry with you. That's why day-to-day time with your child is so valuable.

"Most of the child's basic learning takes place in the many informal situations that occur daily in the life of the family. These informal occasions for learning include all the times the family members are together doing ordinary things, such as getting dressed, taking baths, preparing to leave for kindergarten, eating, and so forth," explains James E. Van Horn, Ph.D., professor of rural sociology at Pennsylvania State.

So talk with your child in the car on the way to school instead of cranking up the music. Take him grocery shopping with you instead of shopping before you pick him up from daycare. Share meals at the table rather than in front of the television, sit together at bedtime for a bit, relaxing with him instead of sending him off to bed "like a big boy." In short, savor your time with him.

Chores Many families assign chores for kids to accomplish each day, and that's a great practice—it builds competency, responsibility, and a feeling of belonging, of being needed. Another option— perhaps occasionally instead of or in addition to his individual chores—is to do chores together with your child.

So instead of having him clean his room while you rake the yard, give his room a once-over together and then head outside as partners. Ask him whether he would like to help you make tonight's dessert or set the table nearby while you cook. You may well double your opportunity to chat with him.

Mealtimes More than 90 percent of parents believe it's important to eat together with their kids, and 60 percent of them pull off a home-cooked meal at least once a day. Meals don't have to be Norman Rockwell events to build family bonds. You might have pizza in front of the television together on Friday nights, or a barbeque on the porch each weekend. It's a good idea to sit together around the meal table often, though, sharing both food and good times as a family. (Long-term studies indicate that the more your child shares dinner with the family, the less likely he is to smoke, drink alcohol, or use illegal drugs.)

Sharing a family dinner also gives you an opportunity to teach your child social skills—everything from how to carry on a conversation to how to use a napkin correctly. Although dinner seems to be the easiest time to get together, stay open to other good options.

Maybe you can make a family date for Sunday brunch, or subs for lunch on Saturday. Whenever you get together, here are some ideas you might consider for optimizing family mealtimes:

- Talk about the day's events. Share anecdotes, including failures as well as successes. Your child will feel safer sharing with you if you share with him.

- Don't make the dinner table a battleground. You might need some rules to keep this from happening. (No complaining or faultfinding at the table, for example—this includes you, too.)

- Involve your child in meal planning. He may enjoy a meal more if the cranberry sauce was his idea.

- Prompt meaningful conversation. Tell about an embarrassing moment. Ask your child about his happiest memory, or whom he admires. Ask everyone at the table what one thing they did this week they would erase if they could.

- If your child is young, don't expect him to sit at the table until everyone is finished. A toddler just doesn't have the attention span or the physical restraint to stay put that long.

- Decide as a family whether there are other rules you want for dinner. No cell phones at the table, for example? No newspapers?

- Foster gratitude in your kids by encouraging them to thank the cook(s) for the meal, whether or not it was their favorite. And whether or not someone recites a religious prayer, you might take a moment before digging in to show appreciation, too.

Bedtime This may not be your first choice for finding extra time to spend with your child. It's understandable that by day's end many parents are ready for a few hours of nonparenting time. But it's well worth the effort. Your evening will likely go a lot more smoothly—and your child will benefit greatly—if you take a little time to reassure him of your love and ease him into slumber.

"One reason children give their parents such a hard time at bedtime is because they can feel that their parents are trying to get rid of them," explains Positive Discipline expert Jane Nelsen. So have a little bedtime ritual. Here are some possibilities:

- Pamper your child with an herbal bath or some special, scented lotion for after his bath.
- Treat your child (old or young) to a foot massage or a backrub to help him unwind at bedtime.
- Ask your child to tell you about the best part of his day when you tuck him in.
- Lie down beside him if he wants you to. Don't worry about spoiling him.
- Fold down his blankets for him and fluff his pillow. If he has a stuffed animal, tuck it in, head on the pillow, waiting for him. It's fun to do this while he's getting in his jammies.
- If your child is afraid of bad dreams, shoo them out of the room for him whenever you tuck him in.
- Make bedtime reading a habit. Not only will it help you bond with your child, it will also help your child bond with books.

If you do what it takes to help your child feel love and a sense of belonging every night, then bedtime is likely to become a pleasant activity. Besides, what better way for him to fall asleep than thinking about your relationship in a loving way?

Special One-on-One Time

You can spend quality time with your child while doing chores or errands, but every once in a while it's important to set aside some time during which your child is your focus. Children love undivided attention.

This is the time you'll write in on the calendar or planner. Your child will count on you, so take it seriously. Take the phone off the hook if you're home, or leave an answering machine message for your child to hear, saying, "I'm having fun with Gage right now. Please call back later!"

WEB TALK: For useful information and tips for addressing big issues (violence, drugs, alcohol, sex, HIV/AIDS) with your 8- to 12-year-old:

↑ www.talkwithkids.org

During your one-on-one time together, you can explore your child's interests. Let him choose what he'd like to do or play. Give him ideas, if he needs some prompting, but respect his choices. Maybe he'll just want to cuddle on the couch or work on a puzzle with you. Or maybe he'll want to make up a new dance together; give it a try. If he wants to shoot hoops down at the park, forget the fact that you can't dribble around your own foot, and join in. Listen to music that he likes and you don't, read his favorite book for the thousandth time, finger-paint even though it's messy. Let your child teach you something—such as how to skateboard on text message. The point is to have fun together on his terms— to connect, to get to know each other better.

One-on-one time is especially important in a busy household and if you have more than one child. When you're alone, focused on one child at a time, that child doesn't have to worry about getting a word in edgewise or shining next to his superstar sibling. You can tackle some ambitious projects together during your special time, or you can just kick back together. Some ideas for one-on-one time:

- Go shopping for new coloring books—one for you and one for him. Let him choose his, of course, along with a new box of crayons. Then color together, talking about your color preferences, what fun it is to color outside the lines sometimes, what makes a good picture, etc.

- Camp out in the living room together.

- Redesign his room together. You can graph it out on paper, ask him to arrange the furniture how he likes it, then follow through. If you're really ambitious, you might have him pick out a new paint color and/or bedding. During your one-on-one times, you can work on the project together.

- Start an ongoing project to pick up during one-on-one time, such as making a quilt or model car, planting a garden bed, or writing a story. It'll give you a great starting point every time.

GET PSYCHED

"It often feels as though playing will not only eat up our precious time, but will deplete our cups …. Actually, fun play refills cups, ours as well as our children's. The play itself is rejuvenating, but the real refill comes from the connection that grows out of the play. We may have to push ourselves at first, especially to play whatever children want to play, but the payoff is worth it."–*Lawrence J. Cohen, Ph.D., author of* Playful Parenting

- Make smoothies together and sit in the backyard drinking them. Just talk for an hour.
- Look at his baby pictures together. Talk about what he was like as a baby, how happy you were when he arrived, what his temperament was like, etc.
- Play old-fashioned games, such as hopscotch, jump rope, tic-tac-toe, and tiddlywinks. Play a brand-new game of his choosing.
- Go car shopping with your teen, even if he's not ready to purchase.
- Take your child to a fancy department store and let her try on the women's hats. (Most store personnel are very obliging.) Or take your teen to try on fancy gowns, even when it's not prom season. Stop for a treat afterward and talk about her favorites.
- Learn magic tricks together and put on a magic show for the rest of the family.

Family Fun

Being part of a loving family helps fulfill your child's sense of belonging. Besides sharing chores, meals, and daily routines together, you can build the family bond with special events now and then. Celebrations—like holidays and birthdays— are great opportunities. These needn't be extravagant to be special. The fact that everyone always wears new pajamas on Christmas Eve or that the birthday person always sits in the decorated chair are examples of rituals that your child will continue to look forward to.

Six-year-old Clare Mangan eagerly anticipates "Love My Feet" night with her mom, Tammy.

"We pamper our feet together," explains Tammy, a busy professional mom who is often away from home. "We soak them in lavender water, moisturize, clip and polish our nails. The lavender scent is relaxing, so we especially enjoy our special time just before bed. This mommy-daughter ritual for just the two of us is something we both look forward to."—*Tammy Mangan, Myersville, Maryland*

You needn't wait for a calendar event to make a special day, of course. Here are some ideas for fun family time:

- Schedule a game night once a week or once a month. Have the kids suggest new games and teach them old ones, too.

- Have an ethnic meal night. Get your child's input on the fare, and ask him whether he'd like to contribute a dish. You can keep it simple, or go all out—by dressing for the occasion in saris or kimonos, for example.

- If Mom and Dad can be there, designate Friday's after-school snack as make-your-own ice cream sundaes.

- Read out loud together. Choose an old classic—such as the *Little House* series—or a new classic—such as the *Harry Potter* series. Or simply take turns choosing the next book.

- Have a pizza night, with everybody chipping in. Depending on their ages, kids can mix and spread dough, grate cheese, chop veggies, or suggest toppings.

- Rent a canoe, cross-country skis, or tandem bicycles. Buy a badminton or croquet set for the backyard.

Family Meetings

Family meetings are a great way to give kids a say and teach them to problem solve, organize, and communicate. Like all of the other time and attention techniques, they also contribute to a child's sense of belonging to the family team. And although it may not (thankfully) feel like a typical business meeting, you may be surprised at how much you can accomplish—handling problems that keep cropping up, planning events, and setting family rules, for example.

You'll want to let the meeting structure evolve in a way that best suits the personality of your family, but an agenda is probably a good idea. You can post it on the family bulletin board or refrigerator and allow any family member to add items to the list—anything from allowance raises to pet acquisition or bathroom etiquette is game. Encourage your child to use the family meeting to solicit advice from other family members, too—on everything from what summer camp he should choose to how to handle his difficult teacher. And when siblings are in the midst of a battle, the agenda can be a tidy solution. Can't untangle whose responsibility it is to clean up the mess in the garage? Put it on the agenda and discuss it when tempers have calmed.

You may have family meetings once a week, once a month, or only occasionally. Some families call an impromptu meeting when they need one; if you want everyone to attend and your family has school-age children, however, you're likely to have better luck scheduling the event. When it comes time for the meeting, tackle the items in the order listed on the agenda, to prevent disagreement about which is the more important item.

Think about guidelines for the meeting, too. Maybe no topic is off limits, for example, but to prevent it from becoming just a gripe session, problems must be addressed in a problem-solving mode. The tone is that the team is working together to solve problems for the family. In his book *Children: The Challenge*, Rudolf Dreikurs talks about the Family Council, a meeting where the parents' voices and the children's voices hold equal weight. Decisions made at these councils hold for one week. They can be discussed again—and changed by the group—the following week, but not before. "The secret of the success of the Family Council lies in the willingness of all members of the family to approach a problem as a family problem," explains Dreikurs. "Solving problems in a Family Council develops mutual respect, mutual responsibility, and promotes equality." Many families try for consensus decision making, which is ideal, but of course it's up to your family to decide what's working best for you.

Consider limiting the length of the meetings. Whether you go casual or formal, you may also want to designate somebody to run the meeting, to keep some kind of order and to ensure that everyone has a chance to speak. Family members who are old enough might take turns chairing the meetings. Some families also assign a secretary to jot down decisions made by the family. It's a good idea to keep a notebook of these, for reference (and fun years from now!).

Although family meetings offer a great opportunity for problem solving, they're also a good time to talk about upcoming events and obligations and to have some fun together. Get everybody's input on Grandma's birthday present, for example. Ask the group what movie they want to rent for family movie night, and decide together where to take next summer's vacation. Jane Nelsen suggests that family meetings begin with each person giving every member of the family a compliment or by sharing what you are each grateful for. If your kids are used to putting each other down, compliments may seem awkward at first. "If this is the case," she explains, "spend some time discussing the kinds of things they could look for to compliment one another about. Parents can model this behavior by beginning with compliments for each member of the family. Also if you see something nice going on between the children, remind them to remember it for a compliment. You might even suggest that they write it on the agenda so they will remember."

Other fun activities you might enjoy at family meetings are show and tell (something especially silly or especially good you did at work this week, something your child made in preschool, something of interest in the news or in the extended family), or joke and riddle telling (ask one person each session to bring a joke or riddle to share). You might end the meeting by playing a card game together or serving snacks. These sessions keep the family meeting from becoming too serious and add to the camaraderie.

What You Can Do

We adults can be obsessed with time—whether we're trying to find better ways to multitask or to complete our assignment by deadline. Spending quality time with kids is necessary for their healthy development, and to establish bonds with which to discipline, but it can be enormously beneficial for parents, too. It can teach us to live with awareness, to demonstrate our love, and to keep our priorities in order.

☐ For one typical day, jot down all the time you spend talking with or doing things with your child. Is the total more or less than you thought it would be?

☐ Encourage your child to keep a diary. Explain that this is another place he can express his ideas and feelings, whether or not he wants to share them.

☐ Introduce Robert's Rules of Order to your family meetings. It can be fun to follow official rules (when you're choosing to), and your kids will learn valuable lessons in meeting skills.

☐ Grandparents are often skilled at giving children their undivided attention. If your child is lucky enough to have such a grandparent, watch her or him in action for tips.

☐ Don't dismiss the possibility that your teen still wants to participate in family rituals. Even if he bristles at the mention of a new Easter outfit, he may still enjoy dyeing Easter eggs or sharing Easter brunch with relatives. And nobody gets tired of being the center of attention on his birthday.

☐ Some children are more affectionate than others. If your child shuns hugs and kisses, don't give him the cold shoulder. Instead, casually give him a little pat on the arm as you walk by, or smooth his collar for him on his way out the door. Or simply offer him your affection with a warm smile.

☐ Help your child collect riddles, jokes, magic tricks, finger rhymes, and other fun things to share at family meetings.

☐ Take photos of times you share—celebrations, of course, but also those Friday-afternoon sundae treats and living room campouts. Looking back, these smaller special times will loom as large as the big bashes.

Modeling

Children learn both positive and negative, healthy and unhealthy, safe and unsafe, kind and unkind behaviors most effectively in a social context. Most often the lessons take place when they're observing or having meaningful interaction with adults or peers. Modeling gives parents the opportunity to provide, by example, the best kind of loving, guiding discipline.

The influence of role modeling can't be overlooked. If you've ever heard your child repeat something you said days ago in the same tone of voice you used, you know how well she observes and how completely the lesson is absorbed. As much as we would sometimes like to think that we can teach our children by *telling* them right from wrong, if we don't follow through with our *actions,* the lessons become hollow.

Our children learn from watching how we take care of our bodies, refrain from risky behaviors, and engage in healthy ones. They notice the way we handle problems, cope with emotions, and act toward others. Through our everyday actions, we convey to our children our approach to life—negative and fearful or positive and enthusiastic.

When your child is a baby, she learns to wave "bye-bye" by watching you wave "bye-bye." She learns to speak—with much the same twang or lilt in her voice as yours—by listening to and copying you. She may even lift her pinky as she drinks from her sippy cup, if you do the same with your teacup. From your approach to fitness and food to your attitude toward life, your child learns by watching you. Your preschooler really does want to grow up to be "just like you!" And whether or not she retains that goal throughout her teen years, your modeling lessons continue.

By being cognizant of the power of modeling, we can use it to positively influence our children in body, mind, and spirit.

Body Builders

If you'd like your child to be active and physically fit, you would do well to get a move-on yourself. Researchers at the University School of Medicine in Massachusetts studied the physical activity levels of 4- to 7-year-olds and found that children of mothers who are more active than the average mother are twice as likely to be active. And children of active fathers are three-and-a-half times as likely to be active than those of inactive fathers.

Consider teaming up, too; when both parents are active, the study reports that the kids are 5.8 times as likely to be active as children of two inactive parents. The researchers cited role modeling as a primary factor, along with genetics and parental support for the children's participation in activities.

Moms have an especially strong influence on their daughters when it comes to body image. Studies show that girls whose mothers frequently diet and are concerned about their weight are more likely to develop unhealthful weight-control practices than other girls. Parenting experts today advise parents—and moms of daughters in particular—not to obsess over weight, especially in front of their children.

Both parents might also consider keeping an eye on their eating habits. Do you snack all day, eat when you're bored or upset, eat in front of the television, skip meals, shun fruits and veggies, and/or diet constantly? A study published in May 2001 in the *Journal of the American Dietary Association* found that children whose parents model healthful eating habits eat more low-fat foods and more fruits and vegetables than other children. The researchers concluded that parents' eating behaviors have the power to affect the development of childhood eating patterns, and in turn the children's ultimate nutritional health.

What should I do when I mess up in front of my child?
"Turn the situation into a valuable lesson. Make it a teachable moment! Here's how.

"Let's say your child catches you using a bad word while you are on the telephone. Your initial reaction may be embarrassment or denial. If only you could take it back! You may even become defensive and scold your child for eavesdropping on your call. Reacting this way won't help. Stay calm. It's time to come clean.

"Admit what has happened and take responsibility for your behavior. Explain that what you said was not a nice word and apologize. 'You're right, Alyssa, that is not a nice word to use. I am sorry that I said it. I made a mistake. I hope that you do not use that word.' You are now providing a good example by accepting responsibility, being honest, admitting you were wrong and apologizing—all the things you want your children to learn to do when they mess up.

"This strategy applies to any situation where your child catches you misbehaving. Remember that being a good role model does not mean you need to be perfect. It means you need to be responsible."—*Sal Severe, Ph.D., author of* How to Behave So Your Children Will, Too!

And before you turn up your nose at the okra, consider the findings of a report published in 2004 in the *International Journal of Obesity.* David Benton in the department of psychology at the University of Wales studied the "role of parents in the determination of the food preferences of children and the development of obesity." Not only is the type of food you eat influential, so is your approach. Parents, siblings, and peers, he found, can act as valuable role models to encourage healthful eating habits as well as the tasting of new foods. Not earth-shakingly surprising, but worth remembering at the dinner table.

Most parents wouldn't dream of telling a child it's okay to do drugs or habitually drink alcohol. Yet when we model these choices, that's exactly the message we're giving our kids. It's no news that alcoholics often grow up in families of alcoholics. In fact, children of alcoholics are four to six times as likely to develop alcohol problems than children from nonalcoholic families.

Studies have found that parents and their grown children tend to have similar drinking habits, based on modeling by the parents. In alcoholic families, the child is exposed to alcohol at an earlier age and more frequently. In one study, preschool children were able to identify a variety of alcoholic beverages simply by smell. Even if none of the adults in your home has an alcohol problem, consider what message you send your child when you drink "to relax" or "to unwind." And, of course, similar messages are sent to your child if you engage in drug use, however occasional.

PsychSpeak

Social learning theory—Initiated by psychologist Albert Bandura, SLT is an explanation of how people learn by watching, remembering, and copying behavior that is modeled by others.

Interestingly, *social learning theory* suggests that modeling has the greatest impact when the child respects the model. For example, in a study identifying the causes of alcoholism, researcher Joan McCord found that children of alcoholic fathers were more likely to develop alcoholism in families where mothers thought highly of the fathers.

Other behaviors that influence your child's safety might seem tame by comparison to addictions, but in fact they can also be dangerous. At the University of North Carolina in 2001, researcher Susan A. Ferguson and colleagues found that young adults between the ages of 18 and 21 whose parents had 3 or more traffic violations were 38 percent more likely to have had a violation. And kids whose parents had 3 or more automobile crashes on their driving record were 22 percent more likely to have had at least 1 crash compared with kids whose parents had no crashes.

Risky behaviors include actions as simple as not wearing sunscreen. A 2003 article published by researchers at the Department of Dermatology at Boston University School of Public Health found that children (ages 5 though 12) whose parents were conscientious about using sun protection were more likely to also be conscientious. Parents who get sunburned have kids who get sunburned.

A report released in April 2005 by the U.S. Surgeon General Richard Carmona, M.D. and Martin Eichelberger, M.D., president of the National Safe Kids Campaign in Washington, D.C., stresses that parents do not consistently role model safe behaviors for their children. It also underlines the effectiveness of role modeling. For example, 98 percent of parents agree that it's important to act as safety role models for their children. And when it comes to seatbelt use, the numbers are pretty good: 86 percent of adults wear safety belts themselves, and 91 percent of children do. But although 78 percent of parents say it is extremely or very important that their child wear a bike helmet, only 25 percent of parents always wear one. As a result, only 40 percent of children do. When it comes to life jackets, 86 percent of parents say it's extremely or very important for kids to wear them, but

WEB TALK: For info on keeping your child safe from accidental injury, visit www.safekids.org

only 39 percent of parents wear them, and only 57 percent of children always do. "Parents can talk about how important it is," the National SAFEKIDS Campaign states, "but if they aren't doing it themselves, their kids aren't likely to either."

Mind Matters

Have you noticed that many libraries these days are plastered with posters of celebrities with books in hand? That's because reading experts and library administrators understand the importance of modeling behavior. And your child may well pick up a book because Julia Stiles or Orlando Bloom has one in hand.

But the people your child is most likely to model when it comes to reading are the folks at home. In fact, a mother's literacy level is the single most significant predictor of children's literacy, according to the Educational Testing Service. And although children in poor families are less likely to be read to daily than children in homes above the poverty line, some researchers have found that the home literacy environment (the literacy of parents and the availability of reading materials) can be an even stronger predictor of literacy and academic achievement than family income.

Adults who rarely read books or newspapers may be less likely to read to their children. "Adults who value reading are more likely to turn off the television, visit the library, and give books as gifts," explains the U.S. Department of Education in "Start Early, Finish Strong: How to Help Every Child Become a Reader." Studies delving into how to help children become good readers have underlined that a positive attitude toward reading at home can help a child become a better reader and that if parents share enthusiasm about books and reading with their children, the children will be more interested in learning to read in the first place.

What's more, the National Research Council reports that when reading gets to be a challenge, children who have learned from their parents that reading is fun may be more likely to sustain their efforts at reading. So if you want your child to be a reader, pick up a newspaper, book, or magazine. Read to her, too, and, when she's able, encourage her to read to you. Share your enthusiasm for reading.

WEB TALK: For tips on reading to children, choosing books for children, developmental milestones related to reading, and literacy links, see
www.reachoutandread.org

You can similarly model a valuable love of learning. Talk at the dinner table about something interesting you learned today. ("I was amazed to read today that about 8 percent of boys are color blind, but less than half a percent of girls have color-vision deficiency, which is the more accurate term. I had no idea that gender was a factor!") Take classes yourself, or read for information. Readily admit when you don't know something, so your child learns to do the same, and then take the time to look up information.

If you want your child to seek answers and enjoy the learning process, you'll want to be a lifelong learner yourself. Expand your areas of learning and interest to include what she's learning in school, and supplement her schoolwork with fun activities when you can. Invite her to join you on a trip to the nearest observatory when she's studying the planets, and drop in at a craft show together when she's taking pottery class. Pick up on her extracurricular interests, too, to enforce that learning happens outside the classroom.

Attitude Adjustments

Teaching children to approach life positively and other people kindly sounds like a more slippery task than teaching her to wear her seatbelt, but modeling makes it much easier. If you want your child to be considerate, let her see you being considerate to others—and to her.

If you want her to be honest, don't ask her to tell the person on the other end of the phone that you're not home when you are. Share your true feelings rather than pretending to be unscathed all the time; admit when you're struggling, and share when you're pleased. Tell her, "I'm upset about the car breaking down again," or "I'm very excited about my promotion!"

Caring and Kindness All parents want their children to act kindly toward other children and adults. And it's always heart-warming when a child throws an arm around your shoulder and asks, "Are you okay, Dad?" Most of us adults are kind, too, so what's the problem?

Well, we don't always make a point of letting our kids *see* us be kind. You don't need to pat yourself on the back all the time, but you might mention that you're going to drop off an extra batch of cookies at the neighbor's today, or that you're delivering groceries to Aunt Sarah, who isn't able to manage the stairs right now. Explain which organizations you choose to donate to and why, and ask your child how she thinks the family might help out at school.

"**A**s a mother of triplets, there are many times when I have all three toddlers shouting at me for three different things at the same time. It would be easy—and ineffective—to shout back. (I'm thinking that would just turn up the volume!)

"Instead, I simply respond as follows: 'I'll be happy to listen to all of you and get you what you are looking for one at a time, when your voice is as calm as mine.' By modeling the voice I'm looking for, I teach them how best to communicate their needs. All three are able to quickly copy me!"–*Jennifer Colecio, mom to Amanda, Alexis, and Antonio (the A Team), Weatherly, Pennsylvania*

Many studies show that parental modeling of caring, empathetic behavior is strongly related to the development of empathy in children. Researchers David J. Bearison and Tricia Cassel, in a study published in *Developmental Psychology* in 1975, investigated children's ability to be empathetic, to take another person's perspective. First the researchers examined how the children's mothers reacted to several disciplinary situations. Some of the mothers were person oriented in their responses; in other words, they mentioned the feelings, thoughts, or needs of the mother or child in the situation. Others were position oriented, which meant that they referred to rules or statuses in the situation. The children of the person-oriented mothers were more successful at taking the perspective of another person than the children of mothers who relied on rules.

Preschoolers and kindergarteners who have watched someone be generous are more generous themselves, and those who have watched helping behavior tend to imitate those behaviors. These

PsychSpeak

Prosocial behavior–
Voluntary, intentional actions that benefit another person. The motive may be empathetic or it may be external (to receive a reward, for example). Altruistic behavior, by comparison, is also intentional and voluntary but is only motivated by empathy.

effects of observing *prosocial* models aren't fleeting, either; they generally persist for days or weeks. In one study, preschool boys who viewed their fathers modeling generosity and compassion (in doll play) shared more than boys who perceived their fathers as less prosocial. And in a study of 1- to 2-year-olds, psychologist Carolyn Zahn Waxler, Ph.D., and colleagues found that children who exhibited more prosocial reactions toward others in distress had mothers who were empathic with them.

Older children continue to follow in our caring footsteps, too. In a study analyzing the traits and motivation of students who became involved in service organizations in college, researchers found that "students felt a greater obligation to be involved in service because of the role models that their parents provided." And in a similar study at the University of Notre Dame in January 2002, researchers found that the parents of their student-service learning program participants were almost three times more likely to be "very active" in community service than non-service-learning participants (35.7 percent versus 14.4 percent). Students not in student-service learning were more likely to have parents who had done no community service.

Research psychologists E. Gil Clary and Jude Miller found that two kinds of parental role modeling help teach children kindness. One is when the parent shows kindness to others, and one is when the parent shows kindness to the child. In other words, you want to think about what behavior you're modeling in front of your child, but also what kind of behavior you're modeling in your exchanges with her.

What is "lending ego"?

"You can help your child stay in control or cope with a difficult situation. The way to do this is by 'lending your ego.' Because your ego (another name for the management and control part of the personality) is stronger than your child's, you can lend it out.

"For instance, if your child is concerned about what he feels is an unfair grade, you may expect him to work this out with the teacher. However, you may need to be present—not to do his talking for him, but for him to know that he has a backup if he isn't sure how to handle the situation.

"When 9-year-old Robert got into an argument on the sidewalk in front of his house, his father watched the situation develop from inside the house. He could see Robert become more animated and frustrated, so he walked outside, and when he approached his son he put his arm on Robert's shoulder. Robert took a deep breath and told the other boy exactly what he was feeling and what he wanted from the boy. Robert didn't lose control, and he didn't hit the other boy. But it was his father's letting Robert borrow his dad's ego temporarily that helped save the situation."—*James Windell, author of* The Fatherstyle Advantage

From the time your child is a baby, suggests William Sears, M.D., author of *The Baby Book* and an advocate of Attachment Parenting, you should model calmness in your interactions with her. Sears explains that the parenting style that your child is most likely to follow when she becomes a parent is the one she learns from you now. "Children pick up nurturing attitudes at a young age," he says, "and those early impressions stay with them."

GET PSYCHED

"The development of successful achievers is greatly facilitated when you possess the qualities that your child needs to learn. This is no less true for emotional mastery. Your child will learn his most basic emotional habits from you through observation and modeling."
—*Jim Taylor, Ph.D., author of* Positive Pushing

Keeping Your Cool When you're tired or exasperated or stressed, you're going to occasionally miss the model parent mark, especially when your toddler is in the midst of a tantrum or your teen is asserting herself over a non-negotiable issue. But overall you'll want to keep in mind that you're the parent and that it's your responsibility to act in a way that warrants modeling. If you speak to your child harshly, she will learn your "script," and if you spank your child, well, watch her play house with her dolls sometime. If you don't want your child to grow up using aggression, you won't want to model violence by spanking her, shaking her, threatening her, or being verbally abusive to her.

When your child is upset and yelling, take the opportunity to teach her by example how to act—especially if you're angry yourself. Rather than yell back, threaten, or resort to physical violence, take some time to calm down, breathe, think about the situation, and then problem solve. "Children need someone older and wiser to be in charge. When adults resort to screaming, saying things they don't mean, falling apart, or losing their cool, children react in many different ways. When they feel that an adult is no longer in control, they are frightened," explains Katharine Kersey in *Don't Take It Out on Your Kids!* "Children imitate our behaviors, and when we yell and go berserk, they usually do the same. The tension escalates and nothing productive is accomplished."

Studies show that children who grow up in families with parents who fight and where anger is the norm tend to be more aggressive and are more likely to grow up to perpetrate violence. According to Judith Kahn, director of the Konopka Institute for Best Practices in Adolescent Health at the University of Minnesota, "Current data suggest that children learn to be aggressive when they are very young. One study found that some of the most important precursors of aggression in boys were harsh attitudes and harsh discipline experienced by age 8. The aggressive 'scripts' that children hear and learn very early become resistant to change." Studies also suggest that when a child witnesses violence at home, it may be as traumatic for her as being victimized herself, with long-term psychological and behavioral consequences.

In addition to showing your child how to relate to others kindly and generously, you also model, consciously or not, how to handle life's turns. How do you react to frustration and setbacks? When your toddler watches you rant and rave over a quirky remote control, you can't blame her for having a tantrum over her broken Lego masterpiece. And your responses to life's big setbacks—a job loss or an illness, for example— are lessons your child will thoroughly absorb. Will they show her how to be calm, positive, and solution oriented? Will she learn that difficulties foster growth? "How your child learns to respond to adversity depends largely on how you respond to adversity," explains Taylor, "and the perspective you teach him about the inevitable setbacks he will experience in his achievement efforts."

GET PSYCHED

"The question for the child is not 'Do I want to be good?' but 'Whom do I want to be like?'"–Bruno Bettelheim, child psychologist

We've outlined just a few of the ways that your behavior instructs your child, but the opportunities to positively influence her in the course of just one day are enormous. You might model healthy risk taking when you try a new sport or while playing a game with her, for example. You'll teach her to delay gratification when you talk about saving up for a new dress or treating yourself to a new magazine after your work is done. She'll learn the importance of good effort when she sees that you give a task your best shot, and she'll learn about persistence and commitment when you try three different solutions for getting the tar off the car and you miss a new movie because you're scheduled for a community service activity. She'll learn how to be generous to others when you show empathy for someone's mishap or mistake. You can show her how to have a good time with friends, how to laugh at herself, and how to enjoy the pleasures of the day—such as the sound of the rain on the attic roof and the smell of her new soap. Working on role modeling is a kind of self-improvement course!

What Kind of Role Model Are You?

Give yourself four points for each question that you answer with a "yes."

Does your child consistently see you ...

- ☐ Eat healthful foods?
- ☐ Exercise regularly?
- ☐ Take responsibility for your mistakes?
- ☐ Apologize when appropriate?
- ☐ Talk about your feelings and show a range of emotions?
- ☐ Show affection?
- ☐ Avoid self-destructive behaviors (such as drug or alcohol use)?
- ☐ Show kindness to others?
- ☐ Develop friendships?
- ☐ Enjoy work?
- ☐ Respect the environment?
- ☐ Practice safety behaviors (such as wearing a bike helmet)?
- ☐ Make your family a priority?

☐ Budget your money and spend it appropriately?

☐ Answer questions honestly?

☐ Tackle hard work with a good attitude?

☐ Get enough sleep?

☐ Read?

☐ Enjoy learning?

☐ Act in a cheerful, optimistic manner?

☐ Forgive yourself and others?

☐ Appreciate your own effort and others' efforts?

☐ Speak in a respectful way?

☐ Take good care of your things?

☐ Show openness to the opinions of others?

Score:

88 to 100 points: Your child is learning good habits from you.

60 to 84 points: You've got pretty good habits and you likely have the hang of role modeling. Once you give it your attention, it'll be easy to boost your score.

40 to 56 points: You might want to spend some time thinking about the items you responded "no" to. If you feel they're a priority for your child, tackle one at a time and make them a priority for you, too.

Below 40: First step is convincing yourself that your actions really matter, that what you do has a profound influence on your child. When you believe that, make a prioritized list of which items you feel are the most important of these, which you most want your child to learn. Then tackle them, one at a time, and change your habits for your child's benefit, and your own.

For Better or for Worse: Other Influences

Although you are your child's first and primary teacher, there will be other influences in her life—good and bad. Your child may look up to athletes, authors, actors, musicians, scientists, artists, designers, and fashion models, for example, depending on her interests and exposure to media and activities.

When she's old enough, talk with her about her choices, and encourage her to be discriminating as she grows. When asked who their role model is, kids most often name a celebrity. Without being critical about her choices, talk with your child about what merits modeling and the difference between celebrity and being worthy of admiration. And don't be too pessimistic about your ability to compete with celebrities as an influence on your child. A student study published by the National Honor Society in *Psychology Journal* found that parental role models had significantly greater influence on college students' purchasing decisions than did celebrity role models. The researchers concluded that advertisers should consider increasing parental visibility and endorsements in ads and decreasing celebrity endorsements.

In an attempt to foster empathic behavior and goals in students, some school programs focus attention on the lives and achievements of famous empathetic people—such as Martin Luther King Jr., Mother Theresa, and Florence Nightingale. A 1980 study by Dorothy Dixon showed that learning activities such as these increase children's desire to be like these people and to take on attitudes and behaviors associated with them.

Every parent knows that peers are potent models, and studies back up peer power in everything from dress to initiation to marijuana use. Because peers are such powerful models, keep in touch with your child's friends and their families. Encourage your child to talk about what she enjoys about each of her friends, and teach her to spend time with people who bring out the best in her. You might also purposely bring other good role models into her life—through books, the community, schools, and your family tree, for example.

Some kids receive a healthy dose of modeling from television, spending more time watching programming than they spend with peers or parents. It's well known that studies have strongly linked violence on television to violent behavior in children. On the other hand, it's possible for selective viewing to have a positive effect. A study funded by the National Institute of Mental Health found that children who see prosocial behavior on television tend to imitate it, and their aggressive behavior decreases. In fact, they tend to have more positive social interactions in general. One researcher, Nancy Eisenberg, Ph.D., at Arizona State University, concludes, "Although filmed models may have less influence on a prosocial responding than do live models … it is likely that prolonged viewing of prosocial programming could result in substantial and enduring changes in children's prosocial behavior."

So if television is going to be part of your child's day, monitor the modeling for her. A daily dose of *Mr. Rogers* won't hurt (and may even be good for her), but a routine stint of violent cartoons may be counterproductive.

What You Can Do

Keep in mind that you're likely the strongest role model in your child's life, and that you can influence what other role models your child embraces, too.

☐ Think about which media personalities your child looks up to. What character traits does this person teach? Talk with your child about what she likes about these personalities.

☐ Who were your positive role models growing up? Does your child have similar role models in her life?

☐ Make a list of your strongest attributes. Do you see these reflected in your child? Now make a list of your weaknesses. Are they also reflected?

☐ Introduce your child to positive role models in her areas of interest. If she's enamored with astronomy, read an inspirational biography of an astronaut; if she's learning sign language, watch a movie about Helen Keller.

☐ Encourage older relatives—grandparents, aunts, and uncles—to share stories of their small and large successes in life with your child. These often inspire children to follow in their big footsteps.

☐ Pay attention to the music your child listens to. Lyrics can provide support for behavior, too.

☐ Teach your child to spot kindness in others. "Wasn't that nice of Jenny to call her sister when she knew she was home alone?" you might ask.

☐ Consider developing family rules about television viewing, if you haven't already. Address the amount of time as well as the program content.

☐ Point out to an older sibling that she's a model for her younger brother or sister and what an important role that is. Tell her how much you appreciate her setting a good example.

Part 3

Loving Discipline Strategies

Now for the nitty-gritty. In Part 3, you'll learn about loving discipline strategies—specific things you can do to guide your child day-in and day-out to successful adulthood. You'll learn the basics of respectful, empathetic communication and how to use consequences in a supportive, loving environment. The typical time-out is transformed into a positive, affirming experience, and your child learns, as you have, how to turn mistakes into problem-solving opportunities that help him grow.

Communicating

Communication is a powerful tool of loving discipline. From the moment your child arrives in your life, she is shaped by your communication with her. At first your interplay is about getting to know one another, about bonding and growing in trust and love. She needs you to understand and respond to her, to be sensitive to her physical needs. As she grows, she continues to need your emotional understanding and support. By communicating in ways that show mutual respect and appreciation, you and your child establish the parent/child bond from which effective discipline grows.

Bonding with Baby

Your baby communicates with you by crying and babbling and cooing and smiling. Her sounds and mannerisms let you know—if you're sensitive to her—when she's hungry or tired or delighted. Experts who advocate Attachment Parenting stress the importance of developing this kind of sensitivity to each other, which they suggest you do by responding to your baby's cries, sharing sleep with her, being affectionate with her, and carrying her close. As you communicate sensitively with your baby, you build the bond between you, teaching her that you are safe and to be trusted.

Communicating with your baby also fosters her intellectual growth. Your child's brain grows to 90 percent of its adult weight in the first 3 years of life. New neural connections are made all the time; as you talk with your baby and facilitate her experiencing the world, you are helping her build these connections. You are turning on her brain cells, reinforcing links, and helping her make new ones. (Research shows that your baby begins to develop language skills long before she can speak, for example.)

As your baby grows, she'll be able to use her language skills to communicate with you. No matter what her age and ability, though, your affection, support, tone of voice, and sensitivity to her needs will still be an important part of your parent/child communication.

WEB TALK: *Mothering* magazine's website offers birth stories; a mothers' writing group; resources for birthing, breastfeeding, and alternative medicine; and an array of articles on natural family living. Visit 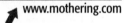 www.mothering.com

Loving Listening

When we talk about communicating with our children, we often think about ways of talking. And that's a crucial issue. But just as important are ways of listening. Remember, communication is a two-way affair.

Passive Listening It's hard to listen to a child talk without butting in. Sometimes we want to fix her problem, or make her feel better, or, well, get to the point. But it's amazing where a child will sometimes take you if you just let her talk.

Imagine your preschooler relating over a snack that she's sick and tired of her best friend and never wants to see her again.

Rather than jump in with "Oh, you're just upset about what happened, you'll be best buds again tomorrow," or "That's not very nice, Jill is good to you," or "You don't really feel that way," find out what happens if you just listen. Stop after the "Oh," and listen. Stay engaged, but without talking.

Stop what you're doing and look at your child while she's talking. Sit with her, or bend down to her eye level, and give her your full attention. Show her with your expressions and body language (nodding your head, acting surprised or concerned) that you're listening and that you care. Try to put yourself in your child's place as you listen to her talk. Maybe your child will go on to tell you that Jill spent her recess with another girl, or that Jill is moving away and your child thinks that she'd better start finding another friend.

By listening quietly and attentively, you let your child know that what she's saying is important enough for you to give it your attention, that you care about her and her feelings, and that it's just fine to feel the way she does. When we don't listen to our children, or we don't take the time to understand their perspectives, we can feed their frustrations and anger. But by teaching your child that you will listen to her concerns, problems, and even everyday events, you show her that you value her and her feelings. When you listen without being judgmental, she's encouraged to come to you more often.

Active Listening Active listening requires the same sensitive, empathetic approach as passive listening, but with more involvement in the conversation. You still want to give your child your complete attention, look at her while she's talking, try to understand her point of view, and let her talk, without offering advice or interrupting.

When you actively listen, though, you also want to take what your child says and reflect it back to her. Your child can then hear that you understand or take the opportunity to help you understand better by correcting you. Your reflecting back can also help her focus on and express her own thoughts, especially when she's young. When you acknowledge what your child has said correctly, you show her that you listened to her and empathize. "Without feeling understood, people will seldom feel accepted," explains Thomas Gordon, Ph.D., author of *Parent Effectiveness Training*.

Q & A

How can I communicate with my child when she's having a tantrum?

"I recommend staying with your child during her tantrums. Get down at her level and give her your loving attention. Hold her if she lets you. Don't let her hurt herself or anybody else. Let her know that you understand. Reflect back her feelings ('You are very angry. You've had a hard day.')

"Let her know that it is okay to cry. She needs the reassurance that she is loved at all times, even when she is sad or angry. Don't try to get her to talk instead of cry. This will not be helpful. Language and emotions are processed in different parts of the brain. If she is crying or raging, she probably needs to do so, and the most useful thing you can do is simply be with her and show her your love and acceptance.

"The tantrum will pass, and you will find a much relieved and relaxed little child who will probably want to snuggle in your arms. Children who have cried and raged as much as needed (with loving support) usually become calm, cooperative, communicative, and nonaggressive. They generally sleep soundly and awaken later bright and alert."—*Aletha Solter, Ph.D., author of* Tears and Tantrums

Let's say your preteen comes home from dance class in tears. When you ask her why she's upset, she blurts out that she's the only one in her class who can't do turns across the floor. And she says she wants to quit dance.

Most parents' knee-jerk reaction would be to try to make it all better. We'll say things like "Turns aren't so important!" or "You're one of the best dancers, you'll get those turns!" or "You don't really want to quit dance over a few turns!" But when we do this, we're denying and contradicting the child's feelings.

Instead, ask yourself how you might feel *en pointe* in front of your peers, twirling dizzily after they executed perfect turns. (Sounds like a bad dream, doesn't it?) Then simply let your child know you heard her by reflecting back what she said. Name her feelings when you can. Sometimes your wider vocabulary and insight can help your child understand her feelings better and express them more easily. At the very least, by *mirroring* the content of her message, you show that you're attempting to understand. "You feel really upset that you can't do what the other dance girls can." No judgment, just observation and understanding.

PsychSpeak

Mirroring is reflecting the content of a message accurately back to the speaker. Often this is done with paraphrasing, or stating what the message means in your own words.

She may go on to say, "Yes, and I think they feel sorry for me. And then I do worse." You might reflect, "When you're upset you can't do your best, can you?" and so on. By providing a safe environment for your child to talk about her feelings and work on her problems, you've given her just the support she needs. "When a child's experiences have been validated," says Katherine Kersey, author of *Don't Take It Out on Your Kids!*, "the child can deal with the difficulties of life."

When a child's feelings are acknowledged, they often begin to soften in intensity. You might find your child saying something like, "Well, I can do splits, at least!" or "Maybe if I practice at home, with nobody watching me, I can get better at turns." And you can facilitate by providing her with a safe place to practice.

You'll want to listen to your child's nonverbal messages, too. Watch her facial expression, her posture, whether she looks at you or her shoes. Listen to the tone of her voice. Open the door for her by reflecting what you think she's feeling, even if she doesn't come out with it herself.

It's important to be sincere while actively listening. It's not a method of manipulation, or of parroting. That means that you need to sincerely want to hear and understand what the child has to say, and you have to want to be helpful. You need to accept her feelings, even if they're not what you want her to feel, and you have to trust that she can handle her feelings and work through them to find solutions.

GET PSYCHED

"We often think our kids aren't listening to us. How often do our kids think no one is listening to them?"
–*Myrna Shure, Ph.D., author of* Thinking Parent, Thinking Child

One of the hardest times to be a good listener is when you're the object of your child's anger. When your teen yells, "I hate you!" it's easy to launch into a tirade about how grateful she should be to have you for a parent, or to guilt trip her about all you've done for her, or to send her to her room for speaking to you "that way."

Instead, a reflective listener would transcend his own point of view for the child's benefit. "Wow, you're pretty angry with me. I wonder why," you might say. No need to attack her back by telling her how nasty she is. Her negative feeling is valid, so focus on that. When you do, you can help your child find a more appropriate way to deal with her anger.

You can validate her feelings and show your empathy by using phrases such as "I can imagine what you must feel ..." or "I understand how that might make you feel ...." You might tell your teen you can imagine that she would feel very angry toward you because you wouldn't let her go on an unsupervised weekend trip with her friends. There's no harm in understanding how terrible it makes her feel to be disappointed and left out. And it can be good to let her know that you understand. (It may also help to keep in mind how transitory feelings can be.)

Q&A

How am I supposed to communicate with my teen when I can't get him to give me the time of day?

It's a myth that kids don't want to talk when they become teens; they will talk, just not at the times that are most comfortable for parents. Some good opportunities:

- When your teen asks whether he can head to the bowling alley, ask a few friendly questions before saying, "Sure." A good time to find out a bit about his buddies and interests is when he wants something.
- Just like when she was little, your teen may open up about why she's upset at bedtime–her "way-too-late" bedtime. It's often worth staying up for.
- Adapt your ritual family get-togethers or after-church lunch for your teen; encourage him to bring a friend or shorten the time commitment. Expect him to attend family dinner. These prime communication times are too good to give up!
- Don't just ask questions–talk about yourself. Listening to you relay an experience with your boss may remind her of a similar incident with her teacher.
- Share pop culture. A favorite television show is likely to inspire discussion. Listen to his favorite music or play his newest video game with him.

–Ron Taffel, Ph.D., author of The Second Family: Dealing with Peer Power, the Pop Culture, the Wall of Silence–and Other Challenges of Raising Today's Teens

Being an empathetic listener doesn't mean that because you understand you give in; you still won't let her go on the trip. But it does let your child know that you care about her feelings. When you validate your child's feelings, mirror her thoughts, and empathize with her situation, you increase her trust in you and foster closeness with her.

If you find that your child is having a hard time expressing her feelings, it may be helpful to talk about what's happening as if it were someone else. You might say, "Lots of people, children and adults, are frightened when they have to move to a new town." Or "Many athletes have a hard time when they lose a game." If you observe that your child is upset but she seems reluctant to talk about it, observe her behavior and facial expressions, and then offer your thoughts. "You seem sad. Can you talk about what's bothering you?" or "Would you like to cuddle on the couch for a little bit?"

In his book *Client-Centered Therapy,* Carl Rogers reviewed studies of listening-based counseling. He found that when therapists used these listening techniques with patients, the patients' positive attitudes increased, along with their acceptance of themselves, their objectivity, and their sense of independence. They were better able to cope with problems, too. Parenting experts report similar results in family settings.

Talking *with* Your Child

Communication is two-way, not just in logistics, but in spirit. To discipline lovingly, you'll want to earn—not demand—your child's cooperation. Speaking *with* her—rather than *to* her— is a pivotal factor.

Lose the Lecture If only we could just tell our children what they need to know and have it stick! Problem is, not only do children need to learn their own lessons (with our loving guidance), when we do all the telling it's easy to turn us off. When it feels like our kids ignore us or don't hear a word we say, it's often because we've been lecturing. Nobody likes a know-it-all, and telling a child how she should and should not feel is disrespectful. It implies that she isn't capable of thinking for herself. Ditto when it comes to problem solving. Give her suggestions if she's asks—or even ask her whether she would like some once in a while—but respect her ability to come up with good solutions on her own.

When your grade-schooler comes home with a failing grade, rather than launch into a lecture about the importance of doing her best—tackling her homework before anything else, making schoolwork a priority, etc., etc.—why not simply ask "Why do you think that happened?" or "How do you feel about that grade?" If she feels bad about it, ask her what she's going to do next time to avoid a repeat. The lesson will be much more valuable if she comes up with these answers herself, and she'll be much more motivated to follow her own advice than yours!

Other times you might help your child work through a problem not by giving her an easy answer, but by asking her pertinent questions. Ask with interest, not challenge. Ask her to explain further or to give you examples. "Are there other things you're afraid of when you're going to sleep in your room? Is there anything you could do in bed to make you feel less afraid?" Sometimes all a child needs is a caring listener for her to arrive at solutions. Maybe your child would actually like to keep her bedroom door shut, so she can hear if somebody comes in, and all the while you thought you were doing her a favor by letting her keep it open while she went to sleep, for example.

Listening can yield valuable information—information that will not only help you understand your child better, but will also help her problem solve. Instead of demanding that your child put her bike in the garage "right this instant," you might ask her why she doesn't want to put her bike away. You might discover that she's afraid of the spider in the garage, or that she wants to keep it where she can see it so it doesn't get stolen. This information can help you help her solve the problem—by taking care of the pesky spider or by giving her a bike lock so she doesn't have to worry about it being stolen. Simply demanding that she put it away now would not be nearly as successful, either in terms of problem solving with her or in terms of communicating your understanding.

GET PSYCHED

"Empathy is the cement that holds together the secret formula for constructing caring and compassionate human beings, and it is as essential for our survival as air and water."–*Jerry Wyckoff, Ph.D., author of* 20 Teachable Virtues

"Dictating to kids (even in a nice way) is far less productive than eliciting ideas and objections and feelings from them. If talking to our children about what they've done wrong fails to bring about the results we were hoping for, it isn't because some stronger form of discipline is required. It may be because we did most of the talking. Maybe we were so busy trying to get them to see our point of view that we didn't really hear theirs," says Alfie Kohn, in *Unconditional Parenting.*

In a 2004 study of adolescent involvement in discipline decision making, researchers at the psychology department of the Citadel in Charleston, South Carolina, found that adolescents appreciated involvement in discipline decision making. After watching video vignettes of disciplinary interactions, high school students rated how close they would feel to the parent, how fair they found the intervention, the degree to which they would feel respected, and how willing they would be to follow the agreed-upon consequences. As a result of the findings, the researchers suggested parents encourage adolescent involvement in discipline.

It's *How* You Say It   Children are sensitive to the way adults speak to them. And although temperament plays a role (one child will cry if you look at her angrily, whereas another will shake off even a stern reprimand), most of them can easily pick up on the feelings behind your approach to them—by your tone of voice, your choice of words, and your manner of speaking. To discipline lovingly, you want to always try to convey your love for your child in your voice. That's a big part of the "kind" in "kind and firm."

Think of how many ways you can tell your preschooler that she cannot play at the park alone. You might be sarcastic—"Right, like I'd let you play at the park by yourself." You might be judgmental or condescending—"Don't you know better than to think I'd let you go to the park by yourself?" Or you might be curt—"No. Now go play upstairs." None of these convey your love or understanding.

On the other hand, if you tell your child, "Honey, I know you'd like to go by yourself, but it's just not safe. I'll be able to take you this afternoon (or tomorrow, or whenever)," or "It'll be nice when you can go places by yourself, won't it? It's not quite time, though," then you are still conveying the same information— that she may not play alone at the park—but in a respectful, kind way. Of course, there will be times when you need to be more firm than others. If your child persists in arguing, for example, you can decide that the discussion is over and state firmly and confidently that you will not be changing your mind.

One of the easiest ways to be more supportive and positive with your child—and often avoid confrontation in the first place—is to look for alternatives to the too-frequent "no." Of course, children need to learn to accept an occasional "no," but it will be more meaningful if it's not a constant refrain. When you can present a positive alternative instead, you actually empower your child instead of overpowering her.

When your child asks for a cookie before lunch, for example, instead of saying "No, you may not have a cookie now," you can say, "Sure, you can have a cookie as soon as we finish lunch." Instead of "Stop kicking the seat," you might say "Please tell your feet to be still," or, if it's an option, "Do your feet need to take a walk?" When she rudely demands a clean shirt, instead of saying, "Don't talk to me that way!" you might say, "Please ask me nicely and I'll be glad to help you find one."

In fact, whenever you can, tell your child what *to* do rather than what *not* to do. Instead of "Don't slam the door!" for example,

you're not alone

"Our 6-year-old daughter, Maya, told us that she brushed her teeth when she hadn't; she didn't want to take the time to brush before leaving with me to visit our close family friends. On the one hand it seemed like a little thing, but on the other we were very concerned that she learn the importance of telling the truth.

"In an effort to impress the gravity of the situation upon her, Dad swiftly told Maya that she couldn't go with me. Tempers flared and Maya was crushed. I thought the consequence was a bit harsh and unrelated to the behavior, but I was at a loss as to what else we might do.

"That night I went online and read about communi-

cating in ways that are respectful—which included both children and parents using a respectful tone of voice and being truthful. The site pointed out that a main reason kids don't tell the truth is that they are afraid of disappointing their parents and getting in trouble.

"I talked with Maya about how telling the truth is part

you might say, "Please close the door gently." By the way, don't ask your child a question when you mean to tell her something. For example, don't ask her whether she's ready to go home if it doesn't matter whether she's ready or not, or if she'd like to clean up now if what you mean is "It's time to clean up now." When you need to give a directive, don't ask. But don't be condescending, either.

Can You Hear Me Now? Practical Tips

We've all heard parents—the grocery store is the clichéd spot—telling their children the same thing over and over, only to be ignored. Children choose to tune out adults for many reasons. Sometimes it's because they get tired of being lectured (or ordered about or yelled at), sometimes it's because the parents never follow through on what they say, and sometimes it's because the child and the parent don't respect each other. Other times, it's the parent who tunes out the child. Children talk and ask and

of being respectful, and I also told her that it really was okay for her to make mistakes. I pointed out that as long as she can admit the mistakes she makes, we could work together to figure out what to do about them. It made sense to her, and she hasn't been afraid of telling the truth since then.

"To address the mutual respect that was lacking in our initial response, we also decided to try a simple way of communicating that I had read about on the same parenting site. When one of us feels that the tension is escalating when we're talking or arguing, that we're no longer being respectful to one another,

then we put our hand on our heart as a reminder to the other person that we love each other and to be respectful. It's so simple, but so vivid and effective."
—*Cindy Wenner, parent*

talk louder and eventually give up or act out because they are ignored. Here are some guidelines for more effective parent/child communication.

Make Sure You're Connecting Before you tell your child to do something or expect her to listen to you, get down at her level and look in her eyes. Use her name, touch her on the arm, or take her hand. These gestures tell your child that you care about her, which will make it easier to convey your message. Encourage her to talk by being patient and supportive. Be attentive and use a gentle voice.

Try "I" Phrases Parent Effectiveness Training (P.E.T.) instructs parents to use "I" phrases rather than "you" phrases to communicate their feelings to their children. So instead of telling your child, "You are so sloppy. This room is a pigsty," you might say, "I feel upset when you leave a room so messy. We're having company and I wanted everything to look nice." Or rather than tell your child, "You can't remember anything!" you might tell her "I feel upset when you don't do what I've asked you to do." Rather than accuse your child, "I" messages help you relay your feelings to your child and give her the opportunity to learn and choose to do better to make you feel better.

Think Before You Speak "One of the most important techniques parents need to implement is that of thinking before they speak," says Katharine Kersey in *Don't Take It Out on Your Kids!* "We are often careless and say what we think without realizing the implications."

We all blurt things out to our children, especially when we're tired or frustrated or angry. If you can make it a habit to think before you speak, however, you'll avoid many unnecessary confrontations, and you'll choose words and tones that will be productive rather than counterproductive. Even if you don't mean it when you say "You wear me out!" and even if your child comes to realize you don't mean it, you'll lose her trust and your credibility. Speaking of credibility, stopping to think may also prevent you from saying things you won't possibly follow through on, such as "I'll never take you shopping again," or "You're grounded for a year."

> **GET PSYCHED**
>
> "As a teacher, I possess a tremendous power to make a child's life miserable or joyous. I can be a tool of torture or an instrument of inspiration. I can humiliate or humor, hurt or heal. In all situations, it's my response that decides whether a crisis will be escalated or de-escalated and a child humanized or de-humanized."–*Haim Ginott, Ph.D., author of* Between Parent and Child

Give Your Child the Benefit of the Doubt When you make the assumption that your child is acting with poor intent, you may well overreact to her behavior. Instead, put yourself in her place and see whether you can understand what's underlying her actions. If your child grabs a doll from another child, it's easy to assume she's just being selfish and needs to learn to share. But maybe she's not developmentally ready to share yet, or maybe the other child agreed to share and hasn't all afternoon and your child just can't take it anymore. In any case, it's highly unlikely that your child is taking the doll just to be mean, so give her the benefit of an understandable motive, at least.

Several studies have shown that mothers who view their child's behavior as negative tend to overreact in their disciplining of the child. In one study, researchers showed abusive moms videos of children they didn't know in daily activities. Compared to the control group, the abusive moms were much more negative in their appraisals of the children's behavior. Even without being abusive, we can discipline our children poorly by assuming the worst.

Don't Decide What Is or Isn't Important to Your Child

What seems insignificant to you might be very important to her. In your child's life, it may be of paramount importance right now that she learn to do a cartwheel or that she write in her diary before turning out the light. Let her decide what matters. You won't always be able to let her decide her course of action, of course. Your grade-schooler may decide it's crucial that she pierce her eyebrow, for example. Being respectful of her doesn't mean that you have to let her get a piercing; it simply means that you accept and acknowledge its importance to her.

Find the Right Environment Dinnertime conversation or family meeting banter is great, but also make time for each of your children individually so that they don't have to vie for your attention. Find a place to talk with few distractions, where you won't be interrupted. Don't try to talk in a room with the television on, for example. And if the phone rings when you and your child are trying to talk, don't answer it.

Don't Try to Trap Your Child If you have knowledge of something, tell her what you know and that you want to talk about it. Don't ask her what she did after school if you know that she went to a movie she wasn't supposed to see. You don't want to convey to your child that you're trying to "catch her" doing something wrong. She will correctly perceive this as adversarial.

You want her to know that she can trust you to be honest with her. So tell her that your friend saw her at the movie and you want to talk about it.

Show Your Appreciation Tell your child that you enjoy talking with her. Encourage her by telling her when she does a good job communicating the facts and/or her feelings.

Ask Questions That Will Draw Her Out Rather than ask her whether she had a good day at school, for example, ask your grade-schooler what her favorite class was today, or who she played with at recess. Ask your teen to explain something you heard about in the news, or ask her opinion about anything in her range of interest—from a new music group to the school policy on skip days.

Don't Overstay Your Welcome If your child looks like she's tired of talking about something, give her an easy out. If she acts like she'd rather not talk about something with you, respect that. Just make sure that she knows you care and that you're there for her if she decides she does want to share.

Explain Yourself

Sometimes it seems the only thing left to say is "Because I'm the parent and I said so!"

Like other authoritarian tactics, however, this one only goes so far. Even if your child complies, you haven't done much to help her understand your decision. That's not to say you need to explain and re-explain over and over just because your child doesn't accept what you say. But by providing her with some background regarding decisions, and by involving her in the actual decision when possible, you'll help her learn to think for herself. You'll also garner respect and, sometimes, even agreement.

Explaining doesn't mean just going on and on about something, though. ("What are you thinking? These clothes are getting all wrinkled and messy and your room looks horrible. You should have put these away as I brought them to you, then you wouldn't have these big piles everywhere. You need to learn to take care of your things. When you get bigger ....") Explain once why it's important to you that your child put away her clothes. Then listen to her thoughts and feelings about it. And if her perspective makes sense, you may even want to compromise. (If she's very busy all week, maybe you can live with her putting all her clothes away twice a week instead of every day, for example. Or maybe when she realizes that you need them picked up so you can sweep the room, she'll be perfectly agreeable about putting them on the shelf in her closet (instead of on the floor) until she can store them where they belong.

Explanations can be useful for your child as well as helpful for you, of course. Give specific instructions when you request something from your child, for example. Don't just tell her to be good at the birthday party. Tell her to remember to say "please" and "thank you," to share, and to help her host clean up. Instead of asking her to get ready for school, tell her to gather her books and her lunch and put them by the door and to put on her shoes and coat.

When you're explaining, try to tackle only one thing at a time, especially for a young child. When she's picking up her clothes, don't also tell her that she needs to organize her desk and pick up her things in the backyard, too. Let her succeed one step at a time rather than feel overwhelmed. Sometimes children really do need to have things spelled out for them. It's all part of teaching your child with loving discipline. Rather than order her to do things, you explain and guide her.

In a study titled "The Altruistic Personality: Rescuers of Jews in Nazi Europe," Samuel P. and Pearl M. Oliner write about the background of people who worked to rescue Jews from the Nazis in Europe. They found that the rescuers were brought up by parents who stressed reasoning, ways of remedying situations, and persuasion and advice, rather than by parents who advocated obedience and punishment. The parents' respectful approach toward the children, the researchers concluded, promoted feelings of empathy toward others.

> **GET PSYCHED**
>
> "Every child needs at least one person who believes in him and does not give up on him. When a child has such a person, he will believe in himself. As long as we live, we have the power to change. Therefore, it is never too late. We need to convey to our children that we will never give up on them."
> —*Katharine Kersey, Ed.D., author of* Don't Take It Out on Your Kids!

Keep in mind, though, that although it's important for you to respect your child enough to be willing to offer her explanations and to listen to her patiently, it's also important that she learn to respect you and listen to you. When you've built a loving discipline framework for her, this kind of mutual respect is automatic. And when you communicate using some of the tools mentioned in this chapter, you foster that mutual respect.

What You Can Do

We have the opportunity to communicate in positive, loving ways with our children every day. When we do, we build our bonds and guide their growth.

☐ See whether you can learn to distinguish between your baby's different cries. Does she sound different when she's tired than when she's hungry? How about when she's afraid?

☐ The next time your child is telling you about something, see how long she will talk with the simplest encouragement—a nod or a "yes," for example. Acknowledge that you're listening, but see what happens if you encourage your child to continue just by being interested.

☐ Do you know an adult who makes you feel lectured to in conversation? How do you feel about your communication with that person?

☐ Listen to your tone of voice when you talk to your child. Would you use the same tone with a friend? If not, why not?

☐ Teach family members to respect conversation between two people, particularly when they've sought a quiet space together.

☐ Watch your child when she communicates with her peers. Is she a good listener? Remember that by being a good listener for your child you're teaching her—through modeling—how to be a good listener.

☐ Sharpen your child's speaking and listening skills (as well as your own) by engaging in storytelling together. Take turns telling parts of the same story.

☐ Research topics that you're uncomfortable talking with your child about. If the idea of chatting about sex makes you squeamish, consult with an organization devoted to sex education; if you don't feel equipped to discuss the dangers of drinking and driving, look up pertinent facts. Sometimes you can simply tell your child your feelings and share your knowledge about an issue, but other times we parents can use a few pointers and/or support, too.

Calling On Consequences

Most parents are comfortable using consequences as a discipline technique. It's that familiar cause-and-effect strategy—"If you whine, you'll be sent to your room." Or "Hit your brother and you'll go to bed an hour early." And "Run over your phone minutes and I'll cancel your service."

Sometimes there's a logical link between the behavior and the consequence; other times the threat or punishment seems arbitrary. Often parents choose the consequence that they know will have the most weight with their child, which is why the denial of a privilege or an anticipated treats are such likely candidates. Teens lose use of the telephone or car. Preteens get slapped with a no-television ordinance. Grade-schoolers wind up without sleepovers and bike rides, and toddlers are deprived of ice cream cones and long-awaited visits to the zoo.

Consequences often get immediate results, and—when used thoughtfully and in a loving context—they can also teach important, long-term lessons. In terms of what children require to learn to grow to their full potential, many would argue that consequences are required teaching. "Children need to develop a sense of competence and mastery over their world," says Jim Taylor, Ph.D., author of *Positive Pushing*. "Most basically, children must learn that their actions matter, that these actions have consequences."

Many proponents of loving discipline techniques agree that, when used within a "firm and loving" framework, consequences are appropriate and effective in the long run. Others have deep reservations about using consequences. It's a touchy subject among loving discipline experts.

In this chapter, we've sorted out a few definitions and a few perspectives, to help you decide what might be a good fit for you and your child. And we've provided some guidelines for using consequences effectively in a loving framework.

Natural Consequences

Natural consequences happen of their own accord. If your preschooler refuses to put on his hat, his ears get cold. When your toddler leaves his game in the yard, the pieces get lost or broken. If your preteen doesn't come to supper when you call him, his food gets cold. A teen who skimps on fuel money runs out of gas half way to the beach. The results aren't prearranged, they happen in the natural course of events.

Natural consequences can be hard for a parent to watch happen, but you don't always need to completely step aside, and you can (in fact, should) use them while maintaining a supportive atmosphere. There isn't always a natural consequence for misbehavior, of course. A child who refuses to be quiet at bedtime isn't likely to suffer any consequences without the intervention of an adult, for example. And, of course, some natural consequences—being hit by a car because of running out into the street—are too extreme to allow to happen. When safe and appropriate, however, most parenting experts agree that a natural consequence can be an effective discipline tool.

Logical Consequences

Logical consequences are linked to action or behavior, but they require some intervention. They often work when an acceptable natural consequence isn't available. For example, if your child fights with his sister, he doesn't get to play with her. If he doesn't finish his homework, he's not allowed to watch television. When he breaks a window, he must earn the money to pay for the repair.

The line between a logical consequence and a punishment can be a fine one, and that's where much of the criticism lies, but a look at the purpose of the consequence will often clarify. Is the consequence meant to hurt your child or to teach him? Angrily sending your preschooler to his room for spilling his milk for the third time will make him feel bad, but it won't do anything to help him learn to be more careful or to fix the specific problems he has caused. Mopping up the floor will, though.

WEB TALK: Catch up on education and healthcare information regarding children from birth through age 12, including recall notices, and book reviews at **www.kidsource.com**

Using Consequences Lovingly

To work in the loving discipline scheme of parenting, you want to make sure of the following:

1. Your child can grasp a clear, reasonable link between his behavior and the consequence.
2. He has choices.
3. The consequences are allowed to occur without interference.
4. You show empathy.

Here's how it comes together.

Keep It Age Appropriate First, as with all methods of discipline, it's important to keep your expectations in line with your child's developmental stage. When it comes to natural and logical consequences, for example, a child who isn't able to reason logically won't be making many meaningful connections. A toddler in the sandbox might never understand—or care—that he's not making any friends when he hogs all the shovels, for example!

Developmental experts have different theories about the ages at which children are capable of understanding concrete and abstract realities and exactly what stages they go through, but many timelines have been based on the work of Swiss psychologist Jean Piaget, who studied the child's path to logical reasoning. According to Piaget, children have an *egocentric* view of the world until they're about 6 or 7 years of age. Even then, when they start to reason logically, they can only reason about concrete objects, not anything as abstract as what will happen if they behave in a certain way. In fact, in Piaget's timeline, not until a child is about 11 years old is he able to think about abstractions such as hypothetical situations and the future.

PsychSpeak

Egocentric view—An egocentric view of the world is an early stage of psychological development in which the child considers himself the center of the universe. Unable to take on another person's perspective, he believes that everyone shares his feelings and desires.

That's not to say that your 5-year-old can't begin to learn about consequences; it's just that you need to keep his developmental stage in mind. Make the links between behavior and results very direct and very obvious, and give him more than one chance. You may not be doing your preteen any favors when you remind him every single morning to pack up his gym shoes, but a friendly reminder to your preschooler that he left his favorite hat on the backyard slide is perfectly reasonable.

Make Direct Links Because natural and logical consequences make sense, they help your child understand the connections between his behavior and the results. If you send your child to his room for lying, or deny him dessert because he didn't do his homework, he has no logical connections to make. In fact, experts believe that a child who is punished illogically, without reasonable links between the consequences and his actions, is more likely to spend time thinking about how to get revenge than about his behavior. He's apt to become angry, to withdraw, and to rebel, or perhaps feel powerless. "These kinds of arbitrary, punitive actions on the part of parents make a child feel humiliated and do nothing to teach him," says Myrna Shure, Ph.D., developmental psychologist who has studied interpersonal problem solving in children.

On the other hand, a child who can clearly see the link between his choices and the outcome learns that appropriate behavior has positive consequences and inappropriate behavior causes problems for him. He learns that he has the power to affect his situation, that his decisions matter and that it's in his best interest to choose the right path. And because a logical consequence has a sense of fairness about it, the child is more likely to focus on the problem rather than on revenge. He learns self-control, cooperation, and accountability for his actions. He develops responsibility, competence, and self-esteem.

"When raised to accept the natural and logical consequences of behaviors, in time young people begin to ask: 'What will be the consequences of my making this decision? Am I willing to accept these consequences?' Or, having made a mistake, they will ask: 'What is my logical responsibility to others for having made this mistake?'" explains Ken West, Ph.D., professor and director of the Center for Family Education at Lynchburg College in Virginia.

Parents who use loving discipline techniques make an effort to teach children the connection between their behavior and the consequences early on, when the stakes are low (such as what happens if he doesn't pick up his marbles before Mom vacuums) rather than later, when the stakes are frighteningly high (such as what happens if he drinks and drives, has unprotected sex, or gets involved with drugs).

By helping your child envision the consequences—specifically how he'll feel when something happens—you're giving him ownership of the problem. Myrna Shure suggests that after you discuss the possible consequences with your child, you ask him, "So what do you think you should do about that?" Making the choice his, and the idea one that he came up with (or at least one he thinks he came up with) is likely to get better results than telling him what to do, Shure explains.

GET PSYCHED

"Keep in mind that the consequences you help your child see don't always have to be negative. Talk about the consequences of earning good grades, of practicing her dribbling, of getting enough sleep, or of doing something nice for a friend. The motivation can be entirely positive."–*Myrna Shure, Ph.D., psychologist and author of* Thinking Parent, Thinking Child

While helping your child consider consequences, you'll often have an opportunity to problem solve, too. "You and your brother always seem to want the same toy at the same time. So you fight about it. What can we do?" Ideally, you and your child will come up with a solution together and not even need a consequence. ("We'll set the timer!") If not, or for added insurance, consequences may be set up. ("And if you do fight, what should we do?") Your child will have a vested interest in complying, especially if he helped come up with the consequences, such as putting the coveted toy away for the rest of the day.

Give Choices Giving your child a choice of decisions is a key component of the loving approach to logical consequences. You can't give your child freedom to make all of his own decisions, of course, but it's a good idea to look for opportunities for him to flex his decision-making muscles. When he's a toddler, it can be as minor as choosing which cookie or fruit to have for a snack; when he's a teen, you might give him the authority to decide which car to buy. Giving your child the authority to make his own decisions demonstrates to him that he is trusted. In turn, he learns self-respect and cooperation.

Q&A

What should I say to my child when he makes a bad decision?
"Ask your child how he's feeling about the decision. Ask him how he thinks others may feel about the decision (his teammates when he gets sidelined for mouthing off to the ref, for example). Ask him how he might handle the same kind of situation differently next time. Show him that you understand and care by taking the time to listen with your undivided attention."–*Myrna Shure, Ph.D., author of* Thinking Parent, Thinking Child

Sometimes the choice isn't as tangible as a cookie or a car; sometimes it's whether or not to do homework or an assigned chore, for example. In two 2004 studies published in *Child Development,* researchers Florrie Fei-Yin Ng, Gwen A. Kenney-Benson, and Eva M. Pomerantz found that when mothers punished their children for poor grades and told them they were disappointed in their academic work, the children performed poorly in school the following day. In addition, the student's grades dropped steadily over the following six months. These mothers, in an effort to force their children to do better, instead taught them that they were incompetent, and the children simply followed through.

Another group of mothers supported the autonomy of their children by discussing the problems, but displaying confidence that the children would succeed, teaching them that they *were* competent. Guess what? These children's grades improved over those following six months! The researchers concluded that to help low-achieving students do better, mothers needed to be less controlling and more supportive.

GET PSYCHED

"What parents must do is create conditions under which children can take pleasure in their own choices and accomplishments because they are theirs."—*Wendy S. Grolnick, Ph.D., associate professor of psychology and author of* The Psychology of Parental Control: How Well-Meant Parenting Backfires

When you give your child the power to make his own choices, his self-worth is boosted by your confidence in him. He learns that responsibility goes hand in hand with privileges and that he must solve his own problems rather than have adults take care of them. On the other hand, if you try to protect your child from his own decisions by insisting that he make a particular "choice," you'll teach him that he's not capable and that he's not responsible for his own actions.

Of course, a child won't always choose right over wrong. Your teen might well choose a motorcycle instead of the sensible sedan. That's why it's a good idea to give choices within a framework of limited options. For the toddler, you can offer a choice of two different fruits instead of an apple or a cookie, if you like. And for the teen, you might give him a set of safety guidelines his choice of wheels must meet, or you might shop together, narrow the choices to a handful, and then let him decide.

When a child makes a bad decision, parents who discipline with love see the mistake as an opportunity for problem solving and learning. They examine together with the child what happened and talk about how it might happen differently—if he acts differently—next time. With his parents' help, the child develops an internal sense of right and wrong.

Step Aside It can be a challenge for a parent to step back and let natural and logical consequences do their job. For a consequence to work, however, you want to let your child experience the results of his choices. It's understandable for you to want to rescue your daughter from the disappointment of losing her new doll at the park, but if you alert her to the possibility, and she insists on bringing it anyway, experts suggest you let her learn "the hard way."

Likewise, if your son repeatedly forgets to bring his papers to school and you repeatedly make a trip to bring them to him, he doesn't learn to be more responsible; he learns that you'll always rescue him. If you explain that it's his job to bring his things to school and that you won't be bringing them anymore, then you set the stage for growth. "You must feel terrible that you'll get a zero for today's work," a loving parent will empathize when he receives the "save me" phone call from school, "but I won't be bringing your things to you today because it's your job to remember them."

> **GET PSYCHED**
>
> "Kids today are often rescued from every struggle—from the consequences of their own mistakes to their responsibilities. This not only raises them to be dependent, helpless, and incompetent in the practical skills of life, it has repercussions for our society and our future."–*Elisa Medhus, M.D.*

It can be especially tough to step aside in a school setting. Parents are eager for their children to do well and often feel that their child's failures reflect poorly on them as parents. Keep in mind that you're aiming for long-term success for your child, not a better grade on today's homework. It might help to talk with your child's teachers so they understand what's going on.

You don't need to be inflexible. If your child is usually conscientious and one day forgets an important paper, there's nothing wrong with doing him a favor by dropping it off at school on your way to do errands. Just don't constantly bail out thoughtless behavior.

Be Empathetic Not giving in doesn't mean not caring. When you tell your child that you're sorry he's unhappy, it doesn't undermine the lesson at all; in fact, your respectful, accepting tone of voice nurtures mutual respect and cooperation. When your child feels your unconditional love, he is stronger and more able to reflect on his situation, confide in you, learn from the lesson, and face the next challenge. "Accepting responsibility for one's choices and behaviors is much easier in an environment of understanding and warmth," says Becky Bailey, Ph.D., professor of early childhood education and development, and author of *Easy to Love, Difficult to Discipline.*

One mother in a parenting chat room was adamant that using natural and logical consequences with her preschooler had sent him the wrong message. "Now he'll step on his sister's hand and tell her that's what happens if you sit on the floor!" Of course, as a loving discipline technique, consequences are used with firmness *and* kindness. (And nobody gets physically hurt!) To provide as much support as possible, experts suggest giving your child a heads-up about consequences rather than looking the other way until the consequences occur. "If you keep ramming your new truck into the concrete wall, it's going to get scratched up," you might point out. Then your child gets to decide whether to stop or not.

you're not alone

Sometimes parents find it necessary to set up consequences to enlist some much-needed help. Of course, along the way kids learn valuable lessons about responsibility and the satisfaction of contributing.

When Beth Crow of Belle Plaine, Iowa, returned to work full-time, she knew she'd need to find ways to streamline some of the housework. She lined up four hampers by the washing machine and explained to her three teen and preteen children (and her husband) that only clothes that were in the hampers would be washed. That meant that they would need to bring their dirty laundry to the laundry area and sort it into the proper hampers instead of leaving it scattered throughout the house. Beth explained that she would no longer have the time to track down dirty clothes before starting up the machine. Then she did her best to keep the hampers empty.

"I do usually tell them when I expect to be doing laundry to prompt them," Beth says, "but they do pretty well. Except, of course, the child who's perfectly comfortable wearing dirty clothes!"

Some parents rescue a child from his actions and then give him a lecture. Positive Discipline advocate and author Jane Nelsen calls this the "bail them out and ball them out" approach. Loving discipline always takes place in a nurturing environment, and that means remaining empathetic. Even if you allow your child to experience the consequence without stepping in, avoid condescension. What won't help is an "I told you so," or a "don't you feel stupid now?" when a doll left out in the rain gets ruined, or when your child gets a flat tire by driving through the construction area despite your warning him not to.

Avoid embarrassing your child or hurting his feelings. Don't point out his lack of judgment in front of his peers, for example. And keep in mind that when things go badly for him, he likely

GET PSYCHED

"Too often we give children answers to remember rather than problems to solve."–*Roger Lewin, scientist and anthropologist*

already feels horrible and doesn't need you to underline his short-fall. It is entirely possible—in fact, loving discipline advocates say it's absolutely necessary—to be both firm and loving while employing natural and logical consequences to teach your child. Although it is challenging to accomplish, parents need to be consistent, matter-of-fact, understanding, and kind all at the same time.

Why Punishment Doesn't Work

A natural or logical consequence is not a punishment. A punishment is something that is done to the child, after the undesirable behavior, in an effort to dissuade him from doing it again. Sometimes punishments are verbal, sometimes physical, sometimes related to the action, and sometimes totally arbitrary. In the worst instances, they are simply an expression of the adult's anger at the child for what he has done. In her 30 years of research on the topic, Martha Pieper, Ph.D., co-author of *Smart Love, The Compassionate Alternative to Discipline That Will Make You a Better Parent and Your Child a Better Person,* found that a child who is punished clearly learns that when he behaves in a certain way, his parents—whom he adores and wants to please—want him to be unhappy. At the very least, she says, negative discipline (constant corrections and punishments) can profoundly discourage a child and do nothing to help him improve his behavior.

Loving discipline advocates agree that punishment doesn't work because ...

- Punishments are external discipline tactics, and they depend on an authority figure being present. They do nothing to teach a child to choose right from wrong when an adult is not around.

- Punishments create a negative state of mind. Think about it. Do you learn work skills by being punished? Are you on your best behavior when you feel miserable or when you feel good about yourself? When the people around you are supportive or when they're cutting you down to size? "Internal states are directly related to outward behavior for both adults and children," says Becky Bailey. "Yet we go on believing in punishment and rewards as the best system of dealing with children."

- A child who is punished usually feels a sense of unfairness and often a desire for revenge. The child continues to misbehave out of anger, or to behave out of fear rather than any real understanding.

- A child who is overpowered often enough, says Dr. Shure, can become immune to the punishment. He may cope by tuning out everything, and as a result, it doesn't matter to him what you do or what he does. "These children become high risk for serious problems as they grow," says Shure, "because they don't care about the consequences of anything."

- Punishment creates a discipline war, with parents thinking of ways to win with punishment and children thinking of ways to not get caught or to get even. "As long as it is important for adults to win, they will make losers out of children," says Jane Nelsen.

- Punishment focuses on past behavior. It doesn't facilitate learning or help a child consider other options for the future.

Loving Discipline Don'ts

There are some don'ts that parents who discipline authoritatively share. Typically, they don't ...

- **Say "I told you so."** This reprimand is completely unnecessary. The child has already learned the lesson from the natural or logical consequences; he doesn't need an adult to rub it in. In fact, he needs empathy. Rubbing it in only shifts his focus from the problem and solution to feeling shamed.

- **Lecture, argue, or preach.** Again, these are unnecessary and put the parent in an adversarial role.

- **Make consequences punitive or unreasonable.** "The mower broke when I ran over your toy; now you can pick up all the sticks and rocks and everything else in the yard!"

- **Add humiliation or degradation.** Loving parents don't put children down. They focus on behavior, without labeling the child. No judgment of good or bad or right or wrong is necessary. Loving parents discuss problems privately with the child, not in front of his peers.

- **Escalate consequences.** Many adults have the mistaken notion that they have to increase consequences (and punishments) when they don't work the first time. Use the smallest consequence you can to make the point.

- **Expect instant success.** Sometimes things get worse before they get better. And teaching takes time and commitment.

When You Need Other Answers

Natural and logical consequences can be very effective, but they aren't always the best discipline choice. You wouldn't let a baby learn not to pull on the kitty's tail by allowing him to get clawed or bit. Likewise, you won't let your toddler learn the natural consequences of climbing the Christmas tree or jamming his fork into the toaster. And a teen can't be permitted to hop on the back of his friend's motorcycle without putting on a helmet.

No matter his age, a child's safety always takes precedence. So do the rights of others. If a baby wants to throw a rock into the middle of the kiddie pool full of toddlers, or a preteen wants to drum his knife and fork on his plate at the restaurant, the consequences—hurting another child and disturbing other diners— aren't acceptable.

What if the logical consequences I think of aren't working? Can I use a consequence that's not related, but that I know will get my child's attention?

"If your logical consequences don't seem to be working, the problem is probably chronic. When chronic problems don't respond to consequences, parents often up the ante, become punitive, impose more and more consequences and become more and more desperate. What you and your child need to try instead of consequences is some problem solving."*—Becky Bailey, Ph.D., professor of early childhood education and development and author of* Easy to Love, Difficult to Discipline

213

Other instances when parents need to look for alternative discipline options are when the consequences really don't matter to the child. If your grade-schooler doesn't want to take a bath and doesn't care if he's dirty, then you won't get very far by letting nature run its course. In each of these instances, other methods of teaching the child—such as encouragement or positive reinforcement, redirection, or reminders—may be more appropriate than trying to dream up logical consequences.

Or you might look for a solution instead of a consequence. Maybe the best way for Mom to handle a child's whining when she picks him up from preschool is to schedule some one-on-one time with him before she starts making dinner. And maybe the best way to win his cooperation at bedtime is to give him a flashlight to keep in bed with him, or take him shopping for a new nightlight for his room. After all, the very positive consequence of a good solution is a discipline problem solved.

What You Can Do

Natural and logical consequences run through every story—in the news, in fiction, in our own daily lives. Being aware of consequences and bringing them to your child's attention can help him learn about their importance. And thinking about consequences for your child in terms of a discipline technique—ahead of time—can help you stay level-headed when your child needs you to discipline him.

☐ Make consequences a frequent topic of conversation at your home. Talk about a character's actions and their consequences in a television show or movie you've just watched together, or a book you've just read. Ask your child how the plot may have changed had the character acted differently.

☐ Tell your child when you have consequences to deal with at work or at home. Explain how you were embarrassed because you hadn't prepared well enough for your presentation or about how you received a bonus for the extra work you did on a project. Tell him how hard it was to stay inside painting this morning when the weather was so beautiful, but how glad you are that you did because the living room looks great and now your weekend is free.

☐ Play a game of "Behavior and Consequences" with your partner—or with the kids. One of you think up possible problem behaviors and the other think of matching natural or logical consequences. Take turns. If your child is old enough, involve him, too.

☐ If your teen enjoys political discussion, explore the actions of politicians or parties in light of major consequences.

☐ Help your child come up with a list of goals. (Even a very young child can do this, if you'll take dictation.) Have him pick his most important goal, and then jot down steps that he'll need to take to reach it. Explain that reaching his goal will be the consequence of his taking these steps.

☐ When your child makes a bad decision that affects someone else, help him explore how he might make amends. Hand in hand with learning about consequences, he can learn that it's sometimes possible to make up for mistakes.

☐ Talk with your child's teachers about the consequences they use in the classroom. Do you find them logical, appropriate, and fair? If not, discuss options with the teacher(s).

Transforming Time-Outs

Time-outs are one of the most popular discipline techniques, and advice about how to give them—down to time specifications—can be found in many parenting books. (In fact, there are even entire books devoted to details of the technique!)

The threat of a typical time-out occasionally achieves a child's immediate compliance. But loving discipline advocates argue that that compliance comes at a steep price. Time-outs are hurtful, not helpful. They convey only damaging messages, and break down, rather than build, your relationship with your child. Typical time-outs do nothing to aid your child in her understanding of the situation or to build her self-calming skills.

So what's the loving alternative? A positive time-out, and the difference between it and a typical time-out is more than a word's worth. Positive time-outs can help your child learn to calm herself and identify her feelings, build your relationship, and, eventually, problem solve.

Here's what the typical time-out looks like, why it's not in your child's best interest, and some guidelines for the loving discipline approach to time-outs.

Typical Time-Outs

Most parents will give a child a time-out by sending her to a designated chair or place (her room, for example) for a certain amount of time. There's even a rule of thumb for timing time-outs: 1 minute for each year of age (5 minutes for a 5-year-old, 7 minutes for a 7-year-old, for example).

Most often, time-outs are given in anger, and the approach is punitive, with a tenuous relationship to the problem behavior. "Go sit in time-out!" a parent might tell a toddler who hits her brother over the head with her doll, or a preschooler who staunchly refuses to pick up her toys. "Go to your room!" a parent might direct a grade-schooler who angrily overturns a game board or a teen who makes one too many smart-aleck remarks when asked about his report card.

Sometimes a child will obediently and quietly sit in time-out for the dictated time. But sometimes (often, in fact) the child will refuse, or fuss about being given the time-out, and the threats will escalate. "If you don't go right now, then you'll be in time-out for twice as long! Okay, now an hour!" And sometimes the child has to be physically taken to the designated spot, or even held in place while she fights and screams. (This becomes increasingly difficult with older children!) Some parents find it necessary to lock their child in a room in order to implement a typical time-out.

GET PSYCHED

"Children are in most need of loving attention when they act least deserving of it."–*Aletha Solter, Ph.D., developmental psychologist*

As the child's already-charged emotions escalate with the added difficulties she's being dealt, the parent's temper often flares, too. The parent's goal may have been to distance herself from her child's behavior, or to put a stop to the misbehavior at hand, but in many cases, both parent and child become more upset and adversarial.

There are endless variations, but in the typical time-out scenario, privileges such as toys, music, television, and telephone are denied. Most important, the child's contact with her parent or caregiver is cut off. This withholding of contact and attention, loving discipline advocates point out, is what makes a time-out such a punitive technique. Parents are advised to completely isolate the child, and usually the parent refrains from touching, talking with, or even looking at her (at least in theory). In an effort to keep the experience as negative as possible, when the time-out is over, some parenting experts explicitly advise parents not to hug their child or tell her that they love her. Others suggest that the child be allowed to "make up." What's the idea behind this typical time-out strategy?

Laboratory Origins

The idea for time-outs originated with the work of *behaviorists* such as B.F. Skinner and J.B. Ferster, who showed in the 1950s that lab animals such as chimps and pigeons would behave in a desired way if given positive reinforcement, or rewards, and that undesirable behavior could be eliminated or reduced by removing the positive reinforcement or by inflicting pain. Some of these experiments were called "time-out from positive reinforcement."

Discipline experts have adapted these findings, using them as the framework for today's typical time-out discipline technique. The positive reinforcement that's either granted or denied the child might be the

PsychSpeak

Behaviorist—Someone who uses a psychological approach based on observable behavior (actions) rather than internal factors (such as emotions). The behaviorist school of thinking was started by psychologist John B. Watson, who claimed that behavior is a physiological reaction to environmental stimuli. Behaviorist theories have led to the use of behavior modification principles—such as rewards and punishments—in disciplining children.

game she's engrossed in (and having a fit over), or the playmate with whom she doesn't want to share her blocks.

Because a child thrives on parental attention, however, the most powerful positive reinforcement that she is denied during a time-out is her parent's attention. Many parents and discipline experts think of time-out as a rather tame discipline method. (It's often suggested in place of spanking, in fact.) But because of the power of the child's connection with her parents, most loving discipline advocates consider it an authoritarian technique that's ineffective, punitive, and hurtful.

The Trouble with Typical Time-Outs

Problem is, loving discipline proponents point out, it's your job as a parent to help your child deal with her problem, not send her away with it. When a toddler has a meltdown because her peas roll off her plate, or a preteen throws her notebook across the floor because her homework is too much of a challenge, for example, the last thing she needs is a distant parent. Sending a child to a time-out by herself in instances like these won't help her learn and it won't do anything for your relationship with her, either.

They Don't Teach Although the threat of a time-out might stop a behavior in its tracks (with a compliant child, anyway), the child only obeys out of fear, not out of any real desire to do the right thing or any attempt to solve her underlying problem. And the time-out typically does nothing to teach the child about the behavior or to help her identify or wrestle with her feelings. You may tell your child, "Go think about what you did," but what are the chances? More likely, loving discipline experts say, the child will harbor bad feelings, become defiant, and/or focus on revenge—hardly a recipe for clear thinking.

And after the typical time-out, it's easy for a parent to take a "glad that's over" attitude and let the child get back to the play or task at hand—with no real lesson under her belt—rather than delve further into just what happened. And so still no meaningful learning occurs.

> ## GET PSYCHED
>
> "Where did we ever get the crazy idea that in order to make children do better, we must first make them feel worse? This power to impose suffering is a common mistake made by many parents and teachers—so much so that they often lose sight of their primary goal of inspiring children to improve their behavior."
> —*Jane Nelsen, Ed.D., co-author of the* Positive Discipline *series.*

They Don't Work   Typical time-outs don't work as a deterrent, either. In fact, even when a child does comply to avoid a time-out, it can exacerbate the misbehavior in the long run. Psychologist Richard A. Dienstbier and other researchers at the University of Nebraska concluded in their 1982 studies of emotion *attribution* that when a child is punished harshly (and children do consider time-outs harsh punishment, despite the fact that parents consider them relatively tame), she is actually more likely to misbehave in similar situations in the future.

WEB TALK: For audio articles, books, workshops, and web links about the Positive Parenting approach, visit **www.positiveparenting.com.**

That's because the child who is harshly punished attributes her bad feelings to the punishment rather than to her own behavior, explains Dienstbier. So when it's time to decide how to act next time, she may well misbehave again, as long as she thinks she can get away with it. The child who doesn't suffer salient punishment, Dienstbier explains, focuses on her misbehavior in the first place; she's more likely to recall those feelings and act in such a way as to avoid them the next time temptation strikes, because the only way she can avoid the bad feelings that she attributes to her misbehavior is to be good.

PsychSpeak

Attribution—A theory used to explain reasons for behavior. External attribution would be factors outside the person (such as punishment), whereas internal attribution would be factors inside the individual (such as sadness or anger).

They're Hurtful Some parenting experts make the distinction between attention withdrawal and love withdrawal, but loving discipline experts point out that for children, especially young children, this distinction rarely exists. A child who is sent away for a time-out, even for just minutes, often feels that she's been abandoned and that she's lost her parent's love—and this can be frightening.

What a child believes when she is given a time-out is that her parents don't want to be around her when she misbehaves, that they don't want to hear about her misery, and that they can use their power to make her suffer alone. These messages can seriously damage the relationship between parent and child. If a parent opts for a time-out because he doesn't want to hear any more about his toddler's broken toy or his

GET PSYCHED

"Nothing is more important to us when we're young than how our parents feel about us. Uncertainty about that, or terror about being abandoned, can leave its mark even after we've grown."—*Alfie Kohn, author of* Uncondiitional Parenting

preschooler's tantrum at not being able to have candy for supper, for example, he will often relay some unfortunate messages to his child about his empathy and his desire to be helpful. Will the child who is sent to time-out when she screams about her broken cookie come to Dad when she's feeling depressed about her lack of friends in grade school or when she's worried about her boyfriend in high school? Not if she's successfully learned her lesson.

"Painful feelings are one consideration; the information conveyed about human relationships to a child in time-out is another," says Aletha Solter. "What message are we giving our children in demonstrating that love and attention are commodities to be doled out or withheld for purposes of controlling others?" she asks.

Time-outs are often used in academic and daycare settings. In these environments, peers play a role in the time-out drama, too. Children who are banished from a group (in a school or at daycare, while at playgroup, or even among siblings) are likely to feel humiliated, says psychologist Myrna Shure, Ph.D., author of *Thinking Child, Thinking Parent.* "In these circumstances," she says, "the period during which the child is isolated is a time when anger and frustration build up, often to the boiling point." Adele Faber, author of *How to Talk So Kids Will Listen and Listen So Kids Will Talk,* agrees. "As an adult you can imagine how resentful and humiliated you would feel if someone forced you into isolation for something you said or did. Imagine what it's like for the child who thinks there is something so wrong with her that she has to be removed from society."

GET PSYCHED

"When parental kindness grows out of genuine love and concern … children cannot get too much of it. When children know that they can engage and hold their parents' committed love, they derive a fundamental and lasting inner happiness."–*Martha Heineman Pieper, Ph.D., and William J. Pieper, M.D., authors of* Smart Love

It's easy to imagine a child feeling hurt and rejected when a caregiver's response to her woes is banishment. Perhaps most detrimentally, however, a time-out may also teach a child to bottle up her emotions. Peter Ernest Haiman, Ph.D., assistant professor of child development and early education, explains, "Upset in time-out and unable to express distress, youngsters desperately need to stop the painful feelings going on inside them. To cope, children learn to ignore and/or distract themselves from the energy of their hurt and angry feelings. Thus, children learn to repress these painful feelings. In the process, nervous habits emerge, such as thumb sucking, fingernail biting, hair pulling, skin scratching, tugging at clothes, self-pinching, and many other similar behaviors. The purpose of these behaviors is to ward off uncomfortable feelings and, in identification with their parents' criticism of them, to punish themselves." (Of course, telling a child to "be quiet!" during her time-out only underlines the fact that you want her to stifle her emotions.)

Positive Time-Outs

Your child isn't going to be irreparably damaged if you had her sit in a chair for taking her brother's favorite fire engine. Still, relying on typical time-outs as a discipline technique can be damaging. And it certainly isn't in line with any long-term positive goals for your child.

So what's the alternative? Well, you can take the opportunity to help your child learn to acknowledge her emotions, regain self-control, and problem solve. The way to do this, of course, isn't by sending her away, but by standing by her, guiding her (disciplining her) as she learns. Take a time-out, but do it positively.

By the way, some experts suggest that the term positive time-out is misleading, or at least burdened with the connotations of a typical time-out. "If anything, this technique is a time-in," says Haiman. "It's time that the parent and child spend working on the problem at hand together," he explains. You might choose to call it cool-down time, time-in, or positive time-out. What's important, of course, is how you carry out the technique.

Strictly Nonpunitive   The first thing to keep in mind is that a positive time-out is *not* a punishment. It's a time to calm down, to step back when things get too charged, to redirect when a child is being aggressive or disruptive, or to take a breather when a problem becomes overwhelming for the child or the parent. A positive time-out can be taken with a parent or alone, depending on the child's age, stage, needs, and desires. (Ideally, a child who experiences positive time-outs eventually learns to calm herself.) When the positive time-out is over, the instigating problem can be addressed with level heads and supportive hearts.

Positive Prep Work   Loving discipline experts suggest that you talk with your child in advance about the value of a positive time-out, explaining that some time to calm down is sometimes very helpful and that it's not a punishment. You might brainstorm in advance with her about things she can do to let off steam safely, or to help her feel better. (Yes, she can play with a toy, or color, or read a book; remember: the goal is not to punish her, but to teach her how to calm herself!)

You and your child might arrange a special place for positive time-outs. No matter the age of your child, sending her to another area of the house isn't necessary. A comfortable corner with big pillow and favorite puzzle or a rocker with a favorite book might work fine. Helping your child discover what comforts her is an important part of the success of the technique.

In the Heat of the Moment When tempers rise, you might simply say to your child, "Let's take a little time-out together to calm down." If your child is playing a game with a sibling and begins to lose control when things don't go her way, for example, you might call for a time-out before things escalate. "We'll come back as soon as you're ready to work this out calmly," you might explain. (Wise parents call for a cooling-off before things get so hot they're boiling over.)

Q&A

How can I teach my child to calm herself?

"Children, even the very young, are capable of learning to cope with frustration, anger, and excitement. But they need to be taught these skills. Each child needs to learn a variety of self-calming techniques, because different strategies are appropriate for different ages, different settings, and different preferences from one day to another. You can model techniques for your child or talk about how a certain technique helps you; for example, you can say, 'I'm so upset about breaking the dish that I'm going to calm myself down by reading quietly for a few minutes.' You can also teach your child a calming activity by doing the activity with her—'Let's relax and do this puzzle together,' for example.

"Be aware that a child goes through three stages when learning self-calming skills. She has to learn how to do the activity so that doing it is easy and reduces anger and frustration rather than increasing them. She notices that doing the activity changes how she feels; ideally, it soothes her. Finally, children realize that they can choose a specific activity to intentionally change how they feel."
—*Elizabeth Crary, author,* The Self-Calming Cards *(Parenting Press, 2004)*

There's no guarantee that your child will happily agree to a time-out by any name, however—especially when you first introduce the technique. In fact, she may be angry and refuse to co-operate. Supporting her does not mean that you let her continue her unacceptable behavior; she may not return to the game in her present state, for example. It does mean that you're patient and clearly willing to help her work through her frustration, anger, fear—whatever is causing the problem. You might sit by her and show her—with your calm, comforting tone of voice—that you're there to help her when she's ready, for example.

Self-Calming Skills Whereas the child who is banished to her room as punishment is likely to spend the time plotting revenge and/or becoming more and more angry instead of calming down, the child in positive time-out with you is encouraged to find ways to comfort herself and deal with her bad feelings. Teaching a child to take a breather when necessary gives her a valuable life skill. "Learning self-regulation is one of the biggest tasks of childhood," says Claire Lerner, LCSW, child development specialist at ZERO TO THREE, a national nonprofit organization promoting the healthy development of young children.

An attentive parent might help by holding her child, reading to her, helping her relax and deal with the problem at hand whenever she's ready. You might suggest deep breaths, coloring, or listening to music. Or you might give your child some time to play quietly by herself, nearby, depending on her age and temperament. An older child might calm herself and decide on her own when she's ready to rejoin the activity, do something else, or problem solve. In any case, the child knows that you're there for her, and that with your support she can work through her situation.

When your child is calm, help her acknowledge her feelings. If she's ready to talk about what led to the time-out, that's ideal. Encourage her to tell you what happened and how she feels about it. (If she isn't, wait until she's ready—even if it's not until tomorrow's car ride home from school.)

you're not alone

Birthday Breather

From the time she was an infant, Claire Lerner's daughter, Jessica, was easily overstimulated. "When she was upset, we'd rock her and walk her, and she'd become more distressed instead of more calmed," Claire, of Bethesda, Maryland, remembers.

When Jessica was a toddler, Claire recognized the need to provide Jessica with a space where she could learn to calm down when her toddler spirit got the best of her. So Claire created a "cozy corner" with pillows and books in the living room. "This was a place where Jessica could go to re-organize herself," Claire says. "I'd peek in and she'd be reading and talking to her animals. It was a good way for her to learn to regroup, to learn strategies for calming herself. Then we could tackle situations that were giving her trouble and problem solve together."

At Jessica's eighth birthday party, Claire saw how her daughter had really mastered the concept of time-outs, and how much this would serve her in life. "She begged to have this sleepover," Claire recalls, "so I finally agreed." A few hours into the party, though, with a basement full of ruckus, Jessica went up to her bedroom, laid down on the bed, and read a book.

When Claire found her there, her first inclination was to tell Jessica to get back downstairs with her long-requested guests! "But I realized that Jessica was wisely taking a needed respite because she was feeling overwhelmed," Claire says. In fact, when asked, Jessica told Mom, "I just need a break." Apparently Jessica learned that sometimes she just needs a time-out, even from too much of a good thing.

Half an hour later, Jessica returned to the party—until bedtime, when she traipsed back up to her room to sleep. "Jessica—12 now—is good at recognizing when she's getting overwhelmed and knows how to settle herself," Claire is happy to report.

The younger your child, the more help she'll need, of course. Eventually, though, if your child has experienced time-outs in a positive context rather than a punitive one, taking time to cool off will be her idea. You'll know your child has learned a thing or two about self-calming when she actively cools off as needed, shifting herself into a better frame of mind when things go wrong.

Taking Your Own Time-Out

Parents often dictate a time-out for a child when they themselves are feeling at their wits' end. But, as Positive Discipline expert Jane Nelsen points out, "Sometimes it may be parents who need to go to their rooms and do something to make themselves feel good enough to work on solutions with dignity and respect." You'll want to explain to your child ahead of time what's going on when you take some time to cool off. You may be able to sit down in the same area and quietly look at a book or close your eyes for a few minutes; if she's old enough, you can teach your child to respect your need for calming-down time, and you'll be providing a good example.

Q&A

What's the biggest discipline mistake parents make?

"When a child misbehaves, most parents think, 'I have to do something right now or I'm not doing my job,' or 'If I don't correct this right now, I'll be letting my child get away with something.' But the worst time to deal with conflict is when you're in the midst of it—when everyone is irrational and nobody can listen. Instead, take some cooling-down time, and then follow up when everyone can access their rational brains and cooperate to find mutually respectful solutions.

"One way to do this is through 'positive time out.' Positive is the operative word. Time-out is not effective when it is used as punishment, but it is very effective for teaching the skill of calming down until the rational brain can be accessed.

"Take some time-out yourself when you're upset. You might say, 'I'm too angry to deal with this right now. I'll get back to you when I feel better.' This is not rewarding bad behavior, and it is not letting your children get away with some-thing. It is modeling a skill that will be useful throughout their lives—waiting until no-conflict time to solve a conflict."*–Jane Nelsen, Ed.D., author of the* Positive Discipline *series*

If you need to be alone, and if your child is old enough to leave unsupervised, you might take a shower or retreat to your bedroom for a while. If your child is too young to leave alone, you might ask a spouse or friend to step in for you. In fact, it's a good idea to make "if ever" arrangements with a nearby friend ahead of time. Explain to your child that sometimes you need to take some time to do something—read, meditate, sing—to help yourself feel better. When you're feeling cooperative again, talk with your child about your cooling-down time. She may even decide on her own to take some next time she gets upset, when she sees how it works.

Meeting Underlying Needs

Instead of declaring a typical time-out, you'll want to identify the cause or causes of your child's misbehavior. "Good parents are diagnosticians," says Haiman. He suggests that when a child acts out, parents examine which of her needs may not be being met. While Positive Discipline parents define the causes of misbehavior in terms of a child's mistaken goals (see Chapter 4), and Aware Parenting advocates take into account a child's legitimate needs, lack of information, or stress and unhealed trauma (see Chapter 3), most loving discipline advocates would agree that this is a valuable place to start.

Of course, a child who misbehaves may well be short on more than one need. But to simplify, and to give you an idea of what you're looking for, here are some typical scenarios.

Normal Developmental Needs of a Child

Based on materials written by Peter Ernest Haiman, Ph.D., for the Contra Costa County Childcare Council.

Need: Love

Scenario: It's time for bed and your child returns to the living room, over and over, insisting that she needs one more this or that.

Cause of Misbehavior: If your child feels that she does not get enough love from you or your partner each day, she may misbehave to get more of it.

What to Do:

- Offer your child lots of hugs, holding, and words of love from you every day.
- Let her know you love to be with her. Show as well as tell. Smile at her and tell her that you love her throughout the day.
- Spend some extra time with her at bedtime, lying down with her, if she likes, and telling her you love her.

GET PSYCHED

"It is not true that you will spoil your young child if you constantly fulfill her needs. In fact, the opposite is supported by the research; you will spoil your child and make child rearing difficult if you regularly fail to satisfy your child's needs. Cooperative independence, achievement, emotional well-being and good behavior patterns develop if you fulfill the needs of your young child."—*Peter Ernest Haiman, Ph.D.*

Need: Health

Scenario: Your child is whining and her tolerance for mishaps is unusually low. After her whining escalates into a meltdown, you discover that she has a fever, or an itchy rash, or a bad bruise.

Cause of Misbehavior: Children who feel sick or suffer minor pains often misbehave.

What to Do:

- Provide regular physical and dental care to your child.
- Give your sick child supportive care to treat childhood injuries and provide comfort. For example, encourage her to drink plenty of liquids and use a cool washcloth to soothe her feverish head, give her an oat bath to soothe her itch, or hold an ice pack on her bruise (while you cuddle, if she likes).
- Let your child stay home and rest rather than go to day-care or school when she's ill.
- Talk to a health-care provider to make sure that you're doing all that you can for your child's illness or pain. Perhaps she can suggest something to help make your child more comfortable. She may recommend that you bring her in for an examination.

Need: Nutrition

Scenario: Your child has a tantrum in the grocery store. She wants something in every aisle. And in every aisle, not wanting to ruin her dinner, you try to put her off.

Cause of Misbehavior: Children grow rapidly and need food for sustenance. They get hungry and need to refuel often.

What to Do:

- Offer your child the opportunity to eat nutritious foods she likes every two to three hours.
- Stock up on healthful snacks and carry some with you at all times.

Need: Vigorous Play

Scenario: Halfway through her older sibling's recital, your grade-schooler decides she absolutely cannot stop kicking the seat in front of her.

Cause of Misbehavior: Children need plenty of active play. If they don't have it, they become restless and act out.

What to Do:

- Let your child play actively several times each day. Running and jumping is fun and healthy and will use up her extra energy. Older children can participate in school sports, take family hikes, ride their bikes, etc.

Need: Rest

Scenario: You have one more errand to run before returning home. Your toddler plops herself on the sidewalk and refuses to move.

Cause of Misbehavior: A tired child will misbehave. (A child who is not tired will misbehave, too, if you try to force her to rest.)

What to Do:

- When you're running errands with your child, keep in mind when your child rested last, the physical and emotional energy expended, and your youngster's need to rest. Schedule time for fun breaks (a stop by the library to read a book or some time on the park bench to feed the birds).

- For a young child, create a restful time in the morning and in the afternoon—even if it doesn't coincide conveniently with your plans for the day. Respect your older child's need to rest after preschool or school. Don't expect her to jump right into doing homework or chores.

- During rest time, ask your child if she'd like to listen to music or lie down and look at a book together. (You need rest, too!)

Need: Attention and Recognition

Scenario: Just home from daycare, and it's time to make supper. But your grade-schooler is causing so many problems, you're not even able to put water on the stove.

Cause of Misbehavior: If your child feels ignored or unimportant, she will likely misbehave. (And if you only pay attention to your child when she misbehaves, she will learn to misbehave to get your attention.)

What to Do:

- Participate and be actively interested in what your child does and says.

- Show an interest in what your child makes and does. Spend some time with her as soon as you pick her up from daycare or a sitter's. Invest your interest in her day and how she's feeling. Then enlist her aid with dinner; ask her whether she'd like to set the table or toss the salad. Talk about how much you appreciate her help.

Need: Independence

Scenario: You've selected an outfit for your preschooler to wear to Grandma's—right down to the matching hair ribbons—but she insists on wearing her comfy sweat suit instead. It's obvious at this point that you can force the issue and deal with her fury all during the visit, or you can let her dress casually.

Cause of Misbehavior: When you frequently tell your child what to do and what not do, she will misbehave. Not giving your little one choices and/or being overly controlling will create a "terrible two." And this behavior can last throughout the adolescent years.

What to Do:

- Give your child choices and decision-making opportunities throughout the day. For example, instead of "Get dressed!" say "Would you like to wear your blue shirt or your red one?" Instead of "Drink your milk!" say "Do you want milk in your blue cup or your red cup?" And instead of "Here's the outfit you'll wear to Grandma's," you might say, "Which of your dresses would you like to wear to Grandma's today?"

Need: Curiosity and Exploration

Scenario: You're at your wits' end because your child can't seem to walk through a store without pawing everything. You even dread a walk through the park with her because she'll stop to examine everything, and you just don't have the time.

Cause of Misbehavior: Your young child is naturally interested in the fascinating world of people and things. Misbehavior happens when your child is not allowed to act out her interest in life.

What to Do:

- Note your child's self-chosen interests. Provide activities that build on those interests. For example, if your child likes to play with toy animals, get a book with pictures of animals. (Don't force your interests on your child, or you'll damage her motivation to learn and cause misbehavior.)

- Allow plenty of time for exploration when you're out and about together. Take that walk in the park when you have time to delight in things with her, and suggest a visit to the zoo or farm rather than a museum, unless it's a hands-on children's museum.
- Keep in mind that what may seem like dawdling to you may be valuable learning time for her. Encourage, don't squelch it.

Need: Security

Scenario: You arrive home late, and, for no apparent reason, your preschooler decides that she can't get ready for bed, even though it's an hour past her normal bedtime. You're tired and cranky, too, so her refusal to cooperate is especially unnerving.

Cause of Misbehavior: If the life you give your child changes a lot from day to day, she will feel her life is unstable and become frightened. The consistency of your demeanor matters, too; if you behave hot-tempered one time, loving the next, close and then withdrawn, your child will learn that you are unreliable. This can cause misbehavior.

What to Do:

- Have routines, so your child knows what to expect. Your child needs to rely on you and to count on a familiar day-to-day life. But keep your schedule a little flexible, so your child doesn't fall apart when there are schedule variations now and then. For example, at bedtime let your child choose what to do first, have a story or brush her teeth.
- Be as even-tempered as possible with your child. This will reduce misbehavior when your life gets hard.

Need: Development of Good Values

Scenario: In the middle of a play date with the sweet kid from next door, you hear your child say, "Stupid, that's not how you play with a doll! Give me that!"

Cause of Misbehavior: Your child may misbehave if you or other members of the family (or even her peers) act and talk harshly.

What to Do:

- Talk about the importance of sharing, cooperation, respect, taking turns, and teamwork.
- Be a good role model; let your child see you practice these values.
- Point out the good behavior of your child, family members, and other children and adults.

Keep in mind that this is a dynamic process, and your child's behavior may have—in fact, likely has—more than one underlying cause. The child who is kicking the seat in front of her at her sibling's recital might need more exercise, and/or more loving attention, for example.

What You Can Do

Preparation is the key to making a positive time-out work, so here are some ideas for setting that stage. When it comes to helping your child hone her self-calming skills, teaching her to recognize and talk about her emotions is an important first step, and it's one you can work on in the course of each day.

- ☐ Talk with the entire family about showing respect for a person who is taking some time to cool off. This isn't the time to ask the person for help, or turn up the music, or put her on the phone with Grandma, for example.

☐ Help your child create a good place to relax. It doesn't need to be in her room or the corner of any room! An area of the living room or den, with a big pillow and some favorite books nearby, will work nicely. Make it pleasant. It should be a place she likes to be.

☐ Role-play a positive time-out with your child when she's in a good mood. "Let's pretend we're upset and need to calm down. Where shall we go and what will help us feel better?" This might make it easier for her to see it as a positive action when it comes time for the real thing.

☐ Stock the location *you're* likely to take a breather with some good magazines, your favorite calming scent, or your ongoing crochet project.

☐ Talk with your child about other kinds of time-outs. Why do coaches and players take time-outs during a basketball game? Why might someone take a time-out during a debate or a contest? Talk about the difference between *taking* a time out and *being given* a time out.

☐ From a young age, help your child learn the vocabulary she needs to name her feelings. When you read picture books together, talk about how the person in the picture looks happy or joyful. When her pet is ill, talk about how sad Rover looks. She'll find it easier when it comes time to identify her own emotions if she knows the lingo.

☐ Make sure your child knows that it's safe to talk about her feelings. Resist the urge to tell her she shouldn't feel a particular way. Instead, validate her feelings by listening carefully and acknowledging that whatever she's feeling, it's good that she can identify it.

☐ Give your child opportunities to try on emotions. Most kids love to act—in skits, with puppets, or just while reading aloud. Suggest that she make a character sound sad or anxious, or tell her that she was very convincing as the angry boss or the frightened kitten.

☐ If you're making the switch from typical time-outs to positive time-outs, consider names that your child will understand and appreciate. For example, maybe you'll say "Time to unwind!" or "Let's refresh!" or "Cool-down time!"

☐ Help your child experiment with different ways of dealing with her emotions. Mister Rogers often told his television viewers that he found playing the piano very helpful when he was angry. Maybe your child would like to try expressing her feelings with an instrument, or or maybe she'd prefer clay, finger-painting, making mudpies, or running around the yard. Then again, maybe she'd just like to talk about it.

Problem Solving

Loving discipline involves guiding children rather than ordering them about or rescuing them from their problems and conflicts. And it teaches children to view mistakes as opportunities to learn. Learning to solve problems, then, becomes a crucial lesson. Whether it's a run-in on the playground or a conflict with his parents about his behavior, a child who is learning to identify and solve problems is empowered and growing in competence. From an early age, parents can help children obtain skills that will help them be good problem solvers. And by exposing them to different techniques, they can help provide them with the tools they need to tackle anything.

Teaching Your Child to Problem Solve

Problem solving sounds like a tall order, but it's something that you can start teaching your child at an early age—by guiding him to take a problem-solving approach to things and giving him the language with which to work.

Myrna Shure, Ph.D., has conducted research on interpersonal problem solving and children for 25 years. She's studied peer and sibling problems (squabbles over grabbing toys and hitting, for example) as well as parent/child conflicts (such as the child not listening). Shure found that 4-year-olds are fully able to recognize and identify their own feelings as well as the feelings of others. They are able to think of alternative solutions to interpersonal problems and to change their behavior based on those alternative solutions. Preschoolers can also recognize potential consequences of actions, setting the stage for genuine empathy. Four-year-olds who are taught basic problem solving have fewer aggressive be-haviors and less social withdrawal, and they are better able to cope with frustration than children without training.

By age 5, Shure found, children with problem-solving skills begin to be guided by their empathetic ability; they make decisions based on how others will be affected and how that makes them feel, rather than by the possibility of external, punitive conse-quences. Learning problem solving also improves their ability to delay gratification and cope with frustration.

Shure's five-year longitudinal study, funded by the National Institute of Mental Health in Washington, D.C., also states that children trained in problem solving improved their academic scores in reading, math, and social studies! Shure concludes that the ability to problem solve actually relieves emotional stress, which allows the students to better concentrate on the tasks demanded in the classroom.

Research published in a 1987 issue of *Developmental Psychology* by Peggy Estrada and colleagues showed a consistent relation over time between mother-child interactions and a child's cognitive competency. When a mother is willing to engage her child in problem-solving tasks, share information, and encourage him to explore, she enhances the child's motivation and persistence when he is faced with a challenging task. Children who benefited from this kind of encouragement, the researchers found, had higher mental ability scores at age 4, school readiness at ages 5 and 6, IQ scores at age 6, and vocabulary and math scores at age 12.

Pre-Problem-Solving Skills One way parents can prepare children for problem solving at a young age is to familiarize them in fun, playful ways with what Shure calls "pre-problem-solving words," words such as *same/different, some/all, might/ maybe, why/because, if/then, before/after,* and *now/later.*

Ask your child "Is that a good idea or *not* a good idea?" or "I have broccoli on my plate. Do you have something *different* on your plate?" or "Do you brush your teeth *before* or *after* you get out of bed?" Then, when the words are used in a problem-solving context, to ask questions, such as "What happened *before* you hit your brother?" your child will be familiar with the words and comfortable using them.

Pre-problem-solving words also include words that describe feelings, such as *happy, sad, mad, scared, proud, frustrated, impatient, worried,* and *relieved.* "Naming emotions is a powerful tool," explains Shure. "Children feel more in control of themselves and their world when they can describe how they're feeling." It's important for your child to be able to name his feelings and others' feelings, because what he does next may depend on that true feeling. If he's frustrated, his solution may be different than if he's worried, for example. You'll want to provide an environment in which your child feels safe exploring his feelings. And by naming and talking about the feelings of others, you'll be setting the stage for empathy, too.

Shure also suggests working with your young child on concepts that can prepare him to problem solve:

- Help him see that there's more than one way to think about things. Ask him about the different ways you might get in touch with Grandma (letter, phone, car, for example). Tell him to think about some of the things that are round. Ask him how many things an empty basket might be used for—a nest, a hat, a bowl, or a doll bed, for example.

- Teach him to identify his emotions. Give him the words he needs to name them. Talk about how the characters in his book feel, how you feel, and how he feels.

- Underline that people have different feelings about the same issue, and that they're all entitled to have these feelings, preferences, and beliefs. Talk about how people like different colors, books, and foods, for example. When he sees a conflict between two people, show him that both people have a perspective.

- Guide him to think about different ways to solve the same problem. He might say that you could buy a beach ball for him and a beach ball for his sister, so they won't fight over toys at the beach; or that they could share the beach ball and also have a pail and shovel to share. Explore how many different ways he might do something, such as build a building with his blocks.

- Explain how a solution might work for some, but not for others. For example, maybe feeding the dog before preschool works well for him, but not for his sister, who can barely eat her own breakfast in time.

- Teach him to be a good listener and to pay attention. You can do this by playing games and by being a respectful listener yourself.

- Encourage your child to find out about others. Ask him his new friend's name and what he likes best at the playground.

Show interest in other people yourself, and report what you discover to your child.

- Teach him an appreciation of timing, of the sequencing of events. "First we'll go to the deli, then we'll have a picnic," or "We want to make the cookies so they'll be ready for your sister when she comes home from school."

Sue Dinwiddie, author of *I Want It My Way! Problem-Solving Techniques with Children Two to Eight,* provides the following example of how a parent might help a young child problem solve.

WEB TALK: The Alliance for Transforming the Lives of Children is devoted to supporting parents, caregivers, professionals, and policymakers in their nurturing of children. The site provides information on education programs, services, products, and public policies.

www.atlc.org

The first step in guiding a young child to problem solve, says Dinwiddie, is to help define what the child actually wants to accomplish: the desire. Wanting something motivates action in healthy young children, and negative actions usually result not from malicious intent or a character deficit, but from choosing the wrong means to achieve the desire.

Dinwiddie gives the example of 3-year-old Kendall who has written on a mirror with Mother's new red lipstick. Mom's first task is to communicate with Kendall to discover the desire. Using an "I" statement, she can let her child know her feelings and the reasons for them. She might say, "Kendall, I feel angry when you draw on the mirror with my new lipstick because it ruins the lipstick and gets the mirror dirty." Now Kendall has some information about how Mom feels, as well as the effects of his behavior.

Mom needs some information about Kendall's motives, so she can encourage more appropriate means to achieve this desire. Instead of punishing Kendall, Mom might try an "I wonder" statement. "Kendall, I wonder what you wanted that made you draw on the mirror with my new red lipstick." Young children who are not intimidated and fearful tend to be quite honest, Dinwiddie points out. So Kendall might innocently say, "I wanted to draw a red picture."

The next step is to help the child find an acceptable choice for accomplishing the desire. "Kendall, I don't want you to draw with my lipstick, and I don't want drawing on the mirror. How else could you draw a red picture?" She is now encouraging some analytical thinking on Kendall's part. The more practice Kendall has in problem solving, the easier it is to generate other choices. If Kendall suggests a choice that's unacceptable to Mother, she can help her child predict the consequences of the actions and ask for more suggestions. Kendall may volunteer, "I could get some paper," or "I could get my drawing book."

Now Mom can help Kendall make amends for the inappropriate behavior—without shaming him. After agreeing that Kendall has found an acceptable choice for drawing a red picture, she could say, "Kendall, drawing a red picture on paper with a red crayon is a good choice. First, let's work together to get the lipstick off the mirror." While they're working she might gently point out that it's hard to remove the lipstick. She may also confide that she's sad about the state of her new red lipstick now. She is not shaming Kendall, nor placing guilt, but she is teaching the consequences of actions and how to find appropriate alternatives.

Working Together There are many patient, loving techniques for teaching a child to problem solve. Becky Bailey, Ph.D., professor of early childhood education and development and author of *Easy to Love, Difficult to Discipline,* outlines this simple method of addressing an ongoing problem and conflicts together with a child.

Step 1. Noticing instead of judging

"I've noticed _____."

"Have you or anyone else in the family noticed this?"

Step 2. Owning the problem instead of blaming

"This is a problem for me because _____."

"Is this a problem for you?"

Step 3. Defining the problem with positive intent

"So the problem is _____."

Step 4. Seeking solutions

"What could we do to _____."

Step 5. Asking for willingness, not obedience

"Are you willing to _____?"

Step 6. Reflecting on the progress

"_____ is working for me."

"Is _____ working for you?"

Here's the process in action:

Step 1, tell your child, in a nonjudgmental tone, using non-judgmental words, what you see happening. "I've noticed that often when we sit down to dinner your voice is very loud, almost like screaming. And you talk a lot in this tone of voice—kind of like this ....” (Demonstrate for the child—not to make fun of him, but so that he can recognize it. It's even okay if it makes you both laugh.) “Then I ask you to talk quieter, then you don't, and then I start yelling at you, like this ....” (Demonstrate how you sound.)

Ask, “Have you noticed this?” Often children (and adults) don't realize what's taking place. If your child says “Yes,” then proceed. If he says “No,” then describe better, again, without judgments. (A judgment would be a comment such as “You demand all of the attention” or “You ruin everybody's dinner.”)

Step 2, say something like, “This is a problem for me because I would like dinner to be fun.” You might say, “When I ask you to be quiet and you do not do what I asked, I feel frustrated and don't know what to do. Then I end up yelling, too, and I don't like myself when I do that. When everyone is yelling, I don't like dinnertime. It is not fun.”

Ask him, “Is this a problem for you at all? Is it fun at dinner when you and I get into a fight?” You must see whether the child perceives it to be a problem. Your child will not be vested in the solution unless he takes some ownership of the problem.

The child at this point (without judgment) might give you some important information. He may say, “Yes, it is a problem. Daddy only listens to you,” or “You won't let me play outside.” (It may be something altogether different from what you thought.)

Step 3, define the problem with positive intent. “So the problem is that we both get too upset to enjoy dinner,” or “So the problem is that you're worried that you won't get a chance to talk to Daddy.” It's important how you state the problem, because it will determine how you'll find a solution. For example, if you state the problem as staying calm, you'll need a different solution than if you state the problem as taking turns talking.

Step 4, ask your child to seek solutions with you. "So the problem is that we get upset. What solutions can you and I both use so that we both stay calmer at dinner?" Or "So the problem is that we both are worried about not getting to talk. What solutions can you and I both use so that we both have a chance to talk?"

Keep it simple. Perhaps your child will suggest that you touch him on the shoulder instead of yelling at him, to remind him to lower his voice. Or together you might decide that everybody will get a chance to talk in turn at the table, to make sure that he does have the spotlight for a bit, but that he doesn't hog it.

Step 5, after you find a solution to try, say, for example, "Are you willing to take turns talking at the table?" If your child is little you might say, "We could use the ketchup bottle as a pretend microphone. Whoever has the microphone can talk and the others listen."

Step 6, if the solution is working, make sure you go back to the child and acknowledge the success. You could revisit it and say, "I'm having a lot more fun at dinner. I enjoy hearing what you have to say and what the others have to say. How about you? Is dinnertime better for you? What do you like most?"

By the way, it's a good idea to try to anticipate problems and brainstorm solutions before the fact whenever you can. Don't wait until you're an hour into your road trip to address the fact that the kids always fight about who gets the window seat, for example. Instead, get them together and start with, "I've noticed that whenever we take a car ride, [this] happens, and we're taking a trip soon, so how can we address [this]?"

> ### GET PSYCHED
>
> "Children who have opportunities to problem solve become adept at generating solutions. They are also invested in the solution, as they have played a part in finding it."—*Sue Dinwiddie, author of* I Want It My Way! Problem-Solving Techniques with Children Two to Eight

Children usually enjoy coming up with solutions. It gives them a handle on their problems and empowers them. "When given the opportunity to become problem solvers, children gain self-knowledge," says Nancy Samalin, author of *Loving Your Child Is Not Enough*.

P.E.T. Problem Solving Here's another technique to try. Many loving discipline experts use the Parent Effectiveness Training (P.E.T.) method of problem-solving conflicts. This is how it works:

1. Identify and define the conflict.
2. Generate solutions.
3. Evaluate the alternative solutions.
4. Choose the best solution.
5. Implement the decision.
6. Follow-up evaluation.

First, you need to get your child's attention and stress that there's a problem that needs to be addressed. State the problem using "I" messages rather than "you" messages. For example, "I am upset when I walk in the door and trip over your backpack," or "I am worried that you're going to be hurt if you keep playing roller hockey with the high school kids," rather than "you are so sloppy," or "you are being reckless," or even "you are not being conscientious enough."

"I" messages tell your child your concerns, whereas "you" messages tend to be critical of the child and adversarial. Tell your child that you're interested in finding a solution that will meet both of your needs.

Next brainstorm a variety of solutions together. Anything goes; don't evaluate the suggestions as you go, just accept all the possibilities at this point. Perhaps your child will suggest that he put his backpack on the kitchen table instead, or that you not watch him play roller hockey anymore. You might suggest that he go to his room with his pack before he does anything else when he gets home and that he finds a group of similarly aged kids to play roller hockey with. Other ideas might include putting a hook just inside the front door for his pack, and his agreeing to always wear protective gear while playing roller hockey.

Together, look at the possibilities and see which ones are workable. Talk about which might work best, which would be too difficult to implement, which would meet both your needs and which wouldn't. Then, decide together which solution you're going to try. Everyone should be committed to the solution, at least for now. You may want to write it down.

Outline how the solution will be carried out. Iron out the specifics of who does what and when to make it happen. If you agreed on the hook for the pack, specify who will buy it and put it up, for example. And if you decided to go with the hockey gear, you might schedule a shopping trip together to purchase the necessary helmet and pads. Or you might help your child organize a grade-school roller hockey group.

Finally, check back with each other to see how the solution is working out. Talk

GET PSYCHED

"Children won't want to be helpful to you when you tell them you have a problem with their behavior, unless they feel you've generally tried to help them when they have had problems. In other words, only if the child feels the relationship to be reciprocal—fair, two-way, just, equitable— will he want to take the trouble to change his behavior to please you."—*Thomas Gordon, Ph.D., author of* Discipline That Works

about things you hadn't thought of the first time around. Delve into what is and isn't working. Modify the initial decision, or start over with another solution—or even another brainstorming session—if you like. Maybe the hook is in somebody's way and needs to be moved, or maybe the kneepads don't fit properly and you'll need to shop for new ones, for example.

Resist Owning the Problem Jim Taylor, Ph.D., author of *Positive Pushing,* emphasizes the importance of making sure that your child does the work when it comes to solving a problem. Help him understand the obstacle, Taylor says, and help him break it down into manageable parts. You can do this by showing him how to restate the problem. "What's another way of describing the problem?" you might ask. "Can you break down the big problem into smaller ones?" Maybe the major problem—your child's being late for school, for example—can be broken down into smaller ones: he turns off the alarm without getting up, he doesn't have his clothes picked out yet, or he finds his brother in the bathroom when he needs to get in there to get ready. By tackling these problems one at a time, your child can solve the big problem. Maybe he'll decide to put his alarm clock on the shelf across the room from his bed, for example, and he'll start picking out his clothes the night before. And maybe he and his sib will come up with a morning schedule for the bathroom.

GET PSYCHED

"Rescuing children from the daily turmoil of life without involving them doesn't help them learn to solve their problems. It only relieves them from having to think any more about them. And as early as age 4, children can turn problems into problems that can be solved."
—Myrna Shure, Ph.D., author of Thinking Parent, Thinking Child

Taking Over

Generally we want to encourage our children to solve their problems on their own, with our support. But sometimes parents should not hesitate to step in and take over on behalf of a child.

Kate Cohen-Posey, author of *How to Handle Bullies, Teasers, and Other Meanies,* was about to present a program on violence in school to ninth and tenth graders, when her daughter mentioned, "By the way, there's this guy in school who keeps threatening to kill me." When Kate asked her daughter to explain, she told how, while playing with a classmate, she had bumped him off a bench.

"I'm never talking to you again," he told her, and she thought he must have been kidding. Sometime later, though, he threatened to kill her, threw rocks at her, scraped her, threatened to stab her, and punched her. Kate found out that this student also had a history of drug use that warranted rehab, and that he had exposed himself to her daughter on another occasion.

Kate spoke with her fellow presenter at the program that day (an agent who had handled the Granite Hills (California) High School shooting incident), who encouraged her to bring the matter to the attention of school authorities. Kate drafted a letter outlining all of the threats and incidents and presented it to the school's School Resource Officer, who promptly handled the matter.

If you think that your child is in any danger at school or anyplace else, you should step in and assure his safety; these are not matters for him to handle on his own. Watching you handle them will assure your child that you will make sure that he is safe, and it will also model for him how serious problems might be addressed.

"This was the one and only time I ever stepped in on my daughter's behalf," says Kate. "Other times I helped her decide what to say, or in one instance I helped her write a letter to a teacher. But this incident required an entirely different approach."

Taylor also advises parents not take credit for the solutions by talking about how "we" figured out the problem. Instead, he advises, let the child take the responsibility and the ownership.

"Like a silent partner," he explains, "you should help in the process, but should get none of the credit."

Ron Taffel, Ph.D., author of *Nurturing Good Children Now,* suggests using hypothetical situations to help a child problem solve. "A hypothetical situation can move the spotlight away from him, allowing your child some breathing room to work out solutions nondefensively with a compassionate adult," he explains.

So you might ask your child, "Jack seems to have a hard time getting along with his little sister. What do you think he might do to improve the situation?" or "What do you think his parents might do to help him get along better?" You can also use fictional characters—in the book you're reading or the television show you're watching together—as a focus of your discussion.

Empathic Understanding Solves Problems A series of questions is a good way to help a child understand how his behavior affects others. Myrna Shure suggests querying that leads a child to choose behavior based on empathic understanding.

For example, if your child leaves his truck on the hallway floor, you might ask him, "What if Dad comes out of the bedroom and walks this way? Yes, he might step on your toy and break it. What else might happen? Yes, he might hurt his foot." And then, Shure suggests, always try to make the consequences relevant to the child by asking something like, "And how would you feel if that happened?"

Wrap up with, "What can you do now to make sure that Dad—or anybody—doesn't step on your truck so that you won't feel sad or mad?"

Q&A

How can I teach my child to be more empathetic?

"Nurturing empathy is an ongoing process. It's not something we teach a child once and for all, like riding a bike or tying his shoes. For some kids it may come quite easily. For others it will take more time and effort. Being a good role model—both by nurturing the child and by showing respect and concern for others—is effective, but it's just the first step. If your child hurts someone, help him to get some ice for her. If she's angered a friend over a toy, have her get another toy, or offer to share. While an apology might sometimes ring hollow, doing something tangible to improve the situation will foster true empathy."—*Kimberlee Whaley, Ph.D., Vice President for Education & Guest Operations, COSI Columbus, adjunct associate professor, The Ohio State University*

Talking with your child by asking him questions such as these, says Shure, can help him focus not only on how the other person will feel, but also on how *he* will feel if that happens. This understanding can motivate him to do the right thing. "When we threaten kids or explain consequences to them, kids usually tune out these demands, suggestions, and explanations. As early as age 4, kids can answer questions that help them care about others while tuning in to their own feelings as well."

Resolving One-on-One Conflict

Positive Discipline expert Jane Nelsen suggests teaching children the following four-step process for resolving conflict on a one-on-one basis (with a classmate at school or a sibling, for example):

- **Ignore it.** Explain to your child that it makes more sense to walk away than to stay and fight. He might find another game or activity to do, or he might leave long enough to cool off.

- **Talk it over respectfully.** Your child might choose to try to work out the problem with the other person. He can start by telling the other person how he feels and that he doesn't like what's happening. Teach him to listen to what the other person says about how he or she feels as well. Then he'll need to share what he thinks he did to contribute to the problem and what he is willing to do differently.

- **Agree together on a solution.** The two might work out a plan for sharing or taking turns, for example, or they might apologize to each other.

- **If they can't work it out together, they can ask for help.** Siblings might put the problem on a family meeting agenda—in fact, they might choose to do this at the start, which is fine—or they can talk over the problem with a parent, teacher, or friend.

To help your child get the hang of the process, it's a good idea to role play different situations in which he might use the technique.

Role Playing

Role playing is simply a rehearsal of a situation. It's easy to do with kids, and it's helpful because it offers the child an opportunity to practice what he's learning. "It's like the difference between talking about how to ride a bike and practicing pedaling and balancing as your parent holds on," explains William Whelan, Psy.D., co-director of the Child-Parent Attachment Clinic at the University of Virginia School of Medicine in Charlottesville.

In fact, says Whelan, role playing is something kids do spontaneously all the time. When a child lectures his teddy bear about how he'll have to go home unless he stops throwing toys, or when he insists that one action figure share with the other, he's role playing—acting out situations that concern him.

To use role playing to help a child through a problem, it's a good idea to take cues from the child, who is likely to bring up situations that are giving him trouble. "Look especially for upcoming events about which he may be apprehensive," advises Mark Wolraich, CMRI/Shaun Walters professor of pediatrics at the University of Oklahoma Health Sciences Center in Oklahoma City. Much of a child's anxiety about a first trip to the dentist, a move, or a hospital stay, for example, stems from not knowing what to expect and not being able to envision himself in the situation. Role playing these events—perhaps using props—can be very comforting. Because he's in a supportive environment, explains Wolraich, he'll feel safe facing his fears and working through them a bit.

Role playing can also encourage a child to be empathetic. Many studies have shown that when children (as well as adults) assume the role of a character and act out that person's feelings or behavior, their empathy for that person is increased. Schools have used this knowledge in programs to encourage understanding of and empathy for those who are physically handicapped, for example.

Trouble spots in a child's behavior are also good candidates for role play, suggests Whelan. "Let's pretend Emerson is here, and he wants to play with your favorite truck. I'll be Emerson," for example. Or, "I'm going to pretend to get a telephone call and I want you to practice being quiet while I'm talking." Such rehearsals will give both you and your child the opportunity to explore options and come up with workable solutions. Of course, plenty of positive feedback for desired behavior during these run-throughs will help ensure similar manners in real situations, too.

Make sure you keep the "play" in role play, too. It's important, stresses Wolraich, that parents be supportive, not critical, and carefully consider whether the child is developmentally up to the task. Common sense is usually the best guide, he says. If your child is disinterested or resistant after a couple of tries at playing through a particular situation, it's time to back off for a while.

Also keep in mind that even if rehearsals have gone well, a young child's success may be limited. "Don't be surprised if the child has trouble transferring what he's learned to slightly different situations," warns Wolraich. If he's practiced with a family member how to share his new truck, for example, he may not automatically translate that information to sharing it with peers. The similarity may not even occur to him.

What You Can Do

As a parent, it's unlikely that you have to go looking for problems to solve! Viewing them as opportunities, however, takes the sigh out of the experience. And with a little attention, you can prepare your child to problem solve with a positive attitude throughout his life.

- ☐ Play "solve the problem" with your child. While driving in the car, for example, take turns thinking up problems and then brainstorming, together, as many solutions as you can. Have fun coming up with silly ideas as well as smart solutions.

- ☐ Ask your child to name all of the different emotions he felt today. Tell him which emotions you felt.

- ☐ Talk with your child about how others solve problems. What does his teacher do about conflicts in the classroom?

☐ Stop in the middle of reading a story to your child and ask him how he thinks a character might resolve a conflict or problem. Then compare his solution to the author's. Talk about how there's no one right answer.

☐ Role play a situation that your child is concerned about—a request for an attendance exemption from a teacher, for example, or a difficult discussion with a girlfriend.

☐ On a regular basis, take stock of how your child is doing. Jot down problems you think need to be addressed and choose a technique for addressing them, one by one.

☐ Solicit your child's problem-solving skills when appropriate. Ask him to help you decide what to do about the fact that you missed a friend's birthday, or that you are scheduled to be in two places at once on Friday.

Epilogue

I hope that you feel excited about your role as a discipline provider in your child's life. Yes, you have tremendous influence and a remarkable responsibility, but don't be daunted.

On the one hand, being well informed about our parenting role makes us sensitive to its importance, while on the other it enables us to enjoy our children more—as we build closer relationships with them and watch them flourish. Like other work, when it's done with focus, good and thoughtful intent, and love, it brings fulfillment to everyone involved.

To those who think that some of the concepts we've outlined are a bit idealistic, please consider that we owe it to our children to do the very best we can. Of course, that's easiest to say when things are running smoothly. We get tired and frustrated and overwhelmed, and so we won't be perfect parents, but we can be parents who try our best—and who, like we're teaching our children to do, see mistakes as opportunities to learn rather than failures. And every time we do succeed in disciplining our children with love, we will be revitalized and encouraged anew.

I also want to encourage you to talk with other parents, to share ideas and offer support to one another. Revisit this book and other loving discipline books. If you find that your positive, consistent discipline strategies have not been effective, or if you have concerns about your child's development, mood, or behavior, please seek professional guidance.

You are the person likely to be the most sensitive to your child's challenges, so be a careful observer and pay attention to your instincts. Share any questions or concerns you have about your child with her health-care provider or other qualified health professional. The resources in the appendix of this book can also point you to loving discipline professionals who are eager to help.

Sources and Resources

If you're interested, here's where to find out more about some of the ideas in this book. Some of the organizations listed offer workshops, networking, and links to other interesting information and groups.

Additional Sources of Help

Active Parenting is an Adlerian-based education program developed by Dr. Michael H. Popkin. It's available on video at www.activeparenting.com.

Alliance for Transforming the Lives of Children. The mission of this group is "to champion a culture of compassionate individuals, family and community who have fun with, learn from, and responsively and lovingly interact with children." Visit www.ATLCWarmLine.org.

Ask DrSears.com offers articles on attachment-style parenting by William Sears, M.D., and Martha Sears, R.N., authors of *The Baby Book*. Two of their sons, also pediatricians, add to the information Dr. Sears provides on this site. Learn about pregnancy and childbirth, feeding, nutrition, discipline, sleep problems, childhood illnesses, and more. See www.askdrsears.com.

ATTACh, or the **Association for the Treatment and Training of Children,** is an international coalition of professionals and families whose mission is to promote healthy attachment. Their focus is helping those with attachment difficulties by sharing knowledge, talents, and resources. See www.attach.org.

Attachment Parenting International (API) is a nonprofit member organization working with parents, professionals, and other organizations around the world. They provide a clearinghouse for educational materials, research, consultations, referrals, and speaker services to promote Attachment Parenting. Visit www.attachmentparenting.org.

The Aware Parenting Institute in Goleta, California, offers workshops by its founder, Aletha Solter, Ph.D., as well as by certified instructors in 12 countries. Dr. Solter also offers telephone consultations for parents who are familiar with her books. The website contains more than 40 articles for parents. Call 805-968-1868, or visit www.awareparenting.com.

BabyCenter.com and its sister site, **ParentCenter.com,** offer an exhaustive array of age-customized articles for expectant and new parents, as well as parents of toddlers, preschoolers, and grade-schoolers. Issues range from adoption to health to work and family, from school success to travel and tradition. A range of discipline techniques (many of which are in the loving discipline vein) are offered in the behavior sections. Visit www.babycenter.com and www.parentcenter.com.

The Center for Effective Discipline provides materials for nonviolent parenting, including articles related to the news, the law, discipline at home and at school, and religious teachings pertaining to discipline. Visit www.stophitting.org.

The Center for Nonviolent Communication offers training in compassionate communication, an approach to communication developed by Marshall B. Rosenberg, Ph.D. The approach emphasizes compassion and focuses on being conscious of what we observe, feel, need, and request. Learn more at www.cnvc.org.

Global Initiative to End All Corporal Punishment. Launched in April 2001, this group aims to speed the end of corporal punishment of children across the world. Learn about them at www.endcorporalpunishment.org.

Kid Source offers a wealth of information to parents, including polls, forums, news about health and safety issues, recall notices, articles on parenting styles, and discipline issues. Visit www.kidsource.com.

La Leche League International promotes breastfeeding among mothers worldwide by providing educational materials and support for breastfeeding women. Visit them at www.lalecheleague.org.

The Liedloff Continuum Network is a nonprofit group dedicated to promoting the attachment principles described in Jean Liedloff's book *The Continuum Concept*. Read about them at www.continuum-concept.org.

Mothering magazine explores health, environmental, medical, and lifestyle issues, including breastfeeding, co-sleeping, midwifery, vaccinations, circumcision, and other issues of importance to a natural family lifestyle. Subscribe to the magazine or read about them at www.mothering.com.

The Natural Child Project offers articles on nonpunitive parenting and other topics of interest to loving discipline parents. "Our vision," they explain, "is a world in which all children are treated with dignity, respect, understanding, and compassion. In such a world, every child can grow into adulthood with a generous capacity for love and trust. Our society has no more urgent task." Visit them at www.naturalchild.org.

News for Parents.org provides up-to-date articles on issues of interest to parents, including pregnancy, education, special needs and medical challenges, health and development, and family and home. Includes breaking news and a poll. See www. newsforparents.org.

Parent Effectiveness Training (P.E.T.) was developed by Nobel Peace Prize nominee Dr. Thomas Gordon. To learn more, find a class in your area, or purchase the home video course, contact Gordon Training International, www.gordontraining.com, or call 1-800-628-8125.

PARENT GUIDANCE WORKSHOP. Nancy Samalin offers introductory and advanced workshops for parents of toddlers through teens in the New York City area, and speeches and seminars throughout the United States and abroad. See www.samalin.com.

PARENTS FORUM, founded in 1992, is a solutions-oriented, assets-based program of networking, skill development, and support for parents and others caring for children. The program handbook, *Where the Heart Listens,* describes their history and approach to parent peer support. They welcome individual members and collaborate with other organizations, local and international, to raise awareness of parents' concerns. They're located in Cambridge, Massachusetts. Call them at 671-864-3801, or visit them at www.parentsforum.org.

Parents Leadership Institute helps parents acquire skills to build and rebuild close connections with their children. They offer parenting talks, classes, support groups, booklets, articles, parent success stories, and videos (in English and Spanish). They also offer phone consultation. Their audience is primarily parents of children age 6 and under, although their booklets are designed to be useful to parents of children of all ages. Their parenting approach is called Parenting by Connection. Learn about it at www.parentleaders.org.

The Positive Discipline Association is a nonprofit organization dedicated to promoting the principles of Positive Discipline in families, schools, businesses, and communities. They are a source for parenting classes, teacher training workshops, articles, speakers, and research. Call them at 866-POS-DISC (1-866-767-3472), or visit www.posdis.org.

Positive Discipline is Jane Nelsen's official site, which promotes Positive Discipline life skills and responsible relationships. Here you'll find answers to questions from teachers and parents, featured articles, success stories, and resources for speakers, workshops, and products. Visit www.positivediscipline.com.

Positive Parenting contains resources and information to "help make parenting more rewarding, effective, and fun." The site contains thoughtful articles for loving parents and teachers about family meetings, alternatives to spanking, keys to successful parenting, and a host of behavioral issues. See www.positiveparenting.com.

Smart Love Parenting Center is a nonprofit, charitable organization based in Chicago. It was founded by parents and child development professionals to provide parents with practical parenting strategies and growth-promoting answers to their childrearing concerns. Its services are guided by Martha Heinemen Pieper, Ph.D., and William J. Pieper, M.D., authors of *Smart Love.* The center offers parenting talks and workshops on a range of parenting topics for businesses, daycare centers, churches, and schools; one-on-one parenting coaching; parenting classes and discussion groups offering in-depth knowledge of Smart Love principles; and publications, such as "Smart Love Answers: A collection of parenting questions and answers to everyday parenting concerns." Call them at 773-665-8052, or visit www.smartlove.com.

ZERO TO THREE is a national nonprofit organization based in Washington, D.C. Its purpose is to support the healthy development of young children by providing up-to-date research, training, and leadership development for parents and professionals. Visit them at www.zerotothree.org.

Bibliography and Further Reading

Following is a chapter-by-chapter list of the books referenced and researched for this book, and a few other books on the relevant topics if you'd like to read more.

Chapter 1

Aquilino, W. S., and A. J. Supple. April 2001. Long-Term Effects of Parenting Practices during Adolescence on Well-Being Outcomes in Young Adulthood. *Journal of Family Issues* 22:289–308.

Lewis, T. J., G. Sugai, and G. Colvin. 1998. Reducing Problem Behavior through a School-Wide System of Effective Behavioral Support: Investigation of a School-Wide Social Skills Training Program and Contextual Interventions. *School Psychology Review* 27:446–459.

Mayer, R., and B. Syulzer-Azaroff. 1991. *Behavior Analysis for Lasting Change.* Fort Worth, TX: Harcourt Brace.

Sears, R. R., E. E. Maccoby, and H. Levin. 1957. *Patterns of Child Rearing.* Evanston, IL: Row, Peterson.

Stormshank, E. A. 2000. Parenting Practices and Child Disruptive Behavior Problems in Early Elementary School. *Journal of Clinical Child Psychology* 29:17–29.

Stormshank, E. A., K. L. Bierman, R. J. McMahon, and L. J. Lengua. March 2000. Parenting Practices and Child Disruptive Behavior Problems in Early Elementary School. *Journal of Clinical Child Psychology* 29 (1).

Straus, M. A. 1994. *Beating the Devil Out of Them: Corporal Punishment in American Families.* Lexington, MA: Lexington Books.

Straus, M. A., D. B. Sugarman, and J. Giles-Sims. August 1997. Spanking by Parents and Subsequent Antisocial Behavior of Children. *Arch Pediatr Adolescent Medicine* 151 (8): 761–767.

Chapter 2

Belsky, J. M. February 1984. The Determinants of Parenting: A Process Model. *Child Development* 55 (1): 83–96.

Crouch, J. L., and L. E. Behl. March 2001. Relationships among Parental Beliefs in Corporal Punishment, Reported Stress and Physical Child Abuse Potential. *Child Abuse & Neglect* 25 (3): 413–419.

Day, R., G. Peterson, and C. McCracken. 1998. Predicting Spanking of Younger and Older Children by Mothers and Fathers. *Journal of Marriage and the Family* 60: 79–94.

Kendler, K. S., P. C. Sham, and C. J. MacLean. May 1997. The Determinants of Parenting: An Epidemiological, Multi-Informant, Retrospective Study. *Psychol Med* 27 (3): 549–563.

Kochanska, G., L. A. Clark, and M. S. Goldman. 1997. Mutually Responsive Orientation between Mothers and Their Young Child: Implications for Early Socialization. *Child Development* 68:94–112.

McCurdy, K. March 2005. The Influence of Support and Stress on Maternal Attitudes. *Child Abuse and Neglect* 29 (3): 251–268.

McLoyd, V. C., T. E. Jayaratne, R. Ceballo, and J. Borquez. April 1994. Unemployment and Work Interruption among African American Single Mothers: Effects on Parenting and Adolescence, Socio-Emotional Functioning. Special issue, *Child Development* 65:562–589.

Pinderhughes, E. E., J. E. Bates, K. A. Dodge, G. S. Pettie, and A. Zelli. 2000. Discipline Responses: Influences of Parents' Socioeconomic Status, Ethnicity, Beliefs about Parenting, Stress, and Cognitive-Emotional Processes. *Journal of Family Psychology* 14 (3): 380–400.

Task Force on the Family. June 2003. American Academy of Pediatrics Report of the Task Force on the Family. *Pediatrics* 111 Suppl: 1541–1571.

Whipple, E. E., and C. Webster-Stratton. 1991. The Role of Parent Stress in Physically Abusive Families. *Child Abuse and Neglect* 15 (3): 279–291.

Chapter 3

Baumrind, D. 1966. Effects of Authoritative Parental Control on Child Behavior. *Child Development* 37(4): 887–907.

———. 1968. Authoritarian vs. Authoritative Parental Control. *Adolescence* 3 (1): 255–272.

———. 1971. Current Patterns of Parental Authority. *Developmental Psychology Monograph*.

————. 1978. Parental Disciplinary Patterns and Social Competence in Children. *Youth and Society* 9 (3): 239–276.

Bredehoft, D. J., S. Mennicke, A. Potter, and J. I. Clarke. Fall/ Winter 1998. Perceptions Attributed by Adults to Parental Overindulgence during Childhood. *Journal of Family and Consumer Sciences Education* 16 (2).

Clarke, J. I., and C. Dawson. 1998. *Growing Up Again: Parenting Ourselves, Parenting our Children,* 2nd ed. Center City, MN: Hazelden.

Cohen, D. A., and J. Rice. 1997. Parenting Styles, Adolescent Substance Abuse and Academic Achievement. *Journal of Drug Education* 272:199–211.

Lamborn, S. D., N. S. Mounts, L. Steinberg, and S. M. Dornbusch. 1991. Patterns of Competence and Adjustment among Adolescents from Authoritative, Authoritarian, Indulgent and Neglectful Families. *Child Development* 62:1049–1065.

Chapter 4

Ainsworth, M., and S. Bell. 1970. Attachment, Exploration and Separation: Illustrated by the Behavior of One-Year in Strange Situation. *Child Development* 40:49–67.

Ainsworth, M., S. Bell, and D. Stayton. 1972. Individual Differences in the Development of Some Attachment Behaviors. *Merrill-Palmer Quarter* 18:123–143.

Bretherton, I. 1992. The Origins of Attachment Theory: John Bowlby and Mary Ainsworth. In *A Century of Developmental Psychology,* ed. R. D. Parke, P. A. Ornstein, J. R. Rieser, and C. Zahn-Waxler, 1994. Washington, D.C.: American Psychological Association.

Chapter 5

A Review of the Research on Corporal Punishment. 2003. Children's Hospitals and Clinics of Minneapolis/St. Paul Primary Prevention Committee.

Aquilino, W. S., and A. J. Supple. April 2001. Long-Term Effects of Parenting Practices during Adolescence on Well Being Outcomes in Young Adulthood. *Journal of Family Issues* 22:289–308.

Baldwin, A., J. Kalhoun, F. Breese. 1945. Patterns of Parent Behavior. *Psychological Monographs* 58 (3).

Baumrind, D. 1967. Child Care Practices Anteceding Three Patterns of Preschool Behavior. *Genetic Psychology Monographs* 75:43–88.

———. February 1991. The Influence of Parenting Style on Adolescent Competence and Substance Abuse. *Journal of Early Adolescence* 111:56–95.

Briggs, D. C. 1970. *Your Child's Self Esteem.* New York: Doubleday.

Carlsmith, J., M. Lepper, and T. Landauer. 1974. Children's Obedience to adult requests: Interactive Affects of Anxiety Arousal and Apparent Punitiveness of Adults. *Journal of Personality and Social Psychology* 30:822–828.

Clarke, J. I., and C. Dawson. 1998. *Growing Up Again: Parenting Ourselves, Parenting our Children,* 2nd ed. Center City, MN: Hazelden.

Cohen, D. A., and J. Rice. 1997. Parenting Styles, Adolescent Substance Abuse and Academic Achievement. *Journal of Drug Education* 272:199–211.

Comstock, M. 1973. Effects of Perceived Parental Behavior on Self-Esteem and Adjustment. *Dissertation Abstracts* 34:465B.

Coopersmith, S. 1967. *Antecedents of Self-Esteem.* San Francisco: W. H. Freeman & Co.

Cowan, P. A., and C. P. Cowan. 2002. What an Intervention about Design Reveals about How Parents Affect Their Children's Academic Achievement and Behavior Problems. In *Parenting and the Child's World, Influences on Academic, Intellectual and Social-Emotional Development,* eds. J. G. Borkowski, S. Landesman Ramey, and M. Bristol-Power. Mahwah, NJ: Lawrence Erlbaum Associates, Inc.

Deslandes, R., and D. Turcotte. 1997. School Achievement at the Secondary Level: Influence of Parenting Style and Parent Involvement in Schooling. *McGill Journal of Education,* 32:191–207.

Dodge, K. 2002. Mediation, Moderation and Mechanisms. In *Parenting and the Child's World, Influences on Academic, Intellectual and Social-Emotional Development,* eds. J. G. Borkowski, S. Landesman Ramey, and M. Bristol-Power. Mahwah, NJ: Lawrence Erlbaum Associates, Inc.

Dornbusch, S., P. Ritta, P. H. Leiderman, D. F. Roberts, and M. Fraleigh. 1987. The Relation of Parenting Style to Adolescent School Performance. *Child Development* 58:1244–1257.

Gershoff, E. T. 2002. Corporal Punishment by Parents and Associated Child Behaviors and Experiences: A Meta-Analysis and Theoretical Review. *Psychological Bulletin* 128:539–579.

Gilmartin, B. 1997. The Case against Spanking. *Human Behavior* 8.

Harris, J. 1998. *The Nurture Assumption: Why Children Turn Out the Way They Do.* New York: Free Press.

Hastings, P., and C. Zahn-Waxler. 2000. The Development of Concern for Others in Children with Behavior Problems. *Developmental Psychology* 36 (5): 531–546.

Hyman. I., E. McDowell, and B. Raines. 1975. Corporal Punishment and Alternative in Schools. *Inequality in Education* 23.

Jackson, C., D. J. Bee-Gates, and L. Henriksen. Spring 1994. Authoritative Parenting, Child Competencies and Initiation of Cigarette Smoking. *Health Education Quarterly* 21 (1): 103–116.

Jackson, C., L. Henricksen, and F. A. Foshee. 1998. The Authoritative Parenting Index: Predicting Health Risk Behaviors among Children and Adolescents. *Health Education and Behavior* 25 (3): 321–339.

Kernis, M. H., A. C. Brown, and G. H. Brody. 2000. Fragile Self-Esteem in Children and Its Associations with Perceived Patterns of Parent-Child Communication. *Journal of Personality* 68:225–252.

Kestenbaum, R., E. A. Farber, and L. A. Sroufe. 1989. Individual Differences in Empathy among Preschoolers: Relation to Attachment History. In *Empathy and Related Emotional Responses*, No. 44 in *New Directions for Child Development* series, ed. N. Eisenber. San Francisco: Jossey-Bass, Inc.

Maurer, A. 1976. Physical Punishment of Children. Paper presented at the California State Psychological Association Convention. Anaheim, CA.

Miller, A., and A. Jenkins. 2005. *The Body Never Lies: The Lingering Effects of Cruel Parenting*. New York: WW Norton & Co., Inc.

Morrison, F. J., and R. R. Cooney. 2002. Parenting and Academic Achievement: Multiple Paths to Literacy. In *Parenting and the Child's World, Influences on Academic, Intellectual and Social-Emotional Development*, eds. J. G. Borkowski, S. Landesman Ramey, and M. Bristol-Power. Mahwah, NJ: Lawrence Erlbaum Associates, Inc.

Radziszewska, B., J. L. Richardson, C. W. Dent, and B. R. Flay. June 1996. Parenting Style and Adolescent Depressive Symptoms, Smoking, and Academic Achievement: Ethnic, Gender, AM and SES Differences. *Journal of Behavioral Medicine* 193:289–305.

Resnick, M. D., P. S. Bearman, R. W. Blum, K. E. Bauman, K. M. Harris, J. Jones, J. Tabor, T. Beuhring, R. E. Sieving, M. Shew, M. Ireland, L. H. Bearinger, and J. R. Udry. September 10, 1997. Protecting Adolescents from Harm. Findings from the National Longitudinal Study on Adolescent Health. *Journal of the American Medical Association* 278 (10).

Simons-Morton, B., D. L. Haynie, A. D. Crump, P. Eitel, and K. E. Saylor. February 2001. Peer and Parent Influences on Smoking and Drinking among Early Adolescents. Special Issue, *Health Education,* 9:37 A.M. Behavior, 281:95–107, 1090–1981.

Sroufe, A. L. 2002. From Infancy Attachment to Promotion of Adolescent Autonomy: Prospective, Longitudinal Data on the Role of Parents in Development. In *Parenting and the Child's World, Influences on Academic, Intellectual and Social-Emotional Development,* eds. J. G. Borkowski, S. Landesman Ramey, and M. Bristol-Power. Mahwah, NJ: Lawrence Erlbaum Associates, Inc.

Steinberg, L., J. D. Emen, and N. S. Mounts. 1989. Authoritative Parenting, Psychosocial Maturity, and Academic Success among Adolescents. *Child Development* 60:1424–1436.

Steinberg, L., S. M. Dornbusch, and N. Darling. 1992. Impact of Parenting Practices on Adolescent Achievement: Authoritative Parenting, School Involvement, and Encouragement to Succeed. *Child Development* 63:1266–1281.

Stormshank, E. A., K. L. Bierman, R. J. McMahon, and L. J. Lengua. March 2000. Parenting Practices and Child Disruptive Behavior Problems in Early Elementary School. *Journal of Clinical Child Psychology* 29 (1).

Straus, M. A., D. B. Sugarman, and J. Giles-Sim. 1997. Spanking by Parents and Subsequent Antisocial Behavior of Children. *Arch Pediatr Adolescent Medicine* 151 (8): 761–767.

Straus, M. A. 1996. Spanking and the Making of a Violent Society. *Pediatrics* 98:837–842.

Watson, G. 1943. A Comparison of the Effects of Lax versus Strict Home Training. *Journal of Social Psychology* 5.

Chapter 6

Buchel, T. L., and F. D. Edwards. January 2005. Characteristics of Effective Clinical Teachers. *Family Medicine* 37 (1): 30–35.

Chapter 7

Aquilino, W. S., and A. J. Supple. April 2001. Long Term Effects of Parenting Practices during Adolescence on Well-Being Outcomes in Young Adulthood. *Journal of Family Issues* 22:289–308.

Carlsmith, J. M., M. Lepper, and T. Landauer. 1974. Children's Obedience to Adult Requests: Interactive Affects of Anxiety Arousal and Apparent Punitiveness of Adults. *Journal of Personality and Social Psychology* 30:822–828.

Comstock, M. 1973. Effects of Perceived Parental Behavior on Self Esteem and Adjustment. *Dissertation Abstracts* 34:465B.

Deci, E. L., A. J. Schwartz, L. Sheinman, and R. M. Ryan. 1981. An Instrument to Assess Adults' Orientations toward Control versus Autonomy with Children: Reflections on Intrinsic Motivation and Perceived Competence. *Journal of Educational Psychology* 735:642–650.

Dunifon, R. May 2001. Study presented at the annual meeting of the American Economic Association, conducted at the Institute for Social Research.

Ginsburg, G. S., and P. Bronstein. 1993. Family Factors Related to Children's Intrinsic/Extrinsic Motivational Orientation and Academic Performance. *Child Development* 645:1461–1474.

Grolnick, W. S. 2003. *The Psychology of Parental Control*. Mahwah, NJ: Lawrence Erlbaum.

Milgram, S. 1963. Behavioral Study of Obedience. *Journal of Abnormal Social Psychology* 67:371–378.

Resnick, M. D., P. S. Bearman, R. W. Blum, K. E. Buoman, K. M. Harris, J. Jones, J. Tabor, T. Beuhring, R. E. Sieving, M. Shew, M. Ireland, L. H. Bearingere, and J. R. Udry. September 1997.

Protecting Adolescents from Harm: Findings from the National Longitudinal Study on Adolescent Health. *Journal of the American Medical Association* 278 (1): 823–832.

Chapter 8

KidsPeace. July 2003. Annual Meaningful Time-Check-Ups on U.S. Children and Families. Washington, D.C.: National Center for Kids Overcoming Crisis, Lee Salk Center for Research study.

Sandberg, J. F., and S. L. Hofferth. 2001. Changes in Children's Time with Parents. Population Studies Center. Dearborn, MI: University of Michigan.

U.S. Census Bureau. 1994. A Child's Day: Home, School, Play (Selected Indicators of Child Well-Being). *Current Population Reports.*

Chapter 9

Anderson, C. A., L. Berkowits, E. Donnerstein, R. L. Huesmann, J. D. Johnson, D. Linz, N. M. Malamuth, and E. Wartella. December 2003. The Influence of Media Violence on Youth. *Psychological Science in the Public Interest* 4 (3).

Bearison, D., and T. Cassel. 1975. Cognitive Decentration and Social Codes: Communication Effectiveness in Young Children from Differing Family Contexts. *Developmental Psychology* 11:29–36.

Beckman, M., and T. A. Trozzolo. 2002. Summer Service Learning—What Distinguishes Students Who Participate from Those Who Do Not? Studies in Social Responsibility. Report 3, 35. Notre Dame, IN: University of Notre Dame.

Benton, D. July 2004. Role of Parents in the Determination of the Food Preferences of Children and the Development of Obesity. *International Journal of Obesity* 28 (7): 858–869.

Carmona, R., and M. Eichelberger. 2005. Follow the Leader: A National Study of Safety Role Modeling among Parents and Children. National Safekids Campaign.

Dixon, D. A. 1980. The Caring Curriculum. *School and Community* 67(4): 13–15.

Ellis, D. A., R. A. Zucker, and H. E. Fitzgerald. 1997. The Role of Family Influences in Development and Risk. *Alcohol, Health, and Research World* 21 (3): 218–226.

Ferguson, S. A., A. F. Williams, J. F. Chapline, D. W. Reinfurt, and D. M. DeLeonardis. March 2001. Relationship of Parent Research Records to the Driving Records of Their Children. *Accident Analysis and Prevention* 33 (2): 229–234.

Gil Clary, E., and J. Miller. 1986. Socialization and Situational Influences on Sustained Altruism. *Child Development* 57:1358–1369.

Harris, J. R. 1995. Where's the child's environment? A Group Socialization Theory of Development. *Psychological Review* 102:485–489.

Harris, J. R. 1998. *The Nurture Assumption: Why Children Turn Out the Way They Do.* New York: Free Press.

Kahn, J. September 2000. Protecting Youth from Harm. *Minnesota Medicine* 83. Minnesota Medical Association.

McCord, J. 1988. Identifying Development Paradigms Leading to Alcoholism. *Journal of Studies on Alcohol* 49:357–362.

O'Riordan, D. L., A. C. Geler, D. R. Brooks, A. Zhang, and D. R. Miller. 2003. Sunburn Reduction through Parental Role Modeling and Sunscreen Vigilance. *Journal of Pediatrics* 142 (1): 67–72.

Rutherford, E., and P. Mussen. 1968. Generosity in Nursery School Boys. *Child Development* 39:755–765.

Tibbs, T., D. Haire-Joshu, K. B. Schechtman, R. C. Brownson, M. S. Nanney, C. Houston, and W. Auslander. May 2001. Parental Eating Attitudes and Obesity in Children. *Journal of the American Dietetic Association* 101 (5): 535–541.

U.S. Department of Education. July 1999. Start Early, Finish Strong: How to Help Every Child Become a Reader. American Reads Challenge.

Wilson, B. J., S. L. Smith, W. J. Potter, D. Kunkel, D. Linz, C. M. Colvin, and E. Donnerstein. 2002. Violence in Children's Television Programming: Assessing the Risk. *Journal of Communication* 52:5–35.

Winniford, C., D. S. Carpenter, and C. Grider. 1995. An Analysis of the Traits and Motivations of College Students Involved in Service Organizations. *Journal of College Student Development* 36:27–38.

Zahn-Waxler, C., M. Radke-Yarrow, and R. A. King. 1979. Child Rearing and Children's Prosocial Initiations toward Victims of Distress. *Child Development* 50:319–330.

Zuckerman, B., M. Augustyn, B. M. Groves, and P. Parker. 1995. Silent Victims Revisited: The Special Case of Domestic Violence. *Pediatrics* 963 (3 pt. 1): 511–513.

Chapter 10

Deroma, V. M., K. S. Lassiter, and V. A. Davis. 2004. Adolescent Involvement in Discipline Decision Making. *Behavior Modification* 28 (3): 420–437.

Eisenberg, N. 1983. The Socialization and Development of Empathy and Prosocial Behavior. Special report. Tempe, AZ: Arizona State University, The National Association for Humane and Environmental Education.

Lorber, M. F., S. G. O'Leary, and K. T. Kendziora. October 2003. Mothers' Overreactive Discipline and Their Encoding and Appraisals of Toddler Behavior. *Journal of Abnormal Psychology* 5:485–494.

Oliner, S. P. and P. M. Oliner. 1988. *The Altruistic Personality: Rescuers of Jews in Nazi Europe.* New York: Free Press.

Reid, J. B., K. Kavanagh, and D. V. Baldwin. September 1987. Abusive Parents' Perceptions of Child Problem Behaviors: An Example of Parental Bias. *Journal of Abnormal Child Psychology* 15 (2): 457–466.

Chapter 11

Ng, F. F., G. A. Kenney-Benson, and E. M. Pomerantz. 2004. Children's Achievement Moderates the Effects of Mothers' Use of Control and Autonomy Support. *Child Development,* 75 (3): 764.

Chapter 12

Dienstbier, R. A. 1982. An Emotion Attribution Approach to Moral Behavior. *Psychological Review* 82 (75): 299–315.

Ferster, C. B., and J. B. Appel. 1961. Punishment of S— Responding in Matching to Sample by Time Out from Positive Reinforcement. *Journal of the Experimental Analysis of Behavior* 4:45–56.

Zimmerman, J., and C. B. Ferster. 1964. Some Notes on Time Out from Reinforcement. *Journal of the Experimental Analysis of Behavior* 7:13–19.

Chapter 13

Estrada, P., W. F. Arsenio, R. D. Hess, and S. Holloway. 1987. Affective Quality of the Mother-Child Relationship: Longitudinal Consequences for Children's School Relevant Cognitive Functioning. *Developmental Psychology* 23:210–215.

Shure, M. 1979. Interpersonal Problem Solving Thinking and Adjustment in the Mother/Child Dyad. In *Primary Prevention of Psychopathology, Social Competence in Children,* eds. M. W. Kent, J. E. Rolf. Kent. 3:201–219. Hanover, NH: University Press of New England.

Shure, M., and K. N. Healey. 1993. Interpersonal Problem Solving and Prevention in Urban 5th and 6th Grades. Presented at the American Psychological Association Annual Convention, Toronto.

Shure, M., and P. A. Spevak. 1982. Interpersonal Problem Solving in Young Children: A Cognitive Approach to Prevention. *American Journal of Comm Psych* 10 (3): 341–356.

Bibliography

Ames, Louise Bates, Ph.D. 1993. *Raising Good Kids: A Developmental Approach to Discipline.* New York: Dell.

Ames, Louise Bates, Ph.D., Frances L. Ilg, and Carol C. Haber. 1983. *Your One-Year-Old* (series runs through *Your Ten- to Fourteen-Year-Old*). New York: Dell.

Bailey, Becky. 2001. *Easy to Love, Difficult to Discipline: The 7 Basic Skills for Turning Conflict into Cooperation.* New York: HarperCollins Publishers, Inc.

———. 2000. *I Love You Rituals.* New York: HarperCollins Publishers, Inc.

———. 1998. *There's Gotta Be a Better Way: Discipline That Works!* Oviedo, FL: Loving Guidance.

Bettelheim, Bruno. 1985. *The Informed Heart: Autonomy in a Mass Age.* New York: Avon Books.

Brazelton, T. Berry. 1983. *Infants and Mothers: Differences in Development.* New York: Dell.

Briggs, Dorothy Corkille. 1975. *Your Child's Self Esteem.* New York: Main Street Books.

Cecil, Nancy Lee. 1995. *Raising Peaceful Children in a Violent World.* San Diego: Lura Media.

Clarke, Jean Illsley, and Connie Dawson. 1998. *Growing Up Again: Parenting Ourselves, Parenting Our Children.* Center City, MN: Hazelden.

Cohen, Lawrence J., Ph.D. 2001. *Playful Parenting.* New York: Ballantine Books.

Cohen-Posey, Kate. 1995. *How to Handle Bullies, Teasers, and Other Meanies: A Book That Takes the Nuisance Out of Name Calling and Other Nonsense.* Highland City, FL: Rainbow Books.

Cohn, Lisa, and William Merkel, Ph. D. 2004. *One Family, Two Family, New Family: Stories And Advice For Stepfamilies.* Ashland, OR: Riverwood Books.

Coloroso, Barbara. 2002. *Kids Are Worth It! Giving Your Child the Gift of Inner Discipline.* New York: HarperCollins Publishers, Inc.

Crary, Elizabeth. 1982. *Kids Can Cooperate: A Practical Guide to Teaching Problem Solving.* Seattle, WA: Parenting Press.

———. 1993. *Without Spanking or Spoiling: A Practical Approach to Toddler & Preschool Guidance.* Seattle, WA: Parenting Press.

———. 2003. *Dealing with Disappointment: Helping Kids Cope When Things Don't Go Their Way.* Seattle, WA: Parenting Press.

———. 2004. *The Self-Calming Cards.* Seattle, WA: Parenting Press.

Dinwiddie, Sue. 1997. *I Want It My Way! Problem-Solving Techniques with Children Two to Eight.* Palo Alto, CA: Better World Press.

———. 1997. *Let Me Think! Activities to Develop Problem-Solving Abilities in Young Children.* Palo Alto, CA: Better World Press.

Dobson, James. 1996. *The New Dare to Discipline.* Carol Stream, IL: Tyndale House Publishers, Inc.

Dreikurs, Rudolf, M.D., and Vicki Solz, R.N. 1990. *Children: The Challenge: The Classic Work on Improving Parent-Child Relations—Intelligent, Humane & Eminently Practical.* New York: Plume.

————. 1989. *The New Approach to Discipline: Logical Consequences: A Practical Guide to Instilling Good Behavior in Your Child—From Toddler to Adolescent.* New York: Plume.

Faber, Adele. 1996. *How to Talk So Kids Can Learn.* New York: Fireside.

Faber, Adele, and Elaine Mazlish. 2004. *Liberated Parents, Liberated Children: Your Guide to a Happier Family.* New York: HarperCollins Publishers, Inc.

————. 1999. *How to Talk So Kids Will Listen and Listen So Kids Will Talk.* New York: Avon Books.

————. 1998. *Siblings Without Rivalry: How to Help Your Kids Live Together So You Can, Too.* New York: W.W. Norton & Company, Inc.

Fisher, Erik, Ph.D. 2004. *The Art of Managing Everyday Conflict: Understanding Emotions and Power Struggles.* Westport, CT: Praeger Publishers.

Gesell, Arnold. 1995. *Infant and Child in the Culture of Today: The Guidance of Development in Home and Nursery School.* Lanham, MD: Jason Aronson Publishers.

Ginott, Haim G., Alice Ginott, and H. Wallace Goddard. 2003. *Between Parent and Child: The Bestselling Classic That Revolutionized Parent-Child Communication.* New York: Three Rivers Press.

Glenn, Stephen H., and Jane Nelsen. 2000. *Raising Self-Reliant Children in a Self-Indulgent World: Seven Building Blocks for Developing Capable Young People*. Roseville, CA: Prima Publishing.

Gordon, Thomas, Ph.D. 1991. *Discipline That Works: Promoting Self-Discipline in Children*. New York: Plume.

———. 2000. *P.E.T.: Parent Effectiveness Training*. New York: Three Rivers Press.

———. 1989. *Teaching Children Self-Discipline at Home and at School*. New York: Random House Value Publishing.

Granju, Katie Allison, and Betsy Kennedy. 1999. *Attachment Parenting: Instinctive Care for Your Baby and Young Child*. New York: Pocket Books.

Greenspan, Stanley, and Beryl Lieff Benderly. 1998. *The Growth of the Mind: And the Endangered Origins of Intelligence*. New York: Perseus Books Group.

Grolnick, Wendy, Ph.D. 2002. *Psychology of Parental Control: How Well-Meant Parenting Backfires*. Mahwah, NJ: Lawrence Erlbaum Associates.

Harris, Judith Rich. 1999. *The Nurture Assumption: Why Children Turn Out the Way They Do*. New York: Touchstone.

Holt, Luther Emmett. 1899. *The Care and Feeding of Children: A Catechism for the Use of Mothers and Children's Nurses*. Out of print.

Hulbert, Ann. 2003. *Raising America: Experts, Parents, and a Century of Advice About Children*. New York, New York: Alfred A. Knopf.

Ilg, Frances L., and Louise Bates Ames. 1992. *Child Behavior: The Classic Childcare Manual from The Gesell Institute of Human Development*. New York: HarperCollins Publishers.

Kennedy, Rod Wallace, Ph.D. 2001. *The Encouraging Parent: How to Stop Yelling at Your Kids and Start Teaching Them Confidence, Self-Discipline, and Joy*. New York: Three Rivers Press.

Kersey, Katharine C., Ed.D. 1994. *Don't Take It Out on Your Kids! A Parent's Guide to Positive Discipline*. New York: Berkley Publishing Group.

Kindlon, Dan, Ph.D. 2001. *Too Much of a Good Thing: Raising Children of Character in an Indulgent Age*. New York: Hyperion.

Kohn, Alfie. 1999. *Punished by Reward: The Trouble with Gold Stars, Incentive Plans, A's, Praise, and Other Bribes*. New York: Houghton Mifflin.

———. 2005. *Unconditional Parenting: Moving from Rewards and Punishments to Love and Reason*. New York: Atria Books.

Leach, Penelope. 1997. *Your Baby and Child: From Birth to Age Five*. New York: Alfred A. Knopf, Inc.

Liedloff, Jean. 1985. *The Continuum Concept: In Search of Happiness Lost.* New York: Perseus Books Group.

Lerner, Claire, and Amy Laura Dombro. 2004. *Bringing Up Baby: Three Steps to Making Good Decisions in Your Child's First Years.* Washington, D.C.: Zero to Three Press.

Maag, John W., Ph.D. 1996. *Parenting Without Punishment: Making Problem Behavior Work for You.* Philadelphia: The Charles Press Publishers.

Marshall, Marvin. 2001. *Discipline Without Stress Punishments or Rewards: How Teachers and Parents Promote Responsibility and Learning.* Los Alamitos, CA: Piper Press.

Marston, Stephanie. 1992. *The Magic of Encouragement: Nurturing Your Child's Self-Esteem.* New York: Pocket Books.

Medhus, Elisa, M.D. 2001. *Raising Children Who Think for Themselves.* Hillsboro, OR: Beyond Words Publishing.

———. 2004. *Raising Everyday Heroes.* Hillsboro, OR: Beyond Words Publishing.

Milgram, Stanley. 1974. *Obedience to Authority.* New York: Harper & Row Publishers, Inc.

Miller, Alice, Ph.D. 1990. *For Your Own Good: Hidden Cruelty in Child-Rearing and the Roots of Violence.* New York: Farrar, Straus and Giroux.

Miller, Alice, Ph.D., and Andrew Jenkins. 2005. *The Body Never Lies: The Lingering Effects of Cruel Parenting.* New York: W.W. Norton & Company, Inc.

Nelsen, Jane, Ed.D. 1996. *Positive Discipline* (revised). New York: Ballantine Books.

———. 1999. *Positive Time Out: And Over 50 Ways to Avoid Power Struggles in the Home and the Classroom.* Rocklin, CA: Prima Publishing.

Nelsen, Jane, Cheryl Erwin, and Carol Delzer. 1999. *Positive Discipline for Single Parents: Nurturing, Cooperation, Respect and Joy in Your Single-Parent Family,* revised 2nd edition. Rocklin, CA: Prima Publishing.

Nelsen, Jane, Cheryl Erwin, and Roslyn Duffy. 1998. *Positive Discipline for Preschoolers: Raising Children Who Are Responsible, Respectful and Resourceful,* 2nd edition. Rocklin, CA: Prima Publishing.

———. 1998. *Positive Discipline: The First Three Years—Laying the Foundation for Raising a Capable, Confident Child.* Rocklin, CA: Prima Publishing.

Nelsen, Jane, and Lynn Lott. 2000. *Positive Discipline for Teenagers: Empowering Your Teens and Yourself Through Kind and Firm Parenting,* 2nd edition. Rocklin, CA: Prima Publishing.

Nelsen, Jane, Lynn Lott, and H. Stephen Glenn. 1999. *Positive Discipline A–Z: From Toddlers to Teens, 1001 Solutions to Everyday Parenting Problems,* revised 2nd edition. Rocklin, CA: Prima Publishing.

Olson, Linda. 1999. *New Psalms for New Moms: A Keepsake Journal.* Valley Forge, PA: Judson Press.

Pieper, Martha Heineman, Ph.D., and William Pieper, M.D. 1999. *Smart Love: The Compassionate Alternative to Discipline That Will Make You a Better Parent and Your Child a Better Person.* Boston: The Harvard Common Press.

Rogers, Carl R. 1995. *Client-Centered Therapy: Its Current Practice, Implications and Theory.* Philadelphia, PA: Trans-Atlantic Publications.

Rosemond, John. 2001. *New Parent Power.* Kansas City, MO: Andrews McMeel Publishing.

Samalin, Nancy. 1992. *Love and Anger: The Parental Dilemma.* New York: Penguin Books.

———. 1998. *Loving Your Child Is Not Enough: Positive Discipline That Works.* New York: Penguin Books.

Sears, William, M.D. 1987. *Growing Together: A Parent's Guide to Baby's First Year.* Schaumburg, IL: La Leche League International.

Sears, William, M.D., and Martha Sears, R.N. 2001. *The Attachment Parenting Book: A Commonsense Guide to Understanding and Nurturing Your Baby.* New York: Little Brown & Company.

———. 2003. *The Baby Book: Everything You Need to Know About Your Baby from Birth to Age Two.* New York: Little Brown & Company.

Segal, Marilyn, Ph.D. 1985–2000. *Your Child at Play* (series). New York: Newmarket Press.

Severe, Sal, Ph.D. 2003. *How to Behave So Your Children Will, Too!* New York: Penguin Books.

Shure, Myrna B., Ph.D. 1996. *Raising a Thinking Child: Help Your Young Child to Resolve Everyday Conflicts and Get Along with Others.* New York: Pocket Books.

———. 2005. *Thinking Parent, Thinking Child.* New York: McGraw-Hill.

Siegel, Daniel, and Mary Hartzell. 2004. *Parenting from the Inside Out.* New York: Jeremy P. Tarcher.

Small, Meredith, F. 1999. *Our Babies, Ourselves: How Biology and Culture Shape the Way We Parent.* New York: Anchor Books.

Solter, Aletha, Ph.D. 2001. *The Aware Baby.* Goleta, CA: Shining Star Press.

———. 1989. *Helping Young Children Flourish*. Goleta, CA: Shining Star Press.

———. 1998. *Tears and Tantrums: What to Do When Babies and Children Cry*. Goleta, CA: Shining Star Press.

Spock, Benjamin. 1957. *The Common Sense Book of Baby and Child Care*. New York: Duell, Sloan, and Pearce.

Steinberg, Laurence, Ph.D. 2005. *The 10 Basic Principles of Good Parenting*. New York: Simon & Schuster.

Straus, Murray A. 2001. *Beating the Devil Out of Them: Corporal Punishment in American Families*. New Brunswick, NJ: Transaction Publishers.

Sullivan, Eve. 2001. *PARENTS FORUM®: Where the Heart Listens*. Cambridge, MA: Colophon.

Taffel, Ron, Ph.D., Melinda Blau. 1999. *Nurturing Good Children Now: 10 Basic Skills to Protect and Strengthen Your Child's Core Self*. New York: St. Martin's Press.
———. 2002. *Parenting by Heart: How to Stay Connected to Your Child in a Disconnected World*. New York: The Perseus Books Group.

Taffel, Ron, Ph.D. and Melinda Blau. 2002. *The Second Family: Dealing with Peer Power, the Pop Culture, the Wall of Silence—and Other Challenges of Raising Today's Teens*. New York: St. Martin's Griffin.

Taylor, Jim, Ph.D. 2002. *Positive Pushing: How to Raise a Successful and Happy Child.* New York: Hyperion.

Watson, John Broadus. 1928. *Psychological Care of Infants and Children.* New York: W. W. Norton & Co.

Williamson, Marianne. 1996. *A Return to Love: Reflections on the Principles of "A Course in Miracles".* New York: HarperPerennial.

Windell, James. 1991. *Discipline: A Sourcebook of 50 Failsafe Techniques for Parents.* New York: Collier Books.

Windell, James, and Kevin O'Shea. 2006. *The Fatherstyle Advantage: Surefire Techniques Every Parent Can Use to Raise Confident and Caring Kids.* New York: Stewart, Tibori & Chang.

Wyckoff, Jerry L., and Barbara C. Unell. 2002. *Discipline Without Shouting or Spanking: Practical Solutions to the Most Common Preschool Behavior Problems,* revised and expanded edition. New York: Meadowbrook.

———. 1991. *How to Discipline Your Six to Twelve Year Old ... Without Losing Your Mind.* New York: Main Street Books.

Index

D

E

T–U–V

W–X–Y–Z

Notes

Notes

Notes

Notes

Notes

Notes

Notes

Notes

psychologytoday.com

You want to
talk to someone...
but how do you find the right person?

FIND A THERAPIST

PROFILES | SPECIALTIES | PHOTOS | FIND THE THERAPIST WHO SUITS YOU

* Review profiles, photos and fees

...ore ...pists' ...ialties, ...eir own ...s

...sands ...ofessionals